ROUTLEDGE LIBRARY EDITIONS: COLD WAR SECURITY STUDIES

Volume 53

THE SOVIET SECRET SERVICES

THE SOVIET SECRET SERVICES

OTTO HEILBRUNN

LONDON AND NEW YORK

First published in 1956 by George Allen & Unwin Ltd

This edition first published in 2021
by Routledge
2 Park Square, Milton Park, Abingdon, Oxon OX14 4RN

and by Routledge
605 Third Avenue, New York, NY 10017

Routledge is an imprint of the Taylor & Francis Group, an informa business

© 1956 George Allen & Unwin Ltd

All rights reserved. No part of this book may be reprinted or reproduced or utilised in any form or by any electronic, mechanical, or other means, now known or hereafter invented, including photocopying and recording, or in any information storage or retrieval system, without permission in writing from the publishers.

Trademark notice: Product or corporate names may be trademarks or registered trademarks, and are used only for identification and explanation without intent to infringe.

British Library Cataloguing in Publication Data
A catalogue record for this book is available from the British Library

ISBN: 978-0-367-56630-2 (Set)
ISBN: 978-1-00-312438-2 (Set) (ebk)
ISBN: 978-0-367-61083-8 (Volume 53) (hbk)
ISBN: 978-1-00-310315-8 (Volume 53) (ebk)

Publisher's Note
The publisher has gone to great lengths to ensure the quality of this reprint but points out that some imperfections in the original copies may be apparent.

Disclaimer
The publisher has made every effort to trace copyright holders and would welcome correspondence from those they have been unable to trace.

ISBN: 978-0-367-61085-2

THE SOVIET
SECRET SERVICES

Otto Heilbrunn

George Allen & Unwin Ltd
RUSKIN HOUSE MUSEUM STREET LONDON

First published in April 1956
Second impression February 1957

This book is copyright under the Berne Convention. Apart from any fair dealing for the purposes of private study, research, criticism or review, as permitted under the Copyright Act 1911, no portion may be reproduced by any process without written permission. Inquiry should be made to the publisher.

ACKNOWLEDGEMENTS

I am indebted to the Monitoring Service of the British Broadcasting Corporation for supplying me with the monitors' reports on certain war-time broadcasts.

I am under a very special obligation to Mr. Gillespie S. Evans, Press Officer, Embassy of the United States of America in London, as well as to the United States Information Service in Washington, D.C., for very kindly providing me with material.

My thanks are also due to Miss A. C. Johnston, M.B.E., of the Foreign Office Library and Research Department, Lt. Edwin Frutiger, Editor of *Der Heerespolizist*, Zurich, and above all to the Librarian of the Imperial War Museum, Mr. J. R. Hillier, and his staff who cheerfully met my heavy demands on the Museum's inexhaustible bookstore.

The responsibility for the contents of the book is of course entirely mine.

CONTENTS

I	The Soviet Stratagem	page	9

THE SOVIET CASE MATERIAL

II	A Classic in Espionage: The 'Red Orchestra', 1941–43	21
III	A Primer in Infiltration: The 'Red Three', 1941–43	33
IV	More About Intelligence: Partisans on Reconnaissance Missions	49
V	A Blueprint for Subversion: The Fall of France, 1940	56
VI	A Study in Political Warfare: The Free German Committee, 1943–45	75
VII	A Plan for Sabotage: Partisans on Operational Missions	81
VIII	A Pattern for Revolution: A Satellite is Born	101
IX	The New Warfare Organization	127

FINAL ARGUMENT AND SUMMING UP

X	A Leaf out of the German Book	147
XI	On a Point of Law	167
XII	The Soviet Sixth Column	172
APPENDIX:	Partisan Operations: Extract from the Field Service Regulations of the Red Army, 1944	183
	Protocol 'M'	192
	The Comintern Appeal for the 1st May, 1940	196
	Memorandum on the German Political Aims in Russia	200
BIBLIOGRAPHY		205
INDEX		210

Chapter I

THE SOVIET STRATAGEM

ONCE upon a time the code of chivalry, and hence diplomatic etiquette and the usages of war, required the attacking power formally to declare war on its opponent before the opening of hostilities. After a suitable interval the opposing forces met on the battlefield, battle was joined, and the last battle decided the war.

We have by now got used to the idea that an aggressor considers civilities such as a declaration of war out of place. Yet we still cling to the notion that battles and wars are necessarily fought or decided on the battlefield.

It is true that even in wars of the past strategic victories have been sought off-stage, particularly by economic blockades, strategic bombing, and psychological warfare. But the final decisions were then still obtained on the battlefield.

Now, however, a new conception of warfare seems to be in the making in which campaigns are fought by civilians far away from the front line. Subversion, espionage by infiltration, sabotage and partisan warfare are the weapons they will use in a future hot war,[1] and the theatres of operations are the home front and the enemy's lines of communication. This is war without a battlefield, a war in which the outcome of a battle or campaign may be decided before battle is joined. Before it commences the opponent is softened up or eliminated.

We have recently heard a lot of Communist infiltration into Allied Government departments, of Communist fifth columns and intelligence organizations abroad, of others abroad actively preparing future 'partisan' work in the event of war, and of Communist-led strikes in vital industries. Yet do we realize that all these activities combine to form the pattern of a new conception of warfare? The Trojan horse, partisan warfare and the fifth column, to be sure, were not invented by the Soviets. But the Russians weave the borrowed threads into a new design,

---

[1] Cf. Julian Amery, *Of Resistance, The Nineteenth Century and After*, March 1949; J. Burnham, *The Coming Defeat of Communism*, London, 1950.

the war without battlefield. By their superiority here they could offset their vulnerability on the battlefield.

This vulnerability is due to two causes.

In the first place, as the London *Times* of 27th August, 1954, points out, while the Soviets have recently relaxed their strict secrecy on atomic weapons,

"in respect to protection against atomic warfare the Soviet authorities have been almost completely silent. There has been no indication from Soviet sources of what kind of *defence*, if any, they are preparing or of the development of defensive weapons of any special type." (Our italics.)

The Red Army has once before found it impossible to adapt itself to the requirements of defence. Before the start of the German invasion of Russia in 1941, the former General Staff of the German Army had formed the opinion—probably correct— that the Red Army had taken up *offensive* positions all along the frontier. This curious feature misled the German General Staff into thinking that the Russians intended to invade Germany. There is little doubt that the German General Staff thought so in all sincerity. On the other hand, it is equally clear that this military appreciation of Russian intentions was politically absurd. Apart from the fact that the German front-line commanders, after their advance into Russia, found no evidence of any aggressive preparations, the leading members of the German Embassy in Moscow were all convinced at the time that Russia had no intention of attacking Germany, and it was quite obvious that Stalin had no desire to enter the war voluntarily on Britain's side at that time. How, in the light of this evidence, could the former Chief of Staff of the German Army still maintain in 1948 that he had in 1941 correctly assessed the enemy's intentions?

It has been hinted in German war literature that the Russians, disappointed with the outcome of Molotov's visit to Berlin in the autumn of 1940, had planned a restricted move against Rumania. But while such an assumption does not seem entirely impossible, there is no evidence whatsoever for it. Yet even if there were, why then should the Russians also have deployed their forces, poised for attack, in far-off Poland?

In reality it appears that we have to look for another solution to this riddle. As a rule the Russians rely on the guidance of their

Marxist scripture and are slow to find the answers to problems which have not been solved for them there for fear of treading the path of deviation. In the political sphere they are therefore masters in the art of cold warfare by infiltration and subversion, so conveniently summarized in one of the Marxist Commandments—never repudiated and frequently practised—that Communists "must be ready to employ trickery, deceit, law-breaking, withholding and concealing of truth, etc." But the method of persuasion is alien to them. Had they known how to apply it and treated their German prisoners of war and the East-German population decently, the whole of Germany might have been converted to Communism. As it was, unable to give psychological treatment not prescribed in the works of the master, the Soviets probably lost the greatest political prize ever within their reach.

Not only their political outlook, but their military strategy, too, suffers from similar limitations and for the same reason. The Russians, before the start of the German campaign, were unfamiliar with the requirements of defence; their military leaders, schooled in the tenets of penetration, tried to meet the coming onslaught with forces poised for attack. Their inability to think and act defensively brought them to the brink of disaster. They learned only by costly experience on the battlefield, and the fact stands out that their initial mistakes were apparently due to their doctrinaire limitations; Marx, after all, had never envisaged Communism in a defensive rôle. Now, once again, it may well be that the Russians are not preparing any kind of defence, this time against atomic warfare.

In the second place, the Red Army is more vulnerable to atomic counter-attack than almost any other army in the world. At a Press conference in the middle of 1954, the Chief of the Imperial General Staff characterized as the main problem of nuclear warfare: how to force the enemy into concentrations presenting good targets for nuclear weapons without presenting good targets ourselves. Obviously nuclear warfare does not mean that large-scale battles are outmoded, but it does mean that the build-up for battle will be fundamentally different. This being so, the Russians will have to revise their battle technique even more radically than the West. In the last war the Russians owed much of their success to the superiority in manpower and equipment which they brought to bear on the Germans; prior to the battle the Russians concentrated their infantry, tanks and artillery to a hitherto unknown extent at the points of attack, and broke through the German lines by sheer weight of numbers. If the first attempt failed, a second, third and fourth followed and, significantly, the concentrations were maintained all the time. If atomic weapons were used in a future World War Russian strategists would have to rid themselves completely of their outdated method of building up that has become known as 'Schwerpunktbildung'.

The problem facing the Red Army in this respect is enormous, because they thus have to abandon their one and only war-winning plan of campaign.

However, in World War II the Soviets employed guerilla forces on a large scale in the German rear and moulded the bands into a highly efficient, hard-hitting movement.[1] After the war each of the satellite countries formed its own guerilla brigades, while in the east guerilla warfare has become a standard device. In the event of another World War it is therefore to be expected that the Soviets will try to divest the front of its supreme importance by conducting clandestine operations in our rear on the largest possible scale. In this kind of warfare their front line can be thinned out, so that it no longer represents an ideal target for nuclear weapons. Instead the Soviets will try to build up their partisan concentrations in our rear, where for obvious reasons atomic weapons cannot normally be used against them. *This, it appears, is their answer to atomic attack.*

The Khokhlov disclosures should be read in this light. We quote from the London *Times* of 23rd April, 1954:

"A Russian, who described himself as Captain Khokhlov, a terrorist agent, was introduced to journalists at the offices of the United States High Commission near Bonn yesterday. It was stated that he and two Germans had been given orders to assassinate Mr. Okolovich, a leading anti-Communist Russian, in Frankfurt.

"Captain Khokhlov said that his conscience prevented his carrying out the murder. . . .

"Captain Khokhlov . . . has given a full account of the history of the Soviet agency to which he belonged . . . which during the war was responsible for partisan activities in the rear of the German armies. It appears that when the war ended its then chief

---

[1] Cf. Dixon and Heilbrunn, *Communist Guerilla Warfare*, London (2nd edition), 1954; New York, 1954; Oslo, 1954; Paris, 1955; Frankfurt, 1956.

persuaded his superiors to keep its senior officers and key agents in service *for the preparation of future 'partisan' work in the event of war.*

"It was planned to send agents to foreign countries to hold themselves ready for use. . . ." (Our italics.)

This statement was fully corroborated by Mrs. Petrova who, as reported in the London *Times* of 8th July, 1954, told the Royal Commission on Russian espionage in Melbourne on 7th July, 1954, that

"the fifth column which Mr. Kislitsin was sent to Australia as an MVD man in 1952 to organize was to be active continuously . . . 'in all kinds of preparatory work'. His work was mainly the transference of illegal agents from abroad into Australia *to organize the fifth column.*" (Our italics.)

We must not take these discloures lightly and console ourselves with the thought that it cannot happen here, because the Russians will never be able to mobilize partisan forces in our rear to the same extent as they did in Russia in the late war. The front line in a future war, if there were one, would not be far away from countries which have not as yet given proof of their immunity from Communist infiltration; in these areas are many of the NATO airfields, oil pipelines and other installations, and near, or in, these areas NATO reserves will be mobilized or landed. There can be little doubt that Communist intelligence in our midst is currently employed in finding out those targets which are most vulnerable to partisan attacks and sabotage operations, and which yield them the greatest possible results. These targets need not necessarily be military objectives: power and transport strikes and sabotage of their installations can delay the mobilization of reserves as well as the production of war material.

The NATO appraisals are based on three assumptions:

(1) The Soviets, before starting a war, will have to build up their forces considerably.

Yet we may have to revise our estimates of the build-up required at the opposite front if and when there are signs of preparations for a partisan build-up in our rear.

(2) The build-up period will allow NATO to mobilize and move the reserves to their assigned positions.

Yet the new warfare makes it possible to hamper the mobilization and play havoc with the time-tables.

(3) The opposing forces will offer a target for nuclear weapons.

Yet in the new warfare the opposing forces will try as far as possible to form the concentrations required for attack, not in their vulnerable front line, but in the immune rear of our forces.

It is not suggested that a re-appraisal of NATO's basic assumptions is necessary, but the 'capabilities studies' should assess the impact of the new technique on conventional and nuclear warfare. Indeed, we must not draw our conclusions on Soviet intentions by fixing our gaze solely on the opposite front line and points east; we must form our appreciation by watching just as closely developments in our rear. In particular, a frontal surprise attack on us would have all the more far-reaching effects if it were accompanied by clandestine warfare in our rear. Conversely, by watching developments of this kind in our rear, we could be forewarned and thus be able to eliminate the element of surprise; if an enemy realized this he might even call off the planned attack. This necessitates on our side a NATO intelligence apparatus widespread enough to cover any such developments in our rear.

But quite apart from any specific functions these weapons of the new warfare may possess, they play a vital part in the Soviet plan of campaign and a detailed weapon study based on their past performance seems therefore overdue.

And finally, irrespective of whether or not we shall in the immediate future be threatened by a hot war, this new concept of war without battlefield is revolutionary. We too must be able to wage such a war.

These words are written immediately after the Geneva Meeting of the Four Heads of Government in July 1955. This is a time when we ought to take stock. The need for vigilance and effort remains as strong as ever.

The Geneva Conference has reduced tension. It has reduced the danger of hot war. It has reduced the dangers of the cold war. But the dangers have not yet been eliminated.

We in the West sincerely believe in democracy. We ought to credit the Russian leaders with a no less sincere belief in Communism. The West strives for peace, the East sponsors peaceful co-existence. We must recognize that a wide and deep gulf separates these two concepts and it is imperative that we are clear in our minds about the meaning of co-existence.

On two very recent occasions, it should be noted, Marshal Bulganin has invoked the policy of co-existence. When the Conference for the formation of the 'Eastern NATO' opened in Warsaw on 11th May, 1955, he said:

"The *invariable* principle of Soviet foreign policy is the *Leninist principle* of the co-existence of the different social systems."[1]

Three days later Russia agreed to attend the Geneva Conference, the 'Eastern NATO' treaty was signed, and Marshal Bulganin stated that this treaty

"was inspired by the *unshakable Leninist principle* of peaceful co-existence of States with different social orders."[2]

What is this invariable, unshakable Leninist principle of co-existence?

It was laid down by Lenin in the Report of the Central Committee at the 8th Party Congress in 1919, and it has been regarded as a classic ever since:

"We are living not merely in a state, but in a system of states, and the existence of the Soviet Republic side by side with imperialist states for a long time is unthinkable. One or the other must triumph in the end. And before that end supervenes, a series of frightful collisions between the Soviet Republic and the bourgeois states will be inevitable. That means that if the ruling class, the proletariat, wants to hold sway, it must prove its capacity to do so by its military organization."

And again, in November 1920, Lenin addressed the Moscow Party Nuclei Secretaries as follows:

"The fundamental thing in the matter of concessions, from the standpoint of political considerations . . . is the rule which we have not only mastered theoretically, but have also applied practically, and which will, until socialism finally triumphs all over the world, remain a fundamental rule with us, namely, that we must take advantage of the antagonisms and contradictions

[1] London *Times*, 12th May, 1955. The italics here and subsequently are ours.
[2] London *Times*, 16th May, 1955.

between two capitalisms, between two systems of capitalist state, inciting one against the other. *As long as we have not conquered the whole world, as long as, from the economic and military standpoint, we are weaker than the capitalist world,* we must adhere to the rule that we must know how to take advantage of the antagonisms and contradictions among the imperialists."[1]

Out of this conception was developed the Leninist-Stalinist thesis on the possibility of temporary co-existence which is to last

"until proletarian revolution ripens in Europe or until colonial revolutions come fully to a head, or finally, until the capitalists fight among themselves."[2]

Peaceful co-existence is therefore a cease-fire, an arrangement of a temporary character made necessary by the ratio of forces in both camps. This, then, is the principle that was endorsed by Marshal Bulganin, and it would be rash to assume that what he regarded as invariable and unshakable in May 1955, had been abandoned by him a month later at Geneva. Indeed, when he addressed the Supreme Soviet after his return from Geneva on 4th August, 1955, he declared that

"Soviet foreign policy was motivated in its main principles by the Leninist idea of co-existence and co-operation of countries with different political systems."[3]

Two conclusions are inevitable: The period of co-existence can be indefinitely extended if, and only if, the united West indefinitely maintains the ratio of forces between the two blocs. This aspect was rightly stressed by the British Secretary of State for Foreign Affairs, Mr. Harold Macmillan, in the House of Commons on 27th July, 1955. There would be a temptation, he said, to relax efforts in all directions in an atmosphere of premature optimism; "if we do that, *all is lost.*"

The second point which we must recognize is that even under the concept of co-existence international Communism may con-

---

[1] Lenin, *Selected Works*, London, 1937, vol. 8, p. 279 f.
[2] Stalin's *Speech to the 15th Congress of the Communist Party of the Soviet Union* of 2nd December, 1927, quoted from *Soviet World Outlook, A Handbook of Communist Statements*, Washington, 1954, p. 226.
[3] London *Times*, 5th August, 1955.

tinue its activities. In Lenin's view, in fact, war can only be avoided by carrying out subversion in the opposite camp. In his "Notes on the Task of our Delegation at the Hague" he stressed that

"we must explain that the only possible method of combating war is to *preserve* existing, and to form new, *illegal organizations* (abroad) in which all revolutionaries in the armed forces shall carry on prolonged anti-war activities."[1]

It was not possible at Geneva to exchange any views on these topics or to include them in the terms of reference of the coming Foreign Secretaries' Conference. While "the American delegation (at Geneva) has made crystal clear American concern about the activities of international Communism",[2] "Marshal Bulganin made it quite clear that the Soviet delegation was not prepared to discuss the activities of international Communism".[3]

Most people expect international Communism to cease its activities[4] but until we receive proof to the contrary, it would be prudent to assume that its organization for peace and war will remain in existence, particularly the latter. Its activities are not prohibited by International Law, as we shall show in Chapter XI, and there is no reason whatsoever why the Soviets should dispense with this highly efficient and well-tried weapon. But there is a very cogent reason why we in the West should take a close look at this weapon. Lenin himself has stated it:

"Everyone will agree that an army which does not train itself to wield all the arms, all the means and methods of warfare

[1] *The Essentials of Leninism*, London, 1947, vol. ii, p. 822. The occasion was the Hague International Peace Congress in December 1922.
[2] So President Eisenhower in his *Broadcast Report to the Nation* on 25th July, 1955. Cf. also the President's Opening Statement at Geneva: International Communism "seeks throughout the world to subvert lawful Governments and to subject nations to an alien domination. We cannot ignore the distrust created by the support of such activities. In my nation and elsewhere it adds to distrust and therefore to international tension."
[3] London *Times*, 19th July, 1955.
[4] "The cold war yield has lately become so small from the Soviet viewpoint that straight diplomacy has taken its place and succeeded where cold war tactics have failed. In Austria the Communists were powerless, but diplomacy has now succeeded in neutralizing the country. The cold war against Yugoslavia was pitifully ineffective; diplomacy has just secured its first result: "Marshal Tito," writes the *Sunday Times* of 31st July, 1955, "used the results of Geneva to put the Balkan pact on ice. In his recent broadcast he stated that 'the military aspect of it is now of a secondary character,' therefore it would be against Yugoslav policy 'to strengthen this military pact'. This would seem to be handing to Moscow the first tangible result in softening the military vigilance of the West." Will in West Germany diplomacy succeed where the cold war failed?

B

that the enemy possesses or may possess, behaves in an unwise or even in a criminal manner. . . . Unless we master all means of warfare, we may suffer grave and even decisive defeat. . . ."[1]

Or, to express the same thought in words more appropriate to the Western mood: At Geneva, as hitherto, the West has steadily maintained that "stability and security depend on the absence of fear which in turn depends on an equilibrium of power"[2] which in turn depends on a parity in *all* weapons of war.

The weapons of the war without battlefield, wielded by international Communism in wartime, are among the most powerful and destructive ones. Nobody in his senses wants another war. Only by being fully prepared can we hope to avoid its outbreak. The purpose of this book is to contribute to the achievement of this aim by exploring the new warfare technique. What has been won by the statesmen at Geneva, can only be preserved by the vigilance of the soldier and the effort of the nation.

---

[1] V. I. Lenin, *'Left Wing' Communism, An Infantile Disorder*, in *Selected Works*, London, 1947, vol. II, p. 629.
[2] London *Times*, 23rd July, 1955.

THE SOVIET CASE MATERIAL

Chapter II

A CLASSIC IN ESPIONAGE: THE 'RED ORCHESTRA',
1941-43

THE following dispatch from Lucerne (Switzerland) appeared in the London *Daily Telegraph* of 3rd November, 1953:

"German-born Rudolph Roessler, fifty-six, *a spy for Russia during the Second World War,* said in a Lucerne court today that he had organized an 'information service' for Czechoslovakia between 1947 and 1953. He is charged with espionage.

"The federal indictment says he used Switzerland as a base for sending secret information on British and United States occupation forces and fortifications in Western Germany and Allied Forces in Denmark to the Czechoslovak secret service. . . .

"Roessler agreed that he had sent military, economic and political reports, but contended these were taken from documents available to anyone. One of his micro-film reports, found in a tin of honey, dealt with plans for R.A.F. airfields in North Rhine-Westphalia."

The *Daily Telegraph* published a further dispatch on 6th November, 1953:

"Rudolph Roessler . . . (was) sentenced to twelve months in prison by a Swiss Federal Court in Lucerne for spying for Czechoslovakia against the Western Allies."

That Roessler was "a spy for Russia during the Second World War" gains significance from the judgment of the Swiss Federal Criminal Court at Lucerne of 5th November, 1953, which found that "Roessler (then) supplied part of his information to the 'Red Orchestra', viz. the Soviet secret service."

Six years earlier the other members of the Soviet spy ring in war-time Switzerland had been in the news. The Bernese daily, *Der Bund*, reported from Lausanne on 31st October, 1947:

"Proceedings before the Divisional Court 1A began on Thursday morning in a big espionage case which goes back to the years 1941–3. Accused are six persons, three of whom are not present. These are: Alexander Rado, Hungarian national, cartographer, present whereabouts unknown, his wife, Helene Rado, and a British subject, Allan A. Foote, engineer, present whereabouts also unknown.

"The following accused appeared before the Military Court: Edmond Charles Hamel, born 1910, from Noirmont (Bernese Jura), radio-technician in Geneva, his wife Olga Hamel, and Marguerite Bolli (now Margrit Schwarz-Bolli), born 1919, at present resident in Basle.

"Alexander Rado, who was an agent of the Soviet Union, is accused of having organized in Switzerland from April 1941 to October 1943, an espionage service in the interest of the Soviet Union and in connection therewith to have installed secret short wave transmitters between Geneva and Lausanne. He had recruited several paid agents whom he had appointed to transmit by wireless information collected by him. . . .

". . . Radio transmitters have been found in the possession of the Hamel couple in Geneva and of Margrit Schwarz-Bolli. Allan Foote worked in Lausanne. His secret transmitter was . . . discovered in Lausanne."

On 2nd November, 1947, *Der Bund* reported the judgment in the case. All the accused were found guilty. Three of them were convicted of espionage or military espionage against a foreign country (Germany) and two of them of military espionage for a foreign country (Soviet Russia).

Thus ended the story of the Red Orchestra in Switzerland.

More scanty are the reports on the final chapter in the story of the Red Orchestra in Germany and German-occupied Western Europe. Seventy-eight agents are said to have been executed in 1943 in Germany, but even this figure is not known for certain; it has been placed as high as 400.[1]

Nor do we know anything definite about the beginning of the story; but it is quite evident that before the start of the German-Russian campaign the Soviet espionage network was firmly established over Western Europe and it kept on working until the end of 1943.

The network was farflung. It had its branches in Berlin, The Hague, Brussels, Paris, Marseilles and Nice. In Switzerland

[1] Paul Leverkuehn, *German Military Intelligence*, London, 1954, p. 176.

the organization was centred in Geneva, with agencies in Lausanne, Lucerne, Berne and Basle.[1] A further network is supposed to have been operating in Sweden.[2] The entire network is commonly known as the Red Orchestra or 'Rote Kapelle', a name given to it by the Germans because 'musicians' was their nickname for wireless operators. The Swiss branch is also referred to as the Red Three or 'Rote Drei', because the Germans located three of their transmitters.

German counter-intelligence had its first success against the network in December 1941 when it discovered and closed down a transmitter in Brussels; a second transmitter was captured there in the summer of 1942.[3] By November 1942, when the battle for Stalingrad started, the Red Orchestra in Germany and German-occupied Western Europe had been almost completely rounded up. But the Red Three carried on and probably used as sources of important information some of the very best Red Orchestra agents who had escaped detection by the Germans.[4]

The Swiss Federal Police, after having made some minor arrests earlier, finally broke up the Red Three towards the end of 1943; in October they raided one station in Geneva during transmission time, a second station closed down because the Police were hot on its trail, and in November a third transmitter in Lausanne and a reserve transmitter were captured, and the agent in Switzerland in control of the German cell was arrested.[5] The chief of the network in Switzerland, Alexander Rado, one of those convicted in absentia in 1947, was never captured, but the network ceased to function.

By then it had done very serious damage to the Germans, as we shall soon see. The Germans were surprised by the existence of these spy rings and were ill equipped to cope with them. It is easy to be wise after the event and try to ridicule German counter-intelligence. It would perhaps be fairer to suggest that hardly any secret service in the world would at that time have suspected the existence of such a widespread spy net and been better prepared to deal with it. We in the West must realize that since then the Soviet spy system has, if anything, been still further improved,

---

[1] Cf. W. F. Flicke, *Agenten funken nach Moskau*, Kreuzlingen, 1954. Alexander Foote, *Handbook for Spies*, London, 1949, p. 72.
[2] Leverkuehn, op. cit., p. 175.
[3] Leverkuehn, op. cit., p. 176.
[4] W. F. Flicke, op. cit., p. 294.
[5] Cf. W. F. Flicke, op. cit., pp. 307, 312 and 332 f.

that we have had our warning, and that we must be prepared to the utmost to deal with this menace in any eventuality.

The difficulties then confronting the Germans were enormous, for which there were several reasons. In the first place, before the outbreak of the German-Russian war, the Soviet spy rings hardly ever went on the air; they sent their messages by courier instead. Couriers using modern methods of clandestine communication are hard to discover, and even if one or the other is discovered, it is almost impossible to locate the sender and addressee of the messages. In the second place, when the campaign began and the Soviet spy rings started their wireless transmissions naturally all messages were coded. Only if, and when, the location of the receiver has been established or the code broken, is it possible to ascertain the significance of the messages and put the cumbersome machinery of the detection service into motion. For the discovery of a secret transmitter long-distance direction-finders are used in the first place in order to determine its area of operation, and only afterwards can close-range detector instruments be used to locate the transmitter itself. Transmitters can be detected only during transmission times. Since the transmitters frequently change them as well as their location, call signs and frequency, it might take weeks of observation to find them. Even then it is hazardous to make arrests; nobody but the wireless operators might be caught, and the bossess would thus be warned to use other transmitters instead. Everybody entering or leaving the house might have to be put under surveillance in order to get a lead to the bosses. But the search does not end there: more important than the bosses are the sources of information; only when they are identified and arrested has the network been finally liquidated. And the identification of all concerned is a tricky task: in the radio messages they are referred to by code names.

At the beginning of the war the radio service of the German counter-intelligence (Funkabwehr) was short of personnel and equipment. Even as late as the end of 1941 German counter-intelligence had only six long-distance direction-finders and had to rely on the co-operation of the Army, Navy and Air Force stations. It had of course its own monitoring and decoding service, as well as close-range detection gear, but the whole apparatus was far too small to deal with the Soviet spy net. The German-Russian campaign began in June, 1941; but it was not until October or November that German counter-intelligence discovered the addressee of the messages to be the 'Director' in Moscow, and not until December did they establish that three transmitters were operating in the Geneva and Lausanne region.[1] It thus took six months to obtain this preliminary information. By then hundreds of messages had already been exchanged.

From then on German counter-intelligence was up against one of the most serious obstacles to its work: this branch of the spy ring worked in Switzerland, and Switzerland was a neutral country. Thus German counter-intelligence could not openly carry out operations against the ring there. The Germans could, of course, have asked the Swiss Federal Police to close down on the ring, whose members would, under Swiss law, be charged with espionage, violating the regulations about the maintenance of Swiss neutrality and illegally operating wireless stations. However, it appears that they did not ask the Swiss for action, and when the Swiss Federal Police later discovered the ring themselves, they—rightly—limited themselves to closing down the stations and arresting all known operators and agents. Being concerned only with safeguarding Swiss interests in the case, they naturally took no steps to discover the cell or cells in Germany which had supplied the Swiss network with information. But for the Germans this was precisely the most important aspect of the case: one cell had survived the round-up of the Red Orchestra in Germany; it had then co-operated with the Red Three and, as it turned out, survived their elimination. Which Soviet network would they supply next?

The Germans apparently realized that official approaches to the Swiss would never lead to the discovery of the German cell, therefore, after having identified a female member of the Swiss network, they tried to infiltrate it, but with no decisive results.[2] Some of the members of the German cell may have been caught in the 1944 purge following the attempt on Hitler's life,[3] but then only accidentally and without suspicion, let alone proof, of their complicity in Soviet espionage.

Again, one can easily find fault with German counter-intelligence—after the event. Since the German cell was never discovered anyway it would have been better to have had the Swiss network closed down by the Federal Police at the end of 1941 instead

---

[1] For the above cf. W. F. Flicke, op. cit., pp. 7, 15, 28.
[2] W. F. Flicke, op. cit., pp. 243, 259.
[3] A. Foote, op. cit., p. 87.

of 1943, and thus have eliminated, if not the source of information in Germany, at least the points of collection and transmission in Switzerland. Even so, the Germans were right in trying to locate the German cell by infiltrating the Swiss net, but they acted too late. Their agent started work in October, or November, 1942.[1]

Here we can learn another important lesson: In a future war the Soviets will again have their networks in neutral countries as well as enemy ones, and for the reasons described only infiltration by Allied agents will make the timely discovery of such traitors possible. In Switzerland, it appears, the network got its original recruits from the ranks of the Communist Party, and this is the circle which must be infiltrated long before the start of any war.

Many books have been written on the campaigns of the last war. Those on the Russian campaign, published in English or French, are not numerous—probably because Allied troops were not involved in it, and contemporaneous documentary evidence is not easily accessible—but they are practically all excellent and serious works which make commendable reading. Yet there is one striking omission in all of them: Russian espionage is not mentioned and its influence on the course of the campaign never assessed. The fact is that we in the West have not even begun to realize the important contribution made by Soviet espionage to the outcome of the campaign during practically all its phases. The Soviets proved in the last war that they were masters of espionage by infiltration. They also showed that as a result their knowledge of the German battle dispositions and plans was often complete to the last detail. And finally, the Soviets knew how to utilize on the battlefield the invaluable information so gained.

Who were the infiltrators? No complete directory exists or will ever be compiled, but there were surprisingly many. Dr. Leverkuehn mentions only a few in his book. The French section was working under a Russian Intelligence officer. "He had succeeded in ingratiating himself with various female employees working in the offices of the C-in-C, Occupied France. . . . The Russian and his principal accomplice were arrested before any serious damage was done."[2] But apart from this small fry Dr. Leverkuehn also mentions agents in the Air Ministry, the Foreign Office, and the Ministry of Economics, adding that the value of

[1] W. F. Flicke, op. cit., p. 243.
[2] Leverkuehn, op. cit., pp. 116–7.

the information passed on to Moscow was enormous.[1] Mr. Foote adds to this list agents in the High Commands of the Wehrmacht and Navy.[2] Mr. Flicke's account leaves no doubt that there were also contacts with somebody highly placed in the Nazi Party Chancery and, unwittingly on the Swiss side, with Swiss Military Intelligence, which had valuable contacts of its own with Germany.[3] That the Swiss spy ring also got some bits of information from German soldiers recuperating in the German clinics at Davos (Switzerland) should be added to complete the picture.[4]

The names of some of the infiltrators are known but others remain anonymous to this day. Some of them realized that they were operating for the Soviets, others believed themselves to be working for the underground against Hitler. Among the members of the Swiss network no such doubts existed. Their method of operation was the usual one: as little contact as possible between the various agents, and, for camouflage, couriers and contact men where feasible.

The Red Orchestra was controlled from Moscow by the 'Director' of the Military Intelligence. He also took charge of the spy ring in Canada, besides Sorge's network in Japan. But whereas in Canada and, as the recent revelations show, in Australia the networks were based on the embassies there, they operated on their own in Japan and in the countries covered by the Red Orchestra. There were, however, special reasons for this independence. Before Dr. Sorge took on his job in Japan, he had made a point of stipulating that he should have as little contact with the Soviet Embassy there as was conceivably possible,[5] and as far as the Red Orchestra was concerned, there were of course no Soviet Embassies from 1941 onwards in Germany or German-occupied Western Europe, while Switzerland had terminated its diplomatic relations with Soviet Russia in 1924. These relations were, however, re-established in 1946, and a future Red Three might therefore adhere to the Canadian and Australian pattern.[6]

The 'Director' in Moscow was in direct contact with the various Resident Directors of the Red Orchestra, Rado in Switzerland,

[1] Leverkuehn, ibidem, p. 176.
[2] A. Foote, op. cit., pp. 81, 82.
[3] W. F. Flicke, op. cit., pp. 149 f., 191, 225.
[4] W. F. Flicke, op. cit., p. 131.
[5] Cf. Major-General Charles A. Willoughby, *Sorge: Soviet Master Spy*, London, 1952, p. 38.
[6] The Soviet war-time spy net in Sofia was also controlled by the Soviet Mission there. Cf. Franz von Papen, *Memoirs*, London, 1952, p. 474.

Coro in Berlin, Kent in Brussels and Gilbert in Paris. The Resident Directors were responsible for the supervision of their network, the channelling of the requests from Moscow, the evaluation of the incoming material, and the enciphering and forwarding of this material. They also looked after finances. Each network was self-contained and, as a rule, had no contact with other rings. This rule was broken when, in 1944, the Red Three appealed to Canada for funds; a matter which is dealt with in the 1946 Report of the Royal Commission which investigated in Canada "the Facts relating to ... the Communication of Secret and Confidential Information to Agents of a Foreign Power."

The Resident Director had also to appoint his contact men and his wireless operators. The contact men had to recruit the agents, who reported to the contact men through couriers. The contact men also kept liaison with the wireless operators.[1] But this arrangement was not always adhered to: 'Kent' in Brussels was on at least one occasion in direct contact with his German agents.[2]

The cipher used for wireless transmissions was carefully guarded; as a rule it was only known to the Resident Director and, of course, Moscow. But, as Mr. Foote reveals, he himself had his own cipher in addition to that used by the Resident Director in Switzerland. No two ciphers were identical: in Canada each of the Embassy sections used its own cipher, which was unknown to the others.

While the Red Three, from the start of the German-Russian campaign, had to rely exclusively on short-wave sets for receiving their instructions and sending their material to Moscow, Sorge in Japan kept up a courier service in addition to his wireless contacts: a courier from Moscow would meet a courier from Japan and exchange messages. Before the start of the campaign the Red Three, as already stated, had also made use of couriers and possibly the mail, the regular peace-time means of communication.

In this respect Roessler's working methods in his post-war activities for Czechoslovakia are probably typical. He had little contact with the local Embassy. His orders were usually received through the man who was later to be his co-defendant, a Swiss citizen by the name of Schnieper, who travelled to Prague and Vienna for meetings with Czechoslovak agents. As the *Neue Zuercher Zeitung* stated on 3rd November, 1953, Roessler then

[1] Cf. for the above, A. Foote, op. cit., p. 52 *seq.*
[2] Cf. Dr. M. Roeder, *Die Rote Kapelle*, Hamburg, 1952, p. 21.

"obtained part of the (required) material in conversation with his acquaintances. He seems to have had regular visits from Germany. . . . His main source, however, consisted of Swiss and foreign publications of all sorts. He had an excellently arranged collection of over 20,000 newspaper cuttings. What the indictment says in this respect is noteworthy: 'These cuttings show that a great deal is published about military matters, even about details which, one would have thought ought to be kept secret. That Roessler, well versed in the military field from his journalistic and former intelligence activities, could deduce a great deal from these publications is plausible.' "

Still according to the *Neue Zuercher Zeitung*, "Roessler wrote his reports in longhand, Schnieper copied them on the typewriter, and usually took them at once to Volf (a captain and secretary to the Czechoslovak Military Attaché) in Berne, where he received money in return. . . . Later on the reports were microfilmed by Schnieper with a camera specially procured for this purpose, and then sent either hidden in letters to a cover address in Prague, or in food parcels to a cover address in Dusseldorf. The indictment specifically names two occasions on which these films were hidden, in a tin of honey, and in a fig."

Unfortunately for the 'Information Service', the cover addressee in Dusseldorf refused to accept a parcel and it was returned to Switzerland. Since the sender's address was fictitious the parcel was opened by the Swiss authorities and the microfilm discovered. In addition to plans for R.A.F. airfields in North-Rhine Westphalia, which we have already mentioned, the Swiss newspaper reveals that information was found on U.S. Army instructors with Korean battle experience, on the manœuvres of U.S. troops in Germany, the organization of the U.S. Air Force in Great Britain, and the operational strength of the French Army. The Swiss newspaper report is based on the indictment and the defendants confirmed that it was substantially correct. Considering that the items selected by the 'Information Service' for closer treatment all analysed Allied strength, it seems rather disturbing that Roessler's source of information was mostly published material.

What the cover addressees were to do with the parcels was not revealed, but it can be assumed that the parcels were supposed to proceed through diplomatic channels to their final destination.

The Red Orchestra did not spring up overnight; it was set up long before Germany invaded Russia and it rendered valuable services to the Soviets, as we shall see in the next chapter. And there can be little doubt that the Red Orchestra or its successor organization is even now in existence and fully prepared to take up its work in the event of war.

In France the revelations about the National Defence Committee, the supreme body on French defence matters, make it clear that it was infiltrated in 1954. It consists of only a few members: the President of the Republic, members of the Government, and the three Service Chiefs. In September, 1954, it was announced that there had been serious leakages of information from meetings of the National Defence Council. Its minutes were supposed to have found their way into the hands of the Communist Party. On 1st October, 1954, "two senior French officials (in the office of the permanent general secretary of the Committee) were charged ... after it was announced they had made statements that are regarded as an admission of responsibility for the leakages of information. . . .

"It was reported . . . that the interrogation had established that both men had acted primarily from ideological motives of a kind that 'could be classified as crypto-Communist'. Their dominating idea had been to oppose, in the first place, a continuation of the war in Indo-China and, secondly, any possibility of an atomic war. It did not appear that they ever communicated directly with the Communist Party. . . . The pattern of espionage seems to have been that (the first official), apparently without thought of gain, passed on information to (the second official) which he in turn sold for cash to (a third man). On what principle the third man shared out the information thus obtained between the Communist Party and the police, only he could reveal; and (he) has for the moment vanished without trace."[1] He was, however, soon traced and arrested, and was reported to have admitted "having passed on this information to the (police) but only after it had been doctored by the Communist Party. . . ."[2]

A few days later, though, one of the officials and the third man went back on vital parts of their evidence, and Mr. Duclos, leader of the French Communist Party, denied that the third man ever supplied the Communist Party with this information.

[1] London *Times*, 2nd October, 1954.
[2] London *Times*, 4th October, 1954.

The fact remains that the leakages did occur and the information was passed on to interested quarters.

So much for France. As far as Germany and Switzerland are concerned, the Roessler case might be regarded as a pointer. It seems rather strange, at first sight, that a man who during the war had been working so successfully in the Red Orchestra for the Russians, should soon after the war be recruited by the Czechoslovaks. But a similar switch was quite recently observed in a spy case in Sweden. Major Communist espionage had been uncovered there in 1951 and 1952. In both cases Soviet Embassy officials in Stockholm were involved and had to leave the country. In March, 1955, another spy ring was discovered in Sweden, and Sweden this time "protested to Czechoslovakia and Rumania after receiving evidence that their Stockholm legations were involved in espionage."[1] As the London *Times* stated on 14th March, 1955, the two earlier cases "made a deep impression on public opinion, and it is considered significant that a satellite is now alleged to have a leading rôle in Communist intelligence work here."

Roessler's antecedents were of course well known in Switzerland; in 1945 he was tried there before a Divisional Court for his Red Orchestra activities for the Russians and acquitted on a point of law. That in Roessler's subsequent activities the Czechoslovaks should appear as his employers is not therefore surprising. But this switch too is not without significance; the veil was lifted during Roessler's trial in 1953. While Roessler and his co-defendant Schnieper were still working for the Czechoslovaks, Schnieper was supposed to meet his employer. "After a first meeting, arranged at the Red Army Monument in Vienna, did not take place, Schnieper, a few days later, went to the flat of an acquaintance whom he knew to be in contact with the Czechoslovaks. His son-in-law then took him (Schnieper) to the *Russian Commandatura* of the district. . . ."[2] This, as the indictment states and Schnieper confirmed, was done "to check his reliability."[3]

The reader will remember that Roessler "seems to have had regular visits from Germany." Who these visitors were was not disclosed, and they remain as anonymous as the war-time contacts who may have survived the 1944 purge.

[1] London *Times*, 15th March, 1955.
[2] *Neue Zürcher Zeitung*, 3rd November, 1953.
[3] *Neue Zürcher Zeitung*, 5th November, 1953.

Since the war there have been innumerable trials in many West-European countries of Communist spies, mostly small fry who relied on their own observations or minor contacts. The Red Orchestra had a different technique; it obtained its information mainly through direct contact with personnel in the enemy's top agencies. The reader, in reviewing the above evidence, may come to the conclusion that the Red Orchestra is playing on. But even if it is not, its successor organization no doubt is.

Espionage by infiltration is Moscow's foremost secret weapon in the war without battlefield.

Chapter III

A PRIMER IN INFILTRATION: THE 'RED THREE',
1941–43

WHEN the Germans attacked the Russians on 22nd June, 1941, the Red Army was completely taken by surprise. How surprised it was is clearly stated in the famous Diary of the then German Chief of the General Staff, Colonel-General Halder, who on that day made the following entry:

"*22nd June, 1941* (Sunday) (1st day).

"*The morning reports* indicate that all Armies (except the 11th) have started the offensive according to plan. Tactical *surprise* of the enemy has apparently been achieved along the entire line. All bridges across the Bug River, as on the entire river frontier, were undefended and are in our hands intact. That the enemy was taken by surprise is evident from the facts that troops were caught in their quarters, that planes on the airfields were covered up, and that enemy groups faced with the unexpected development at the front inquired at their HQ's in the rear what they should do. More effects of the surprise may be anticipated from the assaults of our armour, which have been ordered in all sectors. The Navy reports that the enemy seems to have been taken by surprise also in their zone of action. . . .

"*The overall picture* of the first day of the offensive is as follows:

"The enemy was surprised by the German attack. His forces were not in tactical position for defence. The troops in the border zone were widely scattered in their quarters. The frontier itself was for the most part weakly guarded."[1]

Nobody was more surprised about the surprise of the Russians than the Germans themselves. For weeks there had been rumours about the coming German attack, and the Germans had been anxiously watching Stalin's reaction. After the German invasion of the Balkans the Germans had noticed a stiffening of the Russian

[1] *The Halder Diaries*, vol. vi, February to August, 1941, p. 161.

attitude towards them, but they noted with relief that the German successes soon led to the "return of Russia to the previous correct attitude." As late as 6th June, 1941, German Naval Intelligence reported that the "Russian policy still strives as before to produce the best possible relationship with Germany", on the following day "all observations show that Stalin-Molotov . . . are doing everything to avoid a conflict with Germany", on 14th June the Tass Agency issued an official declaration "which turns against rumours of the coming German-Russian war; emphasizes conscientious fulfillment of the pact by both sides", and one week before the attack, on 15th June, Naval Intelligence records that "Stalin (is) prepared to make extreme concessions."[1]

The rumours about the coming German attack came from two sources, according to German Naval Intelligence:

"11th October, 1940: German entry into Rumania; England attempts by alarming reports to influence Russia's attitude towards Germany.

"24th April, 1941: Naval Attaché in Moscow reports considerable extent of rumours: danger of war Germany-Russia, fed by transient travellers from Germany. English Ambassador predicts as day of outbreak of war 22nd June!"

Let us interpolate here that while the British Ambassador in Moscow had shortly before conveyed such a warning to Stalin, he had not mentioned any date, which must have come from other sources.

"5th May, 1941: English radio speaks of stronger indications of German attack on Russia.

"12th June, 1941: London expects a fundamental change of German-Russian relations."

So indeed it did. After various preliminary warnings the Joint Intelligence Committee had finally reported that day: "Fresh evidence is now at hand that Hitler has made up his mind to have done with Soviet obstruction and attack."[2]

There is just one further entry of interest in the German Naval

---

[1] Document C-170, "A file on Russo-German relations found in the files of the High Command of the Navy", reprinted in *Nazi Conspiracy and Aggression*, vol. vi, Washington, 1946, pp. 977 *seq.*, from which the subsequent quotations are also taken.
[2] Sir Winston Churchill, *The Second World War*, vol. iii, London, 1950, p. 318.

Intelligence files, on 15th June: "Leading army circles (in Moscow) against further policy of compliance."

How, then, could the Red Army be surprised by the German attack? How could Stalin be surprised, especially since he did receive the British Prime Minister's timely warning? During the Moscow Conference in August 1942, Sir Winston Churchill broached the subject:

"In the course of one of my later talks with Stalin I said: 'Lord Beaverbrook has told me that when he was on his mission to Moscow in October 1941, you asked him, "What did Churchill mean by saying in Parliament that he had given me warnings of the impending German attack?" I was of course,' said I, 'referring to the telegram I sent you in April '41,' and I produced the telegram which Sir Stafford Cripps had tardily delivered. When it was read and translated to him Stalin shrugged his shoulders. 'I remember it. I did not need any warnings. I knew war would come, but I thought I might gain another six months or so.' "[1]

But how could Stalin hope to gain time, in the face of the ominous portents, by doing nothing? In fact, he misinterpreted the omens.

He knew, of course, that the German troops were deployed for attack all along the frontier. But so was the Red Army, as we have seen in Chapter I, and the Red Army had at that time no aggressive intentions. It was therefore wrong, in Stalin's view, to conclude that the Germans were going to attack. And so it happened that the German General Staff was misled into thinking that the Red Army's offensive deployment was in preparation for a Russian *attack,* while Stalin must have imagined that the Germans had taken up offensive positions solely for their *defence*. Only thus does Stalin's explanation make any sense: by sitting still he would gain time.

He would hardly take the British warning seriously: at that time, in April 1941, Britain was much too interested in drawing Russia into the fight on her side. But the flying visit of Hess to Scotland a month later must have thoroughly aroused Stalin's suspicion: it was all too obvious, to his mind, that Britain and Germany were concocting the ingredients for a gigantic plot

---

[1]Sir Winston Churchill, op. cit., vol. iv, London, 1951, p. 443.

against Russia, and not even subsequent happenings could shake him in this belief. In 1944 Stalin asked Sir Winston Churchill

"what was the truth about the Hess mission. . . . I (Sir Winston) had the feeling that he believed there had been some deep negotiation or plot for Germany and Britain to act together in the invasion of Russia which had miscarried. Remembering what a wise man he is, I was surprised to find him silly on this point."[1]

Stalin had made up his mind. The British-German plot needed time to materialize, and this reading of events confirmed what his strategic insight had already told him: there would be no German attack at that time. At any rate, in a discussion with Mr. Harry Hopkins in August 1941, he himself stated that he had not believed Hitler would attack.[2]

And so it came about that the first great coup of the Red Three fell flat and their vital information was not acted upon.

Not only had the Red Three informed the 'Director' in Moscow of the exact date of the attack; they also supplied the German Order of Battle: the composition and strength of the German armies in the northern, central and southern sector, with the exact number of divisions, the total Panzer strength and its allocation to the various Army Groups. In addition to the O.B. the intentions of the enemy were disclosed: the directions of attack and the exact objectives. For good measure the names of all C-in-C's down to Corps Commander were passed on as well.[3]

Only two days after Hitler had made his final decision, the Red Three had got hold of this intelligence; it had come to Switzerland by diplomatic courier, having been supplied by an officer in the Wehrmacht High Command.[4] It was at once transmitted to Moscow. Whether Stalin ever saw it we do not know. If he did it might have only confirmed him in his belief in a German-British conspiracy. But since the Red Three never heard about this misadventure, their enthusiasm was in no way diminished. And in any case, this formidable beginning must have made Moscow more attentive to any further information from this network.

[1] Sir Winston Churchill, op. cit., vol. iii, p. 49.
[2] Cf. Robert E. Sherwood, *Roosevelt and Hopkins*, New York, 1948, p. 335, and *The White House Papers of Harry L. Hopkins*, vol. i, London, 1948, p. 337.
[3] W. F. Flicke, op. cit., pp. 86, 89, 95.
[4] W. F. Flicke, op. cit., p. 87. Since Hitler had finally fixed the date for the attack on 30th April, this information must have gone to Moscow on 2nd May, 1941, seven weeks before the attack.

It did, indeed, provide plenty more information. For well over two years there was a constant flow of signals to and fro. How important they were it is not possible to show. A number of messages may be in the German Intelligence files in Washington, but they are "for official government purposes only"; there are also the files of the Swiss Divisional Court 1A in the criminal proceedings against the members of the ring in Switzerland, "but the files were not at the time published and must not be handed over for inspection to third persons", and, finally, and equally inaccessible, a private collection in Germany contains "the original texts of decoded signals from the Archives of the (German) Wireless Counter-Intelligence". As it is, the only ones who know the full story are the Russians.

It would certainly be tempting to re-write the campaign history in the light of these files. The intelligence which reached the Russians from the Red Three, the Red Orchestra, the Sorge ring and the partisans may have had a significant effect on the course of the campaign, and if the evidence were available it might well lead to a reappraisal of Russian generalship.

Only relatively few of the Red Three signals have been published. They are contained in the already quoted *Agenten funken nach Moskau* by W. F. Flicke, a former German Counter-Intelligence officer. The book itself is a fictional account of the activities of the Red Three, but the signals in it are authentic.[1] Even this very limited material, however, permits new light to be thrown on some important battles of the Russian campaign.

In the Germans' original campaign plans the basic objectives were Leningrad, Moscow and the Ukraine, and the final aim was the annihilation of the Red Army in Western Russia. Further details were to be filled in later, depending on the course of the campaign. While the Germans had the initial advantage of selecting their points of attack and targets, the Russians—had they acted on information received—had the chance to deploy their troops accordingly, and they missed this chance.

We do not intend to describe the German drive to the East in 1941, which brought them almost to the gates of Moscow. Up to December 1941, the Russians suffered terrible losses everywhere. But they could at least draw some belated advantage from their precise knowledge of the number and deployment of the enemy's troops, while the Germans had to rely on guesswork, and

[1] Cf. Foreword by the publishers, Neptun Verlag, Kreuzlingen, p. 6.

in this they were far out. How much so is evidenced by Colonel-General Halder's diary entry under the 11th August, 1941:

"The whole situation makes it increasingly plain that we have underestimated the Russian Colossus. . . . At the outset of the war we reckoned with about 200 enemy divisions. Now we have already counted 360. . . .

"And so our troops, sprawled over an immense front line without any depth, are subjected to the incessant attacks of the enemy. Sometimes they are successful. . . ."

This miscalculation proved in the end fateful. In the beginning of December, 1941, the German operations came to a halt. Shortly before this the Soviets had begun their counter-offensive, starting in the south and then, on 6th December, opening up in the centre before Moscow. On 12th December, the Red Three sent a signal to Moscow: it contained the general position of the German defence line.[1] But it was not up to date and it can hardly have helped the Russians much because the German dispositions were in any case obvious; instead of holding a continuous line, for which their forces were insufficient, they had established strong-points round the important communication centres.[2]

In fact, at this time, the Soviets' Japanese network transmitted to Moscow intelligence of very much greater importance, intelligence which made it possible for the Russians to transfer their Siberian reserves to the European theatre of war. Dr. Sorge, a German, was the Resident Director of the Tokyo net. He was Press Attaché at the German Embassy and the German Ambassador's trusted friend. One of his collaborators was Ozaki Hozumi, who was in the confidence of Prince Konoye. The Prince was the key man in the American Japanese negotiations just before the Japanese attack on Pearl Harbour.[3]

Sorge's superior was the supreme intelligence agency of the Red Army, then the 4th Bureau of the Red Army General Staff.[4] He too had informed his masters of the impending German attack

---

[1] Cf. W. F. Flicke, op. cit., p. 124.
[2] *A Military History of World War II*, by Members of the Department of Military Art and Engineering, United States Military Academy, edited by T. Dodson Stamps and Vincent J. Esposito, vol. i, United States Military Academy, West Point, New York, 1953, p. 197.
[3] Cf. Major-General Willoughby, op. cit., pp. 21 and 85.
[4] Major-General Willoughby, op. cit., p. 24.

on Russia. On 20th May, 1941, he had warned them that Germany would begin hostilities on 20th June with about 170 to 190 divisions all along the frontier, the main thrust being directed against Moscow.[1] His prediction was almost correct: the attack started two days later, the number of German divisions involved was about right, and the German General Staff considered Moscow as their most important objective; it was only later, on 21st August, 1941, that Hitler decided otherwise.

After the attack on Russia Germany used every means in an attempt to persuade Japan to join her in this venture and thus involve Russia in a two-front war. It was of the utmost importance for Russia to be correctly informed about the Japanese intentions. It was Sorge's job to discover them.

He performed his mission brilliantly. Did the Japanese intend to move south or north? If they intended to move south, they would obviously leave Russia alone, unless her defeat was a foregone conclusion and she could be finished up with a few troops. But the Japanese were shrewder than the Germans in their assessment of the Russian potential. In any event, as Sorge found out, the Japanese did not consider the German victories in Russia in 1941 to be decisive. In the circumstances it appeared obvious that if the Japanese planned to attack Russia, they would have substantially to reinforce the Manchurian Army for a northern thrust across the Siberian frontier.

On 2nd July, 1941, Sorge could inform the 'Director' in Moscow that the Japanese had decided to push southwards into French Indo-China. In July-August Sorge reported that most of the recently mobilized Japanese soldiers had been sent to China and further south, and only a small proportion to Manchuria. At the end of August he let Moscow know that the Japanese would probably attack in the south. On 15th October he sent Moscow his final message on the subject: the Japanese had definitely decided to move south and there was now no serious danger of a Japanese attack on Russia.[2]

How many men the Russians actually transferred to the European theatre as a result is not known. But this much is certain: Siberian divisions were entrained and did take part in the defence of Moscow.[3]

[1] Major-General Willoughby, op. cit., p. 84.
[2] Major-General Willoughby, op. cit., pp. 85 and 86.
[3] Major-General Willoughby, op. cit., p. 22. Sorge was arrested immediately afterwards by the Japanese and his network was liquidated.

At the end of 1941 the Germans had two obvious possibilities for the further conduct of their campaign: to continue the attack or to go over to the strategic defensive. The latter course was advocated by the German General Staff:

"In face of Russian resources of men and material, in face of the inadequate strength of the German Army and the condition in which its equipment had been left by the severities of the winter, any attempt to force Russia to peace by an offensive was quite hopeless. The most it could have done, even if the whole of the rest of the front had been denuded of its reserves, would have been to have pushed a comparatively small section of the front a certain distance forward; it could never have brought about a strategic decision. The forces we had available were about sufficient to straighten out the deep bulges in the line, which would of course have shortened it and thus made it possible to create the operational reserve we required. This might have enabled us to carry through a successful strategic defensive on which the enemy's strength could have exhausted itself until more favourable conditions had been created for a decisive blow."[1]

Hitler rejected this advice and instead ordered further attacks to be prepared. He decided to hold the central part of the front, to conquer Leningrad in the north, and in the south to break into the Caucasus area, "the objective being to destroy the enemy before the Don in order to gain the oil region in the Caucasian area and to cross the Caucasus Mountains."[2]

In view of the limited forces available and the inadequate transport facilities the operations in the south could only be carried out in stages. It was therefore planned to execute successively three separate encircling movements, starting from the north; each operation would, after its successful completion, release troops for the subsequent operations further south. These three pincer movements would be followed up by the capture of Stalingrad and the drive into the Caucasus.

One might reasonably conclude that these operations were so complex that it was impossible for the Russians to guess the enemy's intentions and foretell his next move. However, it seems that the Red Three, from a source in the Nazi Party Chancery, obtained

---
[1] Colonel-General Franz Halder, *Hitler as War Lord*, London, 1950, pp. 53–4.
[2] Hitler Directive of 5th April, 1942.

the Wehrmacht's strategic plans and promptly passed them on to Moscow.[1] About the last phase of the German plan, the double drive in the direction of Stalingrad and the Caucasus, Moscow was also notified, by its Berlin network of the Red Orchestra; its sources of information were a German Counter-Intelligence officer and a Senior Councillor of the Reich Economics Ministry.[2]

The Germans started their offensive on 28th June and, encountering little resistance in this and the subsequent operations, advanced a hundred miles and more within a few days. Whether the Russians were taken by surprise, as *A Military History of World War II* finds,[3] or whether they merely evaded action, as General Halder believes,[4] it is difficult to say. It could well be—but this is only conjecture—that, knowing the German plans, they had at that time already decided to make their stand at Stalingrad; by the time the Germans reached it they would be able to bring in sufficient reserves to halt the advance and stage an effective counter-attack.

The Caucasus attack and the attack on Stalingrad were intended to take place simultaneously, and the Caucasus attack started well for the Germans. On the 9th August they reached the foothills of the Caucasus and drove on from there. But in September the advance became slow, limited and painful, until it was finally halted altogether. The Russians had brought up reinforcements from the southern Caucasus and Siberia. At the end of August 1942, the Red Three had informed them of the composition, equipment and intentions of the German Army Group 'A' on the Caucasus front under Field Marshal List.[5]

Stalin, with his knowledge of the Germans' strength and dispositions, was confident that he would stop the German drive to the Caspian, as indeed he did. During the Moscow Conference of August 1942, Sir Winston Churchill

"asked about the Caucasus. Was he going to defend the mountain chain, and with how many divisions? At this he sent for a relief model, and, with apparent frankness and evident knowledge, explained the strength of this barrier, for which he said twenty-five

---
[1] W. F. Flicke, op. cit., pp. 160, 183.
[2] Cf. Dr. M. Roeder, *Die Rote Kapelle*, Hamburg, 1952, p. 21.
[3] Op. cit., p. 209.
[4] *Hitler as War Lord*, op. cit., p. 54.
[5] W. F. Flicke, op. cit., p. 224.

divisions were available. . . . He declared himself quite confident. . . ."¹

This was on 13th August. Two days later the Prime Minister returned to the subject:

"I asked particularly whether he would be able to hold the Caucasus mountain passes, and also prevent the Germans reaching the Caspian, taking the oilfields round Baku with all that meant, and then driving southwards through Turkey or Persia. He spread out the map, and then said with quiet confidence, 'We shall stop them. They will not cross the mountains.' "²

Only insignificant German patrols ever reached the Caspian.

The assault on Stalingrad, though it too had started well, soon compelled the Germans to throw in more and more divisions. By the end of August the Red Three had already informed Moscow "of the transfer of the 73rd, 337th and 709th Infantry Divisions and the SS-Division 'Das Reich' to the Eastern Front. . . . Whenever the German High Command had to throw in further reserves in the East, the Organization got to know of it even before the Division in question entrained."³ It may well be that this continuous flow of intelligence enabled the Russians to keep the reinforcements required for the static defence of the city to the absolute minimum, as they managed to do,⁴ and to assemble the bulk of their newly arrived reserves on the flanks of the Germans, in preparation for the counter-offensive. Above all, to put it no higher, it ought to have helped the Russians in reaching their well-founded decisions on the right allocation of reserves as between the Caucasus and Stalingrad fronts.

Yet whatever one may think of the influence of the Red Three's work on the course of the campaign up to this point, there can be little doubt that the Russians, in planning the Stalingrad counter-offensive, did derive substantial benefit from this source of information. On 9th November, 1942, the 'Director' in Moscow sent the following request to the Red Three:

"Where are the German rear defence positions southwest of Stalingrad and along the Don river? Where are defence positions

¹Sir Winston Churchill, op. cit., vol. iv, p. 439.
²Sir Winston Churchill, op. cit., vol. iv, p. 445.
³W. F. Flicke, op. cit., p. 224.
⁴*Military History of World War II*, op. cit., p. 218.

being built in sector Stalingrad-Kletskaya and Stalingrad-Kalach? Their characteristics. Characteristics of work on fortified positions which Germans are carrying out on the line Budenovsk-Divnoje-Verchnetirskaja - Kalach - Kachalinskaja - Kletskaja - Dnieper - Beresina?"[1]

The answer was supplied within a few days. The Russian counter-offensive began on 19th November.

Before we try to evaluate the operational significance of this exchange, it is worth pausing to consider its implications. The 'Director's' signal is remarkable indeed. It reveals the Russians' complete trust in the personal reliability of the Red Three and their German sources of information. It shows the Russians' complete trust in the reliability of the Red Three's information. But above all, it is the clearest possible proof that the German infiltrators had immediate access to the most secret material in all its detail. And so, through them, had Moscow.

Let us now consider the signal against the background of the impending operations. Part of its second half may have been added for future reference or camouflage, but its first half was of immediate importance. Apart from Stalingrad itself, Kletskaya, the Don river and Kalach figure prominently in the Russian counter-offensive. The Russians had planned two main thrusts, one from the north and the other from the south. The northern thrust started from the Kletskaja area; it was to branch off towards Kalach on the Don river, culminating in the attack on Kalach from the west. The southern group was to advance towards the north-west and join forces with the divisions from the north at Kalach. The northern attack started on the 19th November, the attack from the south on the following day, and three days later, after advancing about sixty to seventy miles, the two forces made contact at Kalach. The German 6th Army under Paulus was surrounded.

It seems at first sight that the Red Three's intelligence service materially contributed to sealing von Paulus' fate. But we ought to be careful not to overestimate its contribution to the course of operations. The 'Director's' signal was sent on the 9th of November. He could not possibly have received the reply before the 12th, and perhaps later. The Russian attack began on the 19th. It is therefore obvious that all the plans and dispositions must have

[1] W. F. Flicke, op. cit., p. 248.

been made long before the signal was sent by the Director. It appears that the Russians had made their final decisions on 4th November. According to the Notes to the War Diary of the Wehrmacht Operational Staff, entry of 7th November, their agents had reported that on 4th November "a meeting of the 'Crown Council', at which all the C-in-C's were present, had resolved that a great offensive should take place before the end of the year on the Don front or the Central front."[1] Reading this entry we cannot but wonder at the ambiguity of the German agents' report, compared with the precision work of the Red Three. But the date of the 'Crown Council' meeting was probably right.

In view of these dates it seems obvious that the Red Three's work on this occasion had no influence on Russian strategy, and it might even be questioned whether any tactical importance should be attributed to it. However, it would be wrong to minimize it: the 'Director' would hardly have troubled to send the signal if he had not attached considerable weight to the answer; all the more so since the Germans might have been able to decode it and learn from it as much about the Russian attack as he could hope to learn about the German defence. With this thought in mind we might well conclude that the reply signal enabled the Russians to judge whether and where adjustments were required, and that they did in fact make them where necessary.

At the conclusion of the Stalingrad battle the Russians started their winter offensive in the south. On the 16th February, 1943, they captured Kharkov. As an immediate consequence the tenability of the German Donets front was threatened. On 21st February, the German Army Group South therefore started its counter-attack, and on the 15th March it recaptured Kharkov and advanced towards Bielgorod. On 17th March, the Red Three sent the following signal to Moscow:

"Objective of German pincer attack north of Kharkov is recapture of Bielgorod. In order to retain Kharkov, Germans must conquer positions east of the city previously held by them before summer offensive. Transfer of several divisions of 3rd Panzer Army to south is based on assumption that Army Group Kluge (Centre) is not drawn into heavy Panzer battles, at least not during the next fifteen or twenty days, and that no critical situation arises

[1] Cf. Helmuth Greiner, *Die Oberste Wehrmachtsfuehrung, 1939–43*, Wiesbaden, 1951, p. 417.

for Army Group's left wing, which is being withdrawn to the upper Dvina river and the Smolensk area. Wehrmacht High Command is hopeful, since withdrawal of 9th Army has so far succeeded fairly well and there has been sufficient time for large-scale destruction of railways and billets in evacuated area. . . . Decision very risky on account of Russian Army advancing in Vyazma sector and deployed near Velikie Luki, and particularly because of still existing danger of a Russian break-through in the Bryansk and Konotop sector, which would cut whole Eastern front to pieces."[1]

In this signal the Red Three not only explain the German intentions, but they also pin-point the risks taken at the expense of Army Group Centre and invite a Russian attack on it, which would result in the collapse of the entire German front. The Russians, perhaps on account of the spring thaw, did not avail themselves of this suggestion, and the front remained static until the beginning of July.

On 20th April, 1943, the Red Three procured the following information for Moscow's benefit:

"Present date-line for German attack on Eastern Front is 14th June. Only limited operations are planned."[2]

The German attack was first planned for the first week of May, it was then postponed—as the signal points out—to June, and finally started in July.

This time, as *A Military History of World War II* emphasizes, the Russians were not taken by surprise, as they had been with previous German offensives; they were, in fact, well informed of the German plans.[3] Indeed, according to Mr. Flicke, the Red Three had notified Moscow that the Germans would stage a double attack with limited objectives north of Bielgorod and north of Maloarchangelsk; Moscow also knew how many Panzer Divisions, Motorized and Infantry Divisions would take part in the attack.[4] The Russian defence system was indeed extraordinary. The defence zone extended to a depth of more than sixty miles on the Kursk salient, and it contained everything to stop an attacker, from pre-

[1] W. F. Flicke, op. cit., p. 277–8.
[2] W. F. Flicke, op. cit., p. 280.
[3] Op. cit., p. 235.
[4] Op. cit., p. 298.

pared positions to a system of fortifications. The zone actually held by the troops was several tens of miles deep, and when the Panzers attacked, they found ten and fifteen prepared defence lines, one behind the other, and had still not broken through.[1] On about the 8th July the German offensive had been halted; on the 17th the Russians started their counter-offensive and speedily advanced. On 22nd July the Red Three reported the German losses to Moscow.[2]

Again, was it all the work of the Red Three? Once more it appears at first sight that it was due to their information that the Red Army took the appropriate action at the right place. And yet, there is more to it than that.

In the first place, there was nothing surprising in the fact that Hitler would attack; he had always done so before, and after the débâcle of Stalingrad it was particularly necessary for him to regain the initiative. Nor was it a secret that in view of his depleted forces he could hardly attack on more than one sector; everywhere else he had to try to hold the front line. Next, it was not particularly difficult to pick the sector he had chosen for his offensive: the Soviet salient in the Kursk region invited an attack. Hitler's strategy suited the Soviets down to the ground; their victories so far had been won in counter-offensives, once again Hitler's move would give them their cue, and nothing was more natural than that they would try to stop Hitler's attack from doing them serious damage. It was therefore clear that they would make their defence positions as strong as possible. But this was not all:

"Unlike the operations in 1941 and 1942, those of 1943 started with a complete absence of any element of surprise. On 1st July, 1943, both sides knew perfectly well the imminence of the battle and they knew precisely what the adversary intended and just where and how he had planned his moves. For two or three months both sides had been observing large concentrations both inside and outside the Kursk salient. While the Russians were taking up their positions around the Orel 'bastion' and were deploying in a semi-circle around Kursk, the German divisions

---

[1] General Augustin Guillaume, *Soviet Arms and Soviet Power*, Washington, 1949, p. 134, and W. F. Flicke, op. cit., p. 299.
[2] W. F. Flicke, op. cit., p. 299.

were constantly arriving in the Bryansk-Orel and the Bielgorod regions."[1]

What was obvious, then, became more obvious still when Hitler, as we have seen, twice postponed the attack and thus gave the Russians ample time to make their defence positions strong and deep.

In view of all this the Red Three's signals were simply a confirmation of what the Russians must have known anyway. In addition, the signals may have informed them more exactly of the number and type of German divisions to be employed in the attack—about seventeen Panzer Divisions, a few Motorized Divisions and fourteen or sixteen Infantry Divisions—but even so, this intelligence could not have had much influence on the result.

Not long after this the 'Director' was deprived of the services of the Red Three because the Swiss Federal Police were on their trail, and our survey of the campaign concludes here. Looking back over the work of the Red Three, it appears that they made their most valuable contribution before and during the battle for Stalingrad. If, as we are inclined to assume, this intelligence helped the Red Army to deploy its reinforcements in the required strength at the appropriate place, their work was not without influence on the course of the campaign.

However, it is not yet possible to come to any definite conclusion. As we have pointed out, the available evidence is limited, and even what is still extant but unavailable might not reveal the complete story. Much of the material originally in German hands got lost, some of it was burnt by the Germans to prevent it from falling into Russian hands, and a lot of it defied decoding by the Germans.

Still, however the full story might read, it should not give rise to a new German stab-in-the-back legend. The Germans did not lose the war against Russia because they were betrayed by those working for the Red Orchestra, but because their leadership committed gross strategic errors. These errors have been listed so often that no recapitulation is necessary.

As it was, the work of the Red spy rings may have speeded Germany on her way to disaster, but they did not bring it about.

So much for the German side. As far as the Soviets are con-

[1] Paul Muratoff, *The Third Russian Summer-Autumn Campaign, July–November, 1943*, in *Message*, Belgian Review, January 1944, p. 7.

cerned, there remains the intriguing question of how far their sometimes cunning anticipation of an enemy blow and their skill in attacking his weakest points were due not so much to intuitive generalship than to information received. We shall probably never know the answer.

One conclusion, though, can safely be drawn. In October 1941, Russia was almost down for the count. If the Soviets, warned as they were of the coming German attack and notified of the German Order of Battle, had taken the appropriate action, the campaign would have taken a very much more favourable course for them, and the credit for this would have been due to the Red Orchestra.

Espionage by infiltration may well decide the outcome of a future war.

We can neglect this lesson only at our peril.

Chapter IV

MORE ABOUT INTELLIGENCE: PARTISANS ON RECONNAISSANCE MISSIONS

PARTISAN warfare has been known for almost as long as war itself. Guerillas made their first appearance over 2,300 years ago in China. In more recent times partisans fought in the American War of Independence, the Peninsular War, the American Civil War, the South African War, in World War I with Lawrence, and then in Russia and Ireland. Before World War II guerillas operated under Mao Tse-tung, first against Chiang Kai-shek and subsequently against the Japanese. In World War II partisans fought in many theatres of war: China, Malaya, the Philippines, Indo-China, Timor, Burma, Russia, Poland, Greece, Yugoslavia, France, Italy, Albania and Abyssinia. More recently still they have been active in Malaya, Indo-China, Korea and Kenya.

The operational techniques of partisan warfare have undergone many changes in the course of time, but much that is old is just as applicable today as it was in the past. Today, as then, irregular warfare is frequently the means by which a weaker force can hope to overcome an opponent superior in strength and equipment. But where guerillas fight in support of a regular army, their warfare is hardly any longer 'irregular'. Like regular soldiers, they are commanded by a person responsible for his subordinates, as the Hague Convention puts it, like soldiers they are assigned their missions by, or at least in agreement with, the military, and their discipline is modelled on army lines. The difference lies in their tactical tasks and their theatre of operations: they fight *behind* the enemy's lines.

The partisans 'on the other side of the hill' are therefore the ideal intelligence corps for their master. It seems almost a platitude to say so. Yet they were first deployed for this purpose on a large scale only during the last war, in Russia. We then knew too little about Soviet partisan warfare to take any notice of this novel assignment. Today we realize that it heralded the most fundamental development in partisan warfare in all its long history. The credit for it goes to Stalin.

In 1942 the Soviets issued a *Handbook for Partisans*, which contains a lot of useful information: on how to cross the front line, how to camp, on the destruction of enemy installations, ambushes, attacks on a village, withdrawal from the enemy, how the Fascists try to fight the partisans, on mining, arms, use of enemy weapons, and camouflage. Much of the information is very detailed: there are separate chapters on the destruction of enemy staffs, dumps, columns, transports, individual soldiers, tanks, armoured reconnaissance vehicles, railway tracks, telephone and telegraph wires, and on the mining of high roads. The partisan is told how to step on grass, on soft and hard ground without leaving footprints or being heard, which trees to pick for hiding, how to hide best, and so on. Our particular interest, however, is in the outline the Handbook gives of the partisans' reconnaissance tasks:

"Remember: A partisan reconnoitres not only for his detachment, but *also for the troops of the Red Army*. Help the Red Army to gain information about the enemy and to discover the enemy forces, their positions, minefields, weapons, rear dumps, and so on. Inform also on enemy intentions, his preparations for action, troop transports and so on. Always endeavour to obtain information as precise and concrete as possible.

"Every partisan who is deployed in the enemy's rear is on reconnaissance duty at all times and everywhere. . . .

"Partisans must not be satisfied with carrying out merely military reconnaissance—through observation or in combat. For this reason tested comrades, Soviet patriots from the local population, must also be used to a large extent. Do not be afraid to go on reconnaissance yourself even into enemy occupied villages. Dress for this purpose like a local inhabitant and imitate his manners.

"It is useful to make a prisoner: you can get from him the necessary information. Try to hand over the prisoner to the military.

"Reconnaissance tasks are:

—Information about the enemy: location, number, intentions, staff, petrol dumps, supply stores, officers' billets;

—Territory: covered approaches, condition of roads and bridges, most appropriate weapons;

—Population: morale, attitude towards the enemy, detection of reliable agents.

"Learn to recognize the enemy!

"A partisan on reconnaissance must know the most important

indications from which the presence of the enemy, his auxiliary forces and so on can be deduced.

"A locality is enemy-occupied if trenches have been dug, wire obstacles erected and telephone and telegraph lines installed in its vicinity. Increased traffic, the barking of dogs and so on indicate that the locality is enemy-occupied. But one must be suspicious if the village is absolutely quiet and nobody is about: there may be an enemy ambush."

The Partisan Handbook, it will be remembered, was issued to the partisans in 1942, when the Soviets had as yet had little experience in organizing partisan intelligence. The Handbook is silent on how to transmit the intelligence gathered to the Red Army. Yet it is quite obvious that even the best information in the hands of the partisans is of little use to the Army unless it can be speedily passed on to them. And, conversely, Army Intelligence cannot benefit much from the presence of a partisan detachment on the opposite side of the enemy lines unless it can be quickly contacted. By 1943 this problem was solved: every partisan detachment had been supplied with a radio set for receiving and transmitting intelligence. Every partisan detachment was by then in regular contact with the military staffs in their zone of operations, while larger detachments maintained in addition direct communication with the General Staff of the Red Army.[1]

Furthermore, a number of detachments had in the meanwhile built their own landing strips for aircraft and organized an air-lift system.

The resulting fundamental changes in the technique of transmitting intelligence find their expression in the Field Service Regulations of the Red Army, issued in 1944. According to these regulations:

"The partisan detachments establish and maintain continuous liaison (signal communications):
—between the small units of the detachment;
—between the adjacent detachments;
—with the staff of the Partisan movement;
—*with the military staffs in the zone in which they operate.*
"For the establishment of signal communications, use is made

---

[1] Cf. A. Fedorov, *L'Obkom clandestin au travail*, Paris, 1951, vol. ii, p. 320.

of all available means: foot messengers, carrier pigeons, dogs, *radio, aeroplanes*.

"The reports are transmitted in cipher."[1]

In other ways too the Field Service Regulations represent an advance over the Partisan Handbook. Based on the experience gained with partisan intelligence, they considerably widen the field of action. The partisans no longer gather some haphazard information about the enemy, the territory, and the population; they are now set tasks as precise as those assigned to any regular Intelligence unit:

"Co-operation of partisan detachments with units of the Red Army includes:
—observation and reconnaissance of the numerical strength of the enemy forces, dispositions of his defensive installations and mine fields;
—target designation to combat aviation and long-range artillery; . . .
—reporting to the command of the units of the Red Army concerning the results of bombardment of important objectives (bridges, aerodromes, stations, depots, railway junctions) by our aviation; concerning routes inaccessible or dangerous for tanks; places suitable for landing aircraft and for dropping landing parties."

However, the instructions of the Field Service Regulations on partisan reconnaissance are even more specific than that; in fact it seems almost impossible to name a single aspect of intelligence work which is not enumerated in its lengthy catalogue. The disposition and movement of troops and supplies must be reported, as well as numerical strength, type of weapons, time and direction of movement, strength of security troops, numbering of enemy agencies; on aerodromes the position, number and types of aircraft has to be ascertained, the aerodrome equipment, fuel supplies, guarding arrangement and so on; in towns the numerical strength of the troops, branch by branch of the services, the anti-aircraft defences, depots and military workshops have to be reconnoitred; the defence lines, the signal communication system and

---

[1] The Chapter 'Partisan Operations' of the Field Service Regulations is reprinted in full in the Appendix to this book.

the damage inflicted by air attack has to be determined; and orders, reports, operational maps and other enemy documents have to be captured.

The Partisan Manual comes in handy as a help to the partisan in the fulfillment of his variegated tasks, and a supplementary Guide Book for Partisans provides useful additional instructions:

"A partisan may receive the order to find out where an enemy staff, aerodrome, or depot is located. . . . You may receive the order to observe enemy troop movements in order to ascertain the units (branch of service, number, designation), how strong they are and from where and to where they are moved.

"If you happen to encounter troops on this mission, do not stop and do not show that you observe the enemy. Appear entirely uninterested, turn off the road after having tried to ascertain the colour of their headgear, their collar braid, and the figures on their shoulder straps, and after having estimated the strength of the column. If the enemy troops, when passing through a village, have questioned the inhabitants about something, try to find out what the Fascists have asked, what they wanted to know, and where they went to."

How does a partisan recognize a staff headquarters?

"The enemy staff is as a rule billeted in individual houses. . . . Indications for the presence of a staff are:
(i) A dense net of telephone and telegraph wires, among them many coloured wires and wires thickly insulated;
(ii) The presence in the district of numerous enemy officers;
(iii) On the outskirts, radio stations, information collecting centres, and special staff cars. . . .
"Continuous traffic of runners, motor-cyclists and cars indicates an information collecting centre nearby. Look in this area also for the enemy staff."

Then the partisan is told how to ascertain the enemy's intentions. If an attack is planned, new troops will arrive, the roads and connections with the rivers are hastily repaired, troop transports increase, and the trucks return empty to the rear area. But if the enemy intends to withdraw, the local population knows best; fuel and foodstuffs are transported to the rear, roads and river crossings are demolished, telephone wires are removed, trains and trucks arrive empty and depart full.

For obtaining information, the partisan movement relied not only on the full-timers with the detachments, but also on its numerous part-timers, the agents. Each detachment had its agents. They frequently worked in their normal civilian occupation, as railway personnel, hospital staff and so on. Others took on jobs with the Germans as interpreters, voluntary helpers and servants. Even children were in many cases recruited as agents. Frequently the agents were able to give the partisans most valuable information about troop movements and enemy intentions.[1] Sometimes the Germans found out an agent; more frequently, though, they did not. Communists managed to infiltrate even the dreaded Gestapo.[2]

One typical incident illustrates the activities of these agents. It is taken from a report by the Chief of the German Security Police and Security Service and therefore free from partisan embellishments. Some Russians were employed with the German Commissioner General's Office in Minsk. They informed the partisans that in the Wehrmacht's map room a city plan of Minsk had been drawn which showed all Wehrmacht units stationed in Minsk and all the offices of the civil administration and the police. In addition all undertakings were shown on the map, with special markings indicating whether they worked for the civil administration or the Wehrmacht. The leader of the partisan detachment thereupon instructed an agent who was employed with the Commissioner General to steal the map, a simple assignment, since it was openly displayed in one of the offices. The agent carried out his mission and handed over the plan to the partisan leader, who in turn gave it to a group of parachutists. They evaluated the map and transmitted their findings by radio to Moscow.

To quote from another of these reports, the Security Police managed to capture a short-wave transmitter. It was not a big catch, to be sure, since it had already been destroyed by the operator before the German police arrived. Yet in the opinion of the Divisional HQ this transmitter had directed the Soviet artillery fire on the city. It seems to have been pretty effective, or HQ would not have noticed that partisans in the city had been engaged

[1] Cf. Dixon and Heilbrunn, *Communist Guerilla Warfare*, op. cit., p. 71.
[2] Cf. Oleg Anisimov, *The German Occupation in Northern Russia during World War II: Political and Administrative Aspects*. Research Program on the U.S.S.R., New York City, 1954, p. 20. Mimeographed Series No. 56.

in target designation. But then the partisans did not have much trouble in securing the maps required for their purposes.

The over-all results? Never before in war were so many scouts so densely spread over so wide an area of occupation as during the German campaign in Russia. "It has been found that the enemy is incredibly well informed of troop movements," says a German Corps report of the 5th March, 1942.[1] And, as Mr. Anisimov relates, the Chief of the Russian Section of the German Security Service 'Ostland' stated that the Soviet partisans learned of nearly every German troop movement early enough to plan an attack and set up an ambush.[2]

We need hardly look any further for evidence of the efficiency of Soviet partisan Intelligence. But the lesson would be entirely lost if we were to regard the partisan achievements in this field merely as an interesting contribution to the victory of the Red Army over the Wehrmacht. "There is no doubt that in any future war the threat of Communist guerillas will be even greater than it was in World War II. At that time, after all, the Soviets had neither fellow Communists nor 'partisans of peace' in Germany."[3] "And, in any war against Russia, we must remember that the 'partisans of peace', tools of international Communism, are present in every Western nation. As guerillas, they will be active in the rear areas of the armies of the West and in the homeland, intent on their missions of espionage, sabotage and treason."[4] "The 'guerilla', in the shape of native Communists and agents, is already at his post."[5] "In our own and our allies' territories there will be sabotage, disorders, perhaps even civil war. In the battle zone itself—if the enemy can arrange it—there will be organized guerilla warfare conducted by his partisans."[6]

"If the enemy can arrange it."

In our planning we must assume that he can.

---

[1] Dixon and Heilbrunn, op. cit., p. 93.
[2] Oleg Anisimov, op. cit., p. 20.
[3] Mikhail Koriakov, in *The New York Times Book Review*, 5th December, 1954.
[4] Colonel H. M. Forde in *The Army Combat Forces Journal*, October, 1954.
[5] *Glasgow Herald*, 25th March, 1954.
[6] Lt.-General H. G. Martin, *Daily Telegraph*, 9th April, 1954.

Chapter V

A BLUEPRINT FOR SUBVERSION: THE FALL OF FRANCE, 1940

IN April 1940, just before *la drôle de guerre* turned into a Blitzkrieg, the Labour Publications Department in London issued a letter written by M. Paul Faure, Secretary of the French Socialist Party, to the British Labour Party.

"It is said," the letter reads, "that France is a semi-Fascist country, where all liberties have been abolished, where parliamentary government no longer exists, where the Trade Unions have been suppressed and their leaders imprisoned. . . .
"Need I tell you that we are somewhat surprised and disconcerted by such allegations, which in no way correspond to the truth. . . .
"The cause . . . is to be found, without any doubt, in the measures taken against the Communists. Measures, I do not deny, which are severe. . . ."

At the end of August, 1939, the publication of the Communist newspapers in France had been prohibited, by the decree of 26th September, 1939, the French Communist Party had been dissolved, and many of its leaders were subsequently arrested.

"But," the letter goes on, "how can (these measures) not be considered legitimate? It is, in fact, necessary to understand the magnitude of the danger which the Communists represent to us in France. . . . It had simply to be decided whether a Party, under the orders and in the pay of a foreign Power, could, in time of war, take part, discuss, vote, legislate in a French Assembly, and whether it could be informed, in the parliamentary commissions or secret committees of the Chamber and the Senate, of the military and diplomatic situation of the country and given all the secret intelligence concerning national defence. . . .
"An abominable underground leaflet campaign is being carried on (by the Communists) which describes the present war as having

been desired solely by British capitalism. The Communists thus seek to turn French public opinion against Britain, *to demoralize the mass of the people and the army* in order to provoke moral disintegration and prepare the atmosphere for disorders. After that, no doubt, Hitler and Stalin will have the mission of restoring order.

"That is the situation. . . ."[1]

The sender would not have written, and the addressee would not have published, this letter if the 'situation' had then been known or understood outside France. It would be an exaggeration to suggest that it has in the meanwhile become better known. At the time, the evidence concerning the French Communists' part in the defeat of France was meagre; later, when Russia entered the war on Britain's side, such incidents were not talked about; by the time the uneasy alliance came to an end they had been forgotten. Yet we ought to know and remember them; they are as topical today as they were then. The French case is the leading precedent for Communist subversion in action. The West must be in no doubt as to what it must guard against.

It has always been held by Communists, from the founding father on, that the inherent contradictions of capitalism must lead to war between one capitalist state and another. In such an imperialist war Lenin, as he proclaimed in 1918, considered it his duty, as a representative of the revolutionary proletariat, to prepare for the world proletarian revolution as the only escape from the horrors of war. Only a poor, stupid, nationalist philistine would argue from the point of view of 'my' country; one must argue instead from the point of view of one's share in preparing, propagating, and accelerating the world proletarian revolution.[2]

The necessary tactics for the U.S.S.R. were outlined by Stalin in 1925:

"If war breaks out we shall not be able to sit with folded arms. We shall have to take action, but *we shall be the last to do so*. And we shall do so in order to throw the decisive weight in the scales, the weight that *can turn the scales*."[3]

---

[1] *Communist Activity in France*, Leaflet No. 2 (4/40). The italics are ours.
[2] Lenin, *Collected Works* (1918–19), New York, 1945, vol. xxiii, p. 400.
[3] Speech delivered at the Plenum of the Central Committee of the R.C.P., 19th January, 1925, *Works*, Moscow, 1954, vol. vii, p. 14.

These tactics were specifically endorsed by the Communists for World War II. In 1939 the head of the Comintern circulated the following statement to the Communist Parties abroad:

"The Soviet Government and the Comintern have ... decided that it is best to hold aloof from the conflict, while remaining ready to intervene when the powers engaged therein are weakened by war, in the hope of securing a social revolution."[1]

When Stalin concluded his non-aggression pact with Hitler on 23rd August, 1939, he gave Germany the green light for the start of an imperialist war. Hitler, on the other hand, regarded the agreement as a means to isolate Poland and localize the war. Stalin thought he knew better and proved right. But he too made a fatal mistake: it was not left to him to determine the appropriate moment for unfolding his arms and liberating the oppressed peoples of Europe; Hitler turned on him first. But if Stalin had read *Mein Kampf* and if Hitler had perused Stalin's *Works*, neither of them could have been under any illusion about the sincerity of his treaty partner. It was simply a question of whom it would suit first to break the pact.

Here Stalin was under a severe handicap. He had to make the pact last until the combatants had exhausted themselves, and for this reason the Communists in Moscow had to play ball for the time being; and so did the Communists in France, after the new policy under the non-aggression pact had been explained to them. This explanation was indeed very necessary. The French Communists, not yet grasping the significance of the August 1939 pact, had actually voted in the Chamber on 2nd September for the armed forces budget, while labouring under the delusion that they were supposed to contribute to the defeat of the architect of the anti-comintern pacts.

Molotov hastened to correct such errors. On 1st September, 1939, he declared that

"Russia and Germany were the countries that suffered most in the war 1914–18. Therefore the interests of the peoples of the Soviet Union and Germany do not lie in mutual enmity. On the

---

[1] Cf. *A Military History of World War II*, vol. i, p. 142, quoted by permission of the Department of Military Art and Engineering, United States Military Academy, West Point.

A BLUEPRINT FOR SUBVERSION

contrary, the peoples of the Soviet Union and Germany need to live in peace with each other."[1]

Peace ought not only to prevail between Germany and Russia, but all nations should leave Hitler's Germany in peace, Molotov demanded two months later, after Russia and Germany had carved up Poland.

"As with any other ideological system, one may accept or reject the ideology of Hitlerism—that is a matter of political views. But everyone will understand that an ideology cannot be destroyed by force, that it cannot be eliminated by war. It is therefore not only senseless, but criminal, to wage such a war—a war for the destruction of Hitlerism."[2]

Criminal indeed. Why, Molotov continued,

"today, Germany is in the position of a state which is striving for the earliest termination of the war and for peace, whereas Britain and France, who but yesterday were declaiming against aggression, are in favour of continuing the war and are opposed to the conclusion of peace."

This was the sort of stuff to give out in order to make the *pact* last. But the Soviets had also to make the *war* last, until they could throw in "the weight that can turn the scales". The German General Staff did not favour an attack on France; they considered the Maginot Line a serious obstacle, they were convinced of the high fighting qualities of the French Army, and they could not forget their defeat in the First World War. Moreover, some German front-line commanders had gained the impression during the Polish campaign that the performance of their soldiers had been greatly inferior to that given by their fathers twenty-five years before. A former Chief of Staff, Colonel-General Beck,

---

[1]Molotov's Speech before the 4th Session of the Supreme Soviet of the U.S.S.R. (31st August, 1939), *Pravda*, 1st September, 1939, quoted from *Soviet World Outlook, A Handbook of Communist Statements*, prepared by the Division of Research for U.S.S.R. and Eastern Europe, Office of Intelligence Research, Department of State, for the Coordinator of Psychological Intelligence, U.S. Information Agency, 1954, p. 350, and subsequently referred to here as *U.S. Handbook*.
[2]Molotov, *Foreign Policy of Soviet Union*, Speech made at the 5th Session of the Supreme Soviet, *Pravda*, 1st November, 1939, quoted from *U.S. Handbook*, p. 349 and 350.

considered another German defeat in France as a certainty.

The Russians may or may not have shared these views. But they obviously came to the conclusion that in order to keep the scales balanced some weight had to be thrown into Hitler's scale. With this object in mind they concluded several trade agreements with Hitler for the delivery of strategic materials and foodstuffs, and set out to demoralize the French people and Army.

All that was required was a call to action by the Secretary General of the Comintern. In October 1939 Dimitroff discharged this task in an article printed in the clandestine *Cahiers du Bolchevisme* of the French Communist Party in their edition for the second half of 1939, dated January 1940.[1] World War II, Dimitroff explains, is an imperialist war. The pre-war policy of the Anglo-French imperialists was designed to push Germany into a war against the U.S.S.R., but Germany, conscious of the economic and military might and the moral unity of the U.S.S.R., failed to oblige. Germany's leaders realized that they could not win over the majority of their people for a war against the great country of Socialism. Germany, having to choose between complying with the wishes of the Anglo-French imperialists and putting her relations with the U.S.S.R. on a peaceful basis, decided in favour of the latter course. After the Anglo-French bourgeoisie had failed to embroil Germany and Russia in war, it decided to fight its foremost imperialist rival. As it is, the English and French imperialists have become the outstanding protagonists for the continuation of the war. In the circumstances the working class must fight against the imperialist war, fight in its own country against those responsible for the war, fight against its bourgeoisie.

Thus the stage was set for the Communist conspiracy in France.

"The enemy is within": Lenin's and Liebknecht's clarion call becomes the leitmotif for the French Communists' actions. The big French capitalists, the treacherous French politicians, the financiers in France, the French reactionaries, the French bourgeoisie, they are the enemies of the French working class against whom the fight has to be directed.

Not that the enemy within was the sole enemy; there were others outside. In the first place, of course, the British. The Communist Party proclamation of October, 1939, singles out the British ban-

[1] The full text of Dimitroff's article as well as the complete January, 1940, issue of the *Cahiers* is reprinted in *Les Cahiers du Bolchevisme pendant la campagne, 1939-40*, with a foreword by A. Rossi, published by Dominique Wapler, Paris, 1951. This article is also contained in G. Dimitroff, *Communism and the War*, London, 1939, pp. 3 f.

kers, who imposed the war on France and were making the French people meet the bill. Thorez, from his hiding place somewhere in France, accuses the British imperialists of always having prevented the French from gaining any advantage from their 1918 victory and always having helped Germany at France's expense.[1] Imperialist Britain, he continues, never shares equally in the sacrifices but always claims for herself the biggest share of the profits.

The U.S.A. does not fare much better. That hers is the principal responsibility for Japan's war against China and that she, for selfish reasons, encourages the extension of the present war, is Dimitroff's considered opinion in the article mentioned earlier.

But the Third Reich also figures among the external enemies. According to the Party proclamation the Communists hate Hitler and his régime, but the German workers, the Communist brethren in Germany, will take care of all that and liberate their country. The French workers, the proclamation states, have to fight against the Fascists and their like in France itself.

This proclamation is contained in the *Cahiers du Bolchevisme*, and Mr. Rossi, in his valuable Foreword to the above quoted edition, adduces weighty reasons for the assumption that they were actually printed in Germany.[2] It seems strange at first sight to suppose that Nazi Germany would lend a hand in publishing the proclamation and thus promote, as it were, the Communists' envisaged liberation of Germany from Hitlerism. But then it will be remembered that there was in Nazi Germany no Communist Party to carry out the liberation; Germany was safe from any Communist revolt, as the French Communist leaders knew full well. In fact they and the Nazis joyfully collaborated in a gigantic hoax. A French Communist who wanted to fight Hitlerism would have to support his own people and Army. This was the last thing his leaders and the Nazis wanted him to do. He was therefore told that the German fellow-workers were fighting against Hitlerism—*their* enemy within—and that his own task was solely to fight against *his* enemy within. To this end he had to promote the moral disintegration of France, and to achieve this Nazis and Communist wire-pullers could well unite.

Lenin had long since stated that agitation and propaganda must be carried out precisely in those institutions, societies and associations to which the proletarian or semi-proletarian masses

---

[1] For the full texts cf. *Les Cahiers du Bolchevisme*, loc. cit., pp. 41 and 42.
[2] Loc. cit., pp. ix, xxxiv-viii.

belong. Thorez took the cue: Party members would fight wherever the masses were and wherever they could be influenced and organized. The Communists were therefore allotted their assignments, among the soldiers, the workers, the peasants, the refugees and the soldiers' wives.

In order to accomplish their clandestine tasks, the Communists needed a clandestine organization. With their Party dissolved, most of their members of Parliament arrested or in hiding, and expelled from the Trade Unions and local government, they were faced with a difficult situation; all the more so because the Kremlin's change of front came as a complete surprise to them, and they had not prepared against the day when they would suddenly be driven underground. In the circumstances they managed surprisingly well. The first instructions issued by the Party Centre in December 1939 under the title *Notre lutte contre la guerre*, emphasize the need for cadres imbued with the will to take the initiative and make decisions. The instructions then go on to outline the general plan:

"Organization has become one of the crucial problems of the Party. Without a solid organization which extends to all industries, to all central points, it is impossible to achieve our task. There will therefore be established:

(1) Regional Centres.
(2) Local Centres.
(3) Centres in industries.

There are all over the country many Communists who were dispersed by the call-up or the suppressive measures. No doubt everyone works as best he can. But the necessary regrouping and reorganizing are tasks which have to be tackled without delay. Only thus will it be possible to give effect to the Party's policy. Decentralization to the utmost in order to increase initiative and facilitate the tasks of the regional and local Centres. Special attention must be paid to organization in the big industries and to facilities allowing them to edit and distribute Party literature. Do not neglect the villages, since in view of the soldiers' connexions with the villages the contact with the peasants is of great importance. . . . All security measures must be taken within the organization in respect to clandestine work: skilful directives to escape suppression. Organize the Communists in groups of three or four."[1]

This, then, was the Communists' skeleton organization which, in the words of M. Paul Faure, carried on the "abominable leaflet campaign", with the aim of demoralizing the mass of the people and the Army. Party literature was in fact the predominant weapon of their subversive campaign, and as far as it was possible they preferred to use printed rather than mimeographed copies; the printed texts, the instructions pointed out, could be more explicit and therefore provided the best means for keeping in touch with Communists all over the country and for making known everywhere the Party's stand in its fight against the imperialist war.[2]

L'Humanité, which appeared less than sixty times from the beginning of the war to the end of June 1940 usually dealt with practical questions of the day, while *Les Cahiers*, which came out once during this time in a sixty-four page edition, was devoted more to the doctrine of Communism. In addition there were also regional and local papers. Pamphlets came mainly from the Paris region.[3]

While these publications catered for all alike, others addressed themselves to particular groups, for example, *La Voix des Usines*, the appeals to the *Paysans de France*, and particularly the papers addressed to soldiers and sailors, *Le Trait D'Union*, *L'Humanité du Soldat*, *Ceux de la 31ème* (Le Harve), *L'Etoile Rouge* (Metz), *Cherbourg Naval*, and others.

The general technique applied in these publications was to sow the seeds of disunity and exploit grievances: the capitalists make big fortunes out of the war while the workers are exploited and the soldiers have to shed their blood. This is not a war in defence of democracy and against Fascism, it is an imperialist struggle for the possession of colonies and raw materials. In this war France is degraded to a British dominion; but the British do not share the burden with the French. The working class must bring this war to an end. "Fight against the imperialist war, fight

---

[1] Cf. for the above A. Rossi's fundamental treatise *Les Communistes Français pendant la drôle de guerre*, Les Iles d'Or, Paris, 1951, pp. 94–110, where the above instructions, translated here by permission of the publishers, are also to be found.
[2] For the above cf. A. Rossi, op. cit., p. 100.
[3] Cf. A. Rossi, op. cit., pp. 101 and 171. A number of photostatic copies of Party literature are also to be found in Rossi's work.

for immediate peace!" Only Thorez is able to conclude a just and lasting peace, and he must therefore take over the Government. Long live the Communist International and its French Party.[1]

The then Minister for Internal Affairs, M. Albert Sarraut, reported to the French Chamber on 19th March, 1940, on the counter-measures taken by the French Government and stated that:

"Two thousand seven hundred and seventy-eight elected Communists, city or district councillors, had been deprived of their seats.

"Four hundred and forty-three officials belonging to the Communist Party had been subjected to special measures.

"Six hundred and twenty-nine Trade Unions had been dissolved.

"Six hundred and seventy-five Communist political groups had been disbanded.

"Three thousand four hundred militant Communists had been arrested.

"Eight thousand individual sentences had been passed on Communists."

Furthermore a decree had been passed making the preparation, stocking or supplying of instruments of Communist propaganda a crime punishable by death, and *L'Humanité* and *Ce Soir*, with a combined circulation of 750,000 copies, had been suppressed.

But if these measures had only a limited success, the Government was quite powerless against Communist radio propaganda from abroad. The *Bulletin hebdomadaire du Commissariat de l'Information*, No. 19, of 24th February, 1940, asserted that the stations of *Radio Humanité* and *La Voix de la Paix* were transmitting Communist proclamations in French and that they were located in the Black Forest, Zeesen and Warren in Germany.[2] M. Sarraut, in his report to the French Chamber, was more guarded. He stressed that one could not distinguish between Communist and Hitlerite

[1] Cf. For the texts of these publications A. Rossi, *Les Communistes Français* etc., Planches xxvii, xxviii, xxix-xxxiv and xxxvi, also Paul Reynaud, *La France a sauvé l'Europe*, Paris, 1947, vol. ii, pp. 48–51 for 1st May leaflet and vcl. i, p. 606 for a copy of L'Humanité du Soldat.

The Comintern Appeal of the 1st May, 1940, is reprinted in the Appendix to this book.

[2] Cf. A. Rossi, op. cit., p. 111, Note 25.

propaganda. "The head of this double propaganda is in Germany. German aircraft drop Communist leaflets, and the Communist radio transmitters are on German soil."[1]

The first of these 'double propaganda' broadcasts was monitored by the B.B.C. on 22nd December, 1939. Whether it emanated from Germany has not been definitely established. The announcers, all Frenchmen, declared that they were broadcasting from French soil and that the French radio detection service was trying to locate them; but they quoted too often from foreign newspapers not always obtainable in war-time France to make it sound a likely story. There were five broadcasts daily, starting at 1830 hours and ending at 2300 hours. Each lasted half an hour, of which fifteen minutes were devoted to a talk and fifteen minutes to very short commentaries and slogans, with records played in the intervals. Each broadcast was terminated by the Marseillaise. The network had three wave-lengths at its disposal. The dominant theme of these broadcasts was: "We want peace!"

Not all broadcasts were monitored, and there is a gap during the crucial period 6th May to 4th June, 1940, viz. during the Blitzkrieg. A number of broadcasts were completely or partially inaudible. But sufficient material is available to show the general line of this 'double propaganda'.

According to these broadcasts, the conflict was desired by the capitalists. Peace has never been much good to the capitalists (broadcast of 30th December, 1939), and financiers and bankers are quite content with this war (2nd March, 1940); but what about the simple man in the street? War leads to the enslavement of the working man under the direction of a clique of bourgeois (2nd January, 1940). Only misery and suffering will come to the people out of this war. Despite the mobilization of 5,000,000 Frenchmen the unemployment figure has not gone down. The workers now labour for ten hours or more a day. The mobilized have been thrown out of their jobs; when they return others will have taken their jobs from them (9th January, 1940). Prices rise all the time, many goods are unobtainable (23rd January, 1940), the family allowances are insufficient (9th January, 1940). Reynaud asks us to cut down our consumption. To whom does he speak? To the wives of soldiers at the front, to workmen and peasants who already have not enough to eat? Or to the band of rogues who made this war? Let them cut down their rations who

[1] Cf. Paul Reynaud, op. cit., vol. ii, p. 47.

exploit the people to their heart's content (25th January, 1940).

Our Army is incomparable? Yes, join the incomparable army and march to the slaughter-house under the guidance of its prudent leaders. Our armament is excellent? It is lacking everywhere and out of date (7th March, 1940). The *poilu* frequently has no winter boots, he never has warm underwear (8th February, 1940). Two U.S. newspaper correspondents had been visiting the French front: "Never will I forget this experience and I hope never to see it again, the terrible frost, the poor shivering soldiers in a half frozen condition," one is reported to have said. "How shall I describe to you the misery at the front in this severe winter? Soldiers standing to with their feet half frozen. . . ." was the other's alleged comment (22th February, 1940).

What are we fighting for? "Is it freedom when tens of thousands of Frenchmen are in goal because they have dared to speak in favour of peace? Is it freedom when law courts sentence young women, between sixteen and twenty-three years of age, to terms of imprisonment from three to five years for having voiced their preference for peace? France is governed by a full-blooded dictatorship. Daladier is as much a dictator as Mussolini, Hitler and Stalin, but they admit it while Daladier has the impudence to call himself a democrat." (8th March, 1940)[1]

"We are told that we are fighting to defend our country, our homes and our freedom. Has our country been invaded? Have our homes been attacked? Has our liberty been threatened? Daladier and his colleagues have long ago robbed us of it." (9th January, 1940). "Before we can know who will win the war, we shall have thousands of dead, injured, sick and orphans. All that awaits us is misery. . . . Victory would be a hundred times worse than any kind of peace possible today. . . . That is what would happen if we were victorious. But if you are beaten . . . nothing will remain of France. Whatever the outcome of the war it will be fatal for us." (2nd January, 1940).

"There is another French Army behind the Maginot Line fighting for peace. It will make the French people aware of the nation's true interests. It will spread its propaganda throughout the nation. It fights for peace for France. France was not attacked by Germany. We are all fighting for England." (23rd January, 1940). "Daladier's war has been started to put the workers under

[1] The reference to Hitler and Stalin as dictators, made even more derogatory by the inclusion of Daladier, strongly supports the 'double propaganda' thesis.

the domination of the capitalists, the bankers and the Lords of the City." (26th February, 1940). "England promised to guarantee Czechoslovakia. Where is Czechoslovakia now? England promised her support to Poland. Where is Poland now? What will happen next to France?" (2nd January, 1940). "The British Empire needs a divided Europe in order to subsist. Thus France, who is bearing the brunt of the war, will never receive the guarantees she needs." (15th April, 1940). "The lives of Frenchmen are threatened. We are the avengers of the French *poilus* who are being sacrificed for the English. We have taken up the cause of the French citizens, who are subjected to an unscrupulous capitalist dictatorship. We cry vengeance for the outraged conscience of the French nation, which earnestly desires peace." (7th April, 1940).

On the 10th June, 1940, when the campaign was near its end, the following appeal was broadcast:

"Men of Paris, the choice lies with us. Is Paris to be another Warsaw, or a Brussels? What is our reply to be? We must save Paris as Brussels was saved.

"Frenchmen, the choice is ours—another Warsaw with Reynaud, or another Brussels with the Government of the National Revolution?

"Frenchmen, the National Revolution calls for all your strength. The hour has arrived. Rally round the tricolour and support the National Revolution. Down with Reynaud. This is the French Revolutionary Station.

"Frenchmen, don't you remember how we checked the Boche not long ago, and even then the situation seemed very bad; but we can by no means believe that our enemy is contemptible (?) and held off by the famous Maginot Line. This time it will be much more brutal. Germany is a first-class military power and has at least 2,000 planes for every 1,000 Allied planes. This war has long been prepared by the Allies with fine words but no deeds. Now it is time to start. Reynaud, Mandel and Daladier are far more occupied with their own petty affairs than with the interests of France. That is why in this grave hour Paul Reynaud broadcasts a message calling for resistance to the Germans. Rally round the tricolour—start the Revolution—down with Reynaud! Mandel to the gallows! This is the French Revolutionary Station.

"Frenchmen, patriots of every nation (?) arise as one man and support the revolution. With Reynaud we are lost . . . (inaudible).

... Rothschild ... (inaudible.) Down with the ... and with the Jews. Long live the National Revolution! Mandel to the gallows! Down with Reynaud! Long live Peace!"

Whether this appeal can be ascribed to the Communists is more than questionable. The reference to the Jews might be the tribute paid by the Communists to their hosts, and several of the broadcasts mentioned above contain anti-Jewish remarks. What makes the source of this broadcast really doubtful is its call to revolution; the tricolour is not the banner of Communism, and, above all, there is no appeal for the support of Thorez. It appears that this manifesto ought to be credited to the Germans, who wanted to prevent the French Government from continuing the war in France's oversea possessions. Indeed it is likely that this broadcast emanated from the station which, on 19th June, 1940, urged the French people "to put up slogans in all parts not yet occupied by the Germans"; one of the slogans called for the support of Weygand.

It has never been possible for the monitoring services to ascribe a broadcast to Radio Humanité, or La Voix de la Paix, or a German propaganda station, since all broadcasts were in French, and any such detection work is, of course, entirely outside the B.B.C.'s province. But the other broadcasts referred to above are so completely in line with the Communists' printed propaganda that their designation by M. Sarraut and the Commissariat de l'Information as Communist transmissions seems amply justified.

But no less obvious than the points of conformity are those of divergence between broadcasts and literature. There is no reference in the broadcasts to the imperialist character of the war, no mention of the enemy within Germany, no call for Thorez to power, no appeal in support of Communism. But if we accept the official French view that the stations were located in Germany, the reason for these omissions at once becomes obvious: the Nazis were unwilling to allow references that would provide any Germans who listened to these programmes with an indoctrination course in Communism. No such infection, it should be noted, was to be feared from the Communist literature supposedly printed in Germany, because Germans would have no access to it.

The striking feature of the broadcasts as well as the literature is the constant demand for peace. This call for peace goes against all the rules in the Communist book. Communists are never supposed to put an end to an imperialist war; quite the contrary, their task is to turn it into a civil war of the proletariat against the bourgeoisie in order to gain power. The French Communists were well aware of this standing order. In 1935, M. Duclos, Thorez' second in command, had gone on record as saying:

"You know full well that we Communists have always declared that since the working class cannot prevent an imperialist war ... all our efforts must be directed towards transforming the imperialist war into a revolutionary civil war,"[1]

and Thorez himself had stated before the 7th World Congress of the Communist International, also in 1935, that

"there is only one proven method for taking power, the bolshevist method, the victorious insurrection of the proletariat."[2]

Yet the French Communists did not make any preparations for a "revolutionary civil war" in 1939 and 1940.

Indeed, the goal to which the Communists aspired was much more restricted. It was outlined in the Statement issued by the Executive Committee of the Communist International on the Twenty-second Anniversary of the Socialist Revolution, 6th November, 1939: "The working class cannot support such a war. ... The Communist International calls you to be true to the end to the cause of proletarian internationalism, to the cause of the fraternal alliance of the proletarians of all countries (Stalin) ...", and it concludes:

"Let your battle cry ring out to the whole world:
Down with the imperialist war!
Down with capitalist reaction! ...
No support for the policy of the ruling classes aimed at continuing and spreading the imperialist slaughter!
Fight for the immediate cessation of the plundering, unjust, imperialist war!
Peace to the peoples! ..."[3]

---
[1]Speech of 2nd December, 1935, quoted from Guy Danjou, *La révolution Communiste* Paris, 1939, p. 154.
[2]Cf. Guy Danjou, op. cit., p. 29.
[3]Reprinted in G. Dimitroff, *Communism and the War*, loc. cit., pp. 18 f.

The tenor of French Communist propaganda up to the end of the campaign could hardly be summed up any better. The Statement, in fact, limits the aims of Communist propaganda, and by its silence it deprecates revolutionary uprisings. It thus makes it clear that French Communist propaganda was meant to be comparatively feeble, by Communist standards.

But why was French Communist propaganda toned down?

In the French Communists' view immediate peace was only possible with Thorez in power; he could take power only by revolt; yet the Communists did not incite the masses to revolt. It is therefore quite obvious that the Communists wanted neither peace nor revolt. They did not want at this stage to weaken France too much and strengthen Germany correspondingly. Otherwise the scales of the belligerents would have become too unbalanced to allow Stalin, in his previously quoted words, to enter the war in its last stage and throw in the decisive weight, "the weight that can turn the scales".

It is for this reason—the need to keep the scales balanced—that the French Communists, who soon afterwards were so proficient in guerilla warfare, did nothing to organize it at this stage. It is for this reason that acts of sabotage in factories—in spite of the great number of Communist workers employed there—were comparatively rare.[1] Their subversive activities during the period under review had to strike a medium between too much and too little. They were therefore restricted to 'morale operations', and within these self-imposed limitations they were effective. One result of their nefarious work, however, was unexpected. There can be no doubt that Germany's surprising success in overcoming French resistance, which the French Communists had tried so hard to weaken, contributed to Hitler's decision to attack the U.S.S.R., the very last thing they—or their Russian overlords, for that matter—had wanted.

To assess the immediate effect of the Communists' surversive activities on the French Army is a difficult, if not impossible, task. The evidence of the Riom trial, which was supposed to establish the reasons for the French defeat, throws insufficient light on the subject. The Judges had before them two sets of documents, one of which pertained to Communist activities; copies of this set were not made accessible to the accused at the time nor have they

---

[1] The sabotage of the shipments of arms to Finland during the Russian–Finnish War was a significant exception.

since been published.¹ The testimony of the various general officers, as far as it is accessible, is contradictory. While a number of them stressed the high morale of their troops,² Generals Lenclud and Blanchard testified that morale was lower in June 1940 than in September 1939, and General Requin knew of the existence of some Communist cells in his army.³ General Bourret stated after the war that the Fifth Column did in fact exist but that it exercised little effect on the Army, and could not have been the determining reason for the quick and total defeat.⁴ But then again, it appears that the decisive break in May, 1940, on the 2nd and 9th Army front on the Meuse, was due to the low morale of some of the divisions involved, and that Communist propaganda was responsible for it.⁵

Let us conclude this enumeration by quoting from the London *Times* of 25th June, 1940. The *Times* correspondent had previously interviewed the "General who commanded the Maginot group of armies."

"He talked also of the formidable propaganda with which the Army was being assailed from the rear—Communist propaganda that bore all the marks of Nazi agency—of chain-letters suing for peace presented to soldiers' wives in the villages, and the penalty for a refusal to sign would be an anonymous accusation of infidelity addressed to the husband in the trenches."

The general was well informed: such chain-letters were indeed sent by the Communists to the front and, as we have seen, village people had been designated in the Party's organizational instructions as particularly useful contacts. Moreover, his remarks are unbiased since, as C-in-C Maginot Line, he was in the fortunate position of being one of the few French generals who were not forced by the Germans to retreat and hence, subsequently, to seek an excuse.

---

¹Cf. Pierre Cot, *Triumph of Treason*, Chicago, New York, 1944, p. 128.
²Cf. P. Mazé et R. Genebrier, *Les Grandes Journées du Procès de Riom*, Paris, 1945, p. 219.
³Pierre Cot., op. cit., p. 191.
⁴*La Tragédie de l'Armée Française*, Paris, 1947, p. 100.
⁵Général Bourret, op. cit., p. 101; A. Rossi, *Les Communistes Français pendant la drôle de guerre*, Paris, 1951, p. 295. Cf. also Paul Reynaud, *La France a sauvé l'Europe*, Paris, 1947, vol. ii, pp. 72-3, and especially Général Gamelin, *Servir, Les Armées Françaises de 1940*, Paris, 1946, pp. 348 f.

This much is certain: contemporary reports for public consumption can hardly be taken at their face value; if they praise the morale of the troops it might have been done to keep up morale on the home front. On the other hand bad morale among the troops need not be due to Communist propaganda; the faulty French generalship, the faulty dispositions of men and material, the lack of anti-tank guns and aircraft, and last, but not least, the soldiers' inactivity during the phoney war period and their defective training for a war of positions and defence instead of a war of movement and attack, were all bound to have a depressing effect on the troops. There was also another Fifth Column, that of the French Fascists, which exercised its influence. If one adds other political and sociological factors not connected with Communism, it seems hardly possible to fix the Communists' share in the defeat of the French Army. This applies even more to the last stage of the débâcle.

It is, perhaps, true to say that morale showed an upward trend after the first shocks of impending disaster had been absorbed. Two days before the Belgian capitulation, on 26th May, 1940, General Weygand told M. Baudouin, the Secretary of the War Cabinet, that morale in the army was improving every day, he repeated this statement on 8th June, when all seemed lost, and on the 9th the Minister of Armaments, M. Dautry, informed the Cabinet how pleased he was with the excellent morale of the workers in the factories.[1]

But Sir Winston Churchill is certainly right when he contrasts in his Memoirs the growing strength of the German Army of the time with the deterioration of the French Army "gnawed by Soviet-inspired Communism and chilled by the long, cheerless winter on the front."[2] Just because army morale had never been high, Communist subversive propaganda was bound to have its effect. And while its impact cannot be exactly assessed, we can with reasonable certainty guess at the number of Frenchmen in and out of the Army who were receptive to this type of propaganda.

At the outbreak of war there were seventy-two Communist deputies in a Chamber of 618. If one applies this proportion to the men under arms, over 500,000 French soldiers were Communists or had voted Communist. However, even among the top-ranking

---

[1] Cf. Paul Baudouin, *Neuf mois au Gouvernement, Avril–Décembre, 1940*, Paris, 1948, pp. 89, 134 and 137. Judging from his account of events the Cabinet very rarely took any notice of the problem of morale.

[2] *The Second World War*, London edition, 1949, vol. ii, p. 26.

Communists, there were defections when at the outbreak of war Hitler was suddenly replaced by the " '200 Families' within" as Public Enemy No. 1, and many more at the top would have left the Party fold had it not been for fear of being branded a coward or traitor. In the rank and file, free from such hazards, there must have been many more who turned away from the Party. But, on the other hand, the number of militants in the Army was very much higher than usual because many of them had been weeded out of the factories to stop or prevent sabotage there and sent to the front,[1] and their increasing numbers more than made good the decline in rank and file membership.

But it would be altogether wrong to measure the Communist subversive potential by its effect in the last war. In the first place, there are at present almost 100 Communist deputies in the Chamber. In the second place, in the last war, as we have tried to show, the Communists intentionally limited themselves to subversive propaganda and excluded sabotage and guerilla warfare. If there were a next time their war against the enemy within would be unrestricted and there would be no defections. M. Thorez declared in February, 1949, that if there were another war and the Red Army set foot on French soil, he and his Party would devote themselves to ensuring the active collaboration of the French workers with the new occupying power.[2] No declaration of intentions could warn us more clearly and explicitly.

It would therefore be erroneous to take comfort from the statements of those French generals who consider the Communists' share in the collapse of France to have been negligible; it would be fatal to assume that nothing worse than subversion would be practised by the Communists in a future war; and it would be wrong to think that superior generalship and better censorship will immunize the French Army against the germ of defection. Nor will a new set of prohibitive decrees do the trick. The last war provided the French Communists with two valuable lessons: in the conduct of subversive activities, in the period before the U.S.S.R. was

[1] A. Rossi, loc. cit., p. 215.
[2] *Une déclaration capitale du Maurice Thorez*, L'Humanité, 23rd February and also 25th February, 1949. This statement contains of course nothing new. M. Thorez had already proclaimed in 1935, "We French Communists . . . declare that if the Soviet Union is attacked we shall defend her with all (sic!) means." "To be for the defence of the U.S.S.R., with all means, in every area and not a single one excepted (!), that is the formula of the Communist Party," added M. Cachins in 1936. Both statements are quoted in Guy Danjou, op. cit., pp. 172 and 173. For a similar statement in 1949 by an Italian Communist cf. John Baker White, *The Red Network*, Lower Hardress, 1953, p. 18.

attacked by Germany, and, above all, in the waging of guerilla warfare subsequently. They now have the experience in clandestine operations which they previously lacked.

In this type of warfare without battlefield we can never hope to achieve a decisive victory against an enemy by suppression alone. In order to be successful we must be able to reciprocate: subversion for subversion. What an enemy can do to us, we must be able to do to him. This is the lesson of the 1940 campaign in France.

Chapter VI

A STUDY IN POLITICAL WARFARE: THE FREE GERMAN COMMITTEE

COMMUNIST subversive propaganda was effective in France, as we have tried to show. Soviet attempts at political warfare against Germany, with which we shall now deal, were not successful in their aims.

It seems at first sight surprising that the effects of what are after all only different species of warfare by propaganda should be so disparate. But the explanation is simple: French morale had never been high since the beginning of the war, while Germany's determination to fight became even stronger with each successive victory. Psychological warfare against Germany had a chance of success only after the tide had turned, but it was up against obstacles which proved to be insurmountable: Goebbels' persuasiveness, the Hitler myth, Himmler's grip, and the lack of mass support for Communist ideas.

The Soviets could always play on Bismarck's and von Seeckt's traditional policy of friendship with Russia, but this meant little to the German people, schooled as they were to regard Communism as the arch-enemy of Germany, and even less to the German soldier in the East, who had seen Communism at work.

There was really only one body on which Soviet propaganda could make any impression, and this was the German resistance movement. The Russians knew that men like Count Werner von Schulenburg, the German Ambassador to Moscow until 1941, favoured a rapprochement with the Soviets, and that the propaganda had to be attuned to people in this select circle.

It is for this reason that Soviet propaganda called on the German resistance, in whose existence they had always shown an interest (whereas the Western Allies took no notice of this movement); after all, some resistance members had unwittingly been working for the 'Red Orchestra'. And for the same reason Russian propaganda did not try to appeal to the suppressed workers but to the propertied classes. In order to make the propaganda more effective still, it was entrusted to German prisoners of war in Russian hands.

As early as October 1941, a conference held by German prisoners of war at Camp No. 58 had decided to call on the German people to assist in the military defeat of Hitler, and three months later the first German broadcasts by P.O.W.s started.[1] But Soviet propaganda received its real impetus only after the battle for Stalingrad. In July 1943 German officers captured there and resident German Communists formed the National Committee for Free Germany, which was followed in September of the same year by the founding of the German Officers' Bund. After the German Army Group Centre had been smashed in 1944, sixteen captured German Generals of this Army Group joined together in another appeal to the German people and soldiers.[2]

"If the German people allows itself to be led further into ruin," states the 1943 Manifesto to the German Army and the German people, "then it will become, with every day of the war, not only weaker, but also more guilty. Then Hitler will only be overthrown by the arms of the coalition. That would be the end of our national liberty, of our State. It would mean the dismemberment of our Fatherland. . . . But if the German people takes heart before it is too late and proves by deeds that it wants to be a free people and is determined to free Germany from Hitler, then it wins the right to decide its fate itself and to be listened to by the world. This is the only way to save the existence, the liberty and honour of the German nation. The German people needs and wants immediate peace. But no one will conclude peace with Hitler. No one will even negotiate with him. Therefore the formation of a truly German Government is the most urgent task of the people."[3]

What the German people needs, the appeals stress, is a Government founded on the people and entrusted with saving Germany from chaos and catastrophe. The appeals hold out the promise of

---

[1] Cf. Frederick L. Schuman, *Soviet Politics at Home and Abroad*, London, 1948, pp. 458–9.
[2] Cf. John W. Wheeler-Bennett, *The Nemesis of Power*, London, 1953, where the appeal is reproduced on pp. 720–3.
[3] The above quotation is taken from John W. Wheeler-Bennett, op. cit., pp. 716 f. The Manifesto of the Committee is also published by F. L. Schuman, op. cit., p. 460 and Count H. von Einsiedel, *The Shadow of Stalingrad*, London, 1953, p. 64 f. The Appeal by the German Officers' Bund of 14th September, 1943, is to be found in John W. Wheeler-Bennett's book, pp. 718–20.

democracy and, significantly, private property and free enterprise.

There were daily broadcasts by the Committee. It also printed a weekly called *Freies Deutschland*, which was dropped by aircraft over Germany.

But whatever the effect may have been on the members of the resistance movement, it was lost when the Red Army approached the Reich's frontiers. As Mr. Wheeler-Bennett puts it, "an ominous silence fell upon the broadcasts of the National Free German Committee. In place of the promises of a rosy future for the German Army and people who overthrew Hitler, there was heard the stark demand that the entire Wehrmacht should be employed as slave labour by the victorious Allies...."[1]

Yet it was not only the approach of the Red Army that was responsible for the switch in Soviet propaganda but also another event. After the abortive attempt on Hitler's life by the resistance movement (20th July, 1944) it became clear that the National Committee had failed. As one of its former supporters, Count Heinrich von Einsiedel, puts it, "all our hopes that the country would free itself by its own strength were now gone."[2] And Jesco von Puttkamer, one of his colleagues, voices the same feelings when he states that "the terror wave which flooded all over Germany after 20th July, made any hope of a turn of events illusory. It was now clear to everybody that the war would be decided in Berlin and fighting would not cease until Hitler and his system had been removed by the Allies."[3] The political warfare campaign thus came to an end without having achieved anything.

What did the Soviets expect to gain from the National Committee and the resistance movement? Count von Einsiedel, a few days after the *putsch*, had a conversation with a resident Communist who had just returned from a visit to the Central Party Committee in Moscow. When asked by von Einsiedel about his attitude towards the National Committee, he replied: "The (National) Committee is controlled by us, and in the event of a successful German opposition movement it would have ensured us some influence. We had to be prepared for such a possibility and could not isolate ourselves."[4]

[1] John W. Wheeler-Bennett, op. cit., p. 619.
[2] Count Heinrich von Einsiedel, *The Shadow of Stalingrad*, London, 1953, p. 138.
[3] Jesco von Puttkamer, *Von Stalingrad zur Volkspolizei*, Wiesbaden, 1951, p. 72.
[4] Count Heinrich von Einsiedel, op. cit., p. 140.

How the Soviets would have exercised the influence which the National Committee was meant to ensure them is convincingly explained by Jesco von Puttkamer:

"Had a *putsch* succeeded in Germany and a military dictatorship, even just a temporary one, been established, the Soviet Union would have stepped in and declared that the members of the National Committee, who had pursued a similar aim, had a claim to inclusion in a future German Government. It was unlikely that the Generals who had executed the *putsch* in Germany would reject a man like (General von) Seydlitz (one of the National Committee leaders). But Seydlitz had already collaborated with the Communists, and in this way the Communists could have entered the Government."[1]

The Soviet propaganda campaign was therefore very much more than the usual psychological warfare. It was designed not only to help win the war but also to win the peace, on Soviet terms. It was an attempt at converting post-war Germany to Communism.

The activities of the National Committee were not restricted to newspaper propaganda; it also carried out propaganda at the front. For this type of psychological warfare loudspeakers and transmitters were used. These transmissions usually started with military and political news items, after which came a comment on the war situation, and, finally, an appeal to the German soldiers to put an end to the hopeless defence and go over to the side of the National Committee.[2] On one occasion, in February 1944, General von Seydlitz himself was brought to the front line in order to address the German troops on the other side, encircled in the Tcherkassy area, and ask them to surrender. But the encircled units did not capitulate; with heavy losses to themselves they broke through the ring instead.

Finally, the National Committee sent Germans recruited from the 'Free Germany' movement across the lines. Dressed in German uniforms and supplied with German papers, they had to "establish themselves in some base towns behind the (German) front whence they were to carry out their illegal work."[3] But it appears

[1] Jesco von Puttkamer, op. cit., p. 73.
[2] Count Heinrich von Einsiedel, op. cit., pp. 97, 107 and 118.
[3] Count Heinrich von Einsiedel, op. cit., p. 98.

that relatively few Germans embarked on these missions and the damage done by them was slight. Nonetheless, when it became fashionable in Germany during the 1944 débâcle on the Eastern Front to blame every setback on the activities of traitors, the work of these infiltrators was singled out as having caused the disintegration of the German Army Group Centre.

Whether the Soviets also used peace offers to the Germans as ammunition in their political warfare cannot be established. According to Herr Fritz Hesse the Soviets made peace overtures to the Germans before the battle of Moscow.[1] In view of the military situation this offer may have been meant seriously, if it was made at all. But any such speculation is useless, because no documentary evidence has ever come to light. Herr Hesse also states, however, that further peace overtures were made by the Russians after the battle of Stalingrad, and a former official of the German Foreign Office and Ministry for the East, Herr Peter Kleist, has given a very extensive account of these negotiations, which he conducted in Stockholm.[2] It is possible, of course, that this Soviet peace feeler was part of their political warfare, and was aimed at fostering disunity within the Nazi leadership. It seems more likely, however, that these manipulations had quite a different purpose. Great Britain and the United States were at that time unwilling to accede to certain Russian requests, particularly in regard to the Polish question and the early opening up of the Second Front; Stalin's threat to conclude a separate peace might have been meant to make Britain and the U.S. more willing to yield to his demands. This, at any rate, seems to be the accepted German interpretation of Stalin's peace moves.[3]

Lastly, the Red Army also indulged in the usual front-line propaganda, with the wine-women-and-song promise to German deserters. Since it was as a rule followed up by a terrific bombardment, German soldiers seem to have preferred the uncomfortable safety of their foxholes to the alluring prospects of captivity, and there are no known cases of German mass desertion. Nor did the Red Army propaganda leaflets make any impression on the German soldier.

Yet we have no reason to feel reassured by the failure of the Soviet political warfare campaign against Germany. Because the

[1] Cf. Fritz Hesse, *Hitler and the English*, London, 1954, pp. 144 and 154.
[2] Cf. Peter Kleist, *Zwischen Hitler und Stalin*, Bonn, 1950, pp. 230 *seq*.
[3] The view held, in particular, by Boris Meissner, *Die sowjetische Deutschlandpolitik*, Europa Archiv, 1951, pp. 4526 *seq*.

German people were then proof against subversion, the Soviets chose to make contact with the German resistance. The subtlety of approach should not disguise the fact that it was meant to push the frontiers of the Soviet orbit to the Rhine.

Had Hitler died on 20th July, 1944, and the resistance movement taken over, the Soviets might have succeeded.

Chapter VII

A PLAN FOR SABOTAGE: PARTISANS ON OPERATIONAL MISSIONS

THE Soviet plans for sabotage apparently envisage three types of operation, viz.:

(*a*) The formation of factory workers in the West into partisan sabotage groups.

(*b*) The organization of sabotage cells in the West by trained infiltrators from the East.

(*c*) The preparation of partisan warfare in the West.

We shall deal with these topics in the above sequence.

(*a*) *Factory sabotage groups*. It seems that the first preparations in the post-war years for sabotage actions of this kind were made in 1947 in the United States. According to the *New York Herald Tribune*

"a complete sabotage survey of every major industrial centre in the United States was made by the Communist Party in 1947. It was exhaustively reviewed by the Party in every important city in the nation in 1948. The Party's extensive work on the surveys is known to the Federal Bureau of Investigation.

"The study was made by Communist Party sabotage squads or 'cells'. . . .

"As a result of their surveys, the nation's Communists possess a catalogue of strategic installations earmarked for destruction or capture in a showdown fight with Russia."[1]

In 1952, it appears, Australia received similar attention. As we have seen in Chapter I, Mrs. Petrova, in her evidence before the Royal Commission on Russian espionage in Melbourne, named Mr. Kislitsin of the Soviet Embassy as the MVD officer responsible in 1952 for bringing into Australia agents who were to organize a fifth column there. These agents, she stated in her

---

[1] *Vital U.S. Plants Marked for Destruction in Event of U.S.–Soviet Showdown*, Herald Tribune, 30th November, 1950. Reprinted in *The Threat of Red Sabotage*, published by the *Herald Tribune*, New York, 1951, pp. 7 f.

evidence, had to be ready to undertake any mission which Moscow might decide on, "sabotage and anything".[1] While we may wonder what 'anything' stands for, there can be little doubt that in its context with sabotage it also includes factory sabotage.

At about the same time Captain Khokhlov revealed to the United States authorities in Western Germany that in 1952 specific plans had been developed by the Soviet authorities in Karlshorst for a partisan sabotage group of factory workers in the northern part of the German Federal Republic. The author of this plan was supposed to be one Major Meshcheryakov, who had at various times been acting chief, or deputy chief, of the Karlshorst advanced base of the 9th Section for Terror and Diversion of the MVD. "The last time Khokhlov saw him in 1953, his partisan group plan had not yet been approved by Moscow, but Meshcheryakov was confident it would be."[2]

Details of the plan are not available for publication, and from the scanty evidence it is impossible to say how far it has materialized. But sufficient is known of other, similar, plans to outline the general idea.

Even during the last war the French Communists, in their clandestine resistance news-sheets, issued instructions on how to sabotage production. They informed their readers of the usual ruses for slowing down production. But their main weapon, not only for harming the Germans but also for furthering their own cause, was the general strike. *L'Humanité* of 15th April, 1943, published the General Directives of the Communist Party for the National Insurrection: "Intensify sabotage, destroy machines, burn down factories and enemy dumps, put locomotives and wagons out of order.... Paralyse the economic life through general strikes, cut quickly the lines of communication...."

On 1st August, 1943, Thorez contributed an article to *L'Humanité* in which he stated that "the hour of preparation for the National Insurrection has come.... Without waiting for directives from the central organizations, those in charge of patriotic organizations must from the moment of the Allied landing ... paralyse economic activity through a general strike."

Another Communist underground news-sheet, *L'Étinelle*, in

---

[1] Cf. Commonwealth of Australia, *Royal Commission on Espionage*, Official Transcript of Proceedings, taken at Melbourne, 7th July, 1954, p. 163.
[2] *Khokhlov Briefing Papers*, prepared at the offices of the United States High Commission in Bonn, and issued on 22nd April, 1954, when Captain Khokhlov was introduced to journalists there.

its issue for January February 1944, gave more specific instructions for preparing the strike and for using it as an efficient sabotage weapon. After reproaching those who say that one should wait before calling out a general strike, it goes on: "To speak of a general strike at some future time and do nothing about it now is empty talk. The first step for preparing and making possible the insurrectional general strike consists in engaging in daily activities in the factories. . . . Such a strike makes it necessary for the workers to take possession of the factories. To remain passive would be equivalent to a dispersion of our forces . . . and would allow the enemy to liquidate the movement.

"It is necessary to protect the strike, viz. to be prepared to repel by force any intervention by the enemy. It is necessary to form in every factory a *patriotic workers militia* which acts in liaison with the armed patriots' organization and reinforces the army of liberation. Enemy transports must be stopped. . . . An ordinary strike of railwaymen is not sufficient for this purpose. They must occupy the main stations and important railway junctions, in co-operation with the militia and the armed patriots, and stop enemy convoys carrying arms and ammunition. . . . In every factory a strike committee must be chosen which directs the movement and establishes liaison between its members and also with the patriotic committees." Then follows a paragraph on the special importance of a general strike by iron and steel workers.

These instructions are significant in as much as they show that the strike, far from being a means of passive resistance, is turned into a device for active sabotage, and in the process the factory becomes a 'hedgehog' for armed resistance. At the same time there is a notable omission in these instructions: they make no effort at co-ordination.

This deficiency is to some extent remedied by Protocol 'M'. This Protocol, which was published in full by the West-German newspapers of 15th January, 1948, is supposed to be a peace-time plan, made by the Cominform, for fostering unrest and strikes in Western Germany and for capturing key positions in production. The East-German (Communist) Socialist Unity Party has described the document as a forgery, and while its authenticity is doubtful, Mr. Hector McNeil, speaking for the Government, declared in the House of Commons on 19th April, 1948, that there have been developments in Germany which correspond to some of the statements in the document, "and there are strong indications that even if the document is not itself authentic, it has been compiled from authoritative Communist sources, and this is corroborated by information already in our possession."[1]

According to this document, "it must be ensured that the workers' risings occur simultaneously in transport and production. The trade unions of the transport and iron and steel workers will carry out a succession of strikes. . . . The co-ordination in time of delays in the arrival of food transports and the organization of wild strikes, leading to a loss of production, is an essential feature of the operation." Again, like the resistance directives, the document emphasizes the importance of the metallurgical industries and outlines plans for the cutting of railway communications.

The time-table for the operation envisaged three stages: by December a common Communist basis for a plebiscite had to be arranged, by the end of February strike cadres had to be organized, and from then on the general strikes themselves had to be prepared. The accent, it appears, is on co-ordination in time, viz. the synchronization or staggering of strikes for maximum results.

However, in a country like Western Germany, where there are only a few Communists, strikes and sabotage in general can only be put into effect by the Soviets on a restricted basis, and that means that they have to concentrate on a few targets. The sabotage survey in the United States suggests that in that country, and most likely in others, they will put the selective method into practice, and assign to the factory sabotage groups the most sensitive objectives. We have learnt from the last war how difficult it is to pick the proper targets: it took some time before we realized that strategic bombing ought to be directed against power, oil refining, ball-bearing factories, and transport, among others. The Russians, on the strength of their surveys, try to ascertain the most sensitive sabotage targets, region by region—it might be power here, some raw material or semi-finished product there, and transport elsewhere. Then, in the event of war, they would try to paralyse the strategic production of their opponents by highly selective, co-ordinated sabotage actions.

The detailed plans for each country, it appears, are drawn up locally and based on exhaustive surveys of the major industrial centres; they are then submitted to Moscow for approval. The preparation of future sabotage work is in the hands of the MVD—although Protocol 'M' names the Cominform as the planning

[1] For the text of Protocol 'M' cf. the Appendix to this book.

agency—while their execution rests with infiltrated foreign agents and groups of indigenous factory workers. They are the special shock groups within the wider sabotage network of Soviet design. This wider network is made up of sabotage cells and partisan bands.

(*b*) *Sabotage cells.* We have already mentioned the 9th Section for Terror and Diversion. Its mission is the carrying out of special action tasks. Its functions become obvious from the training curriculum. According to the Khokhlov Briefing Papers, "training is carried out at an operational base at the corner of Metrostroyevskaya Ul. and Turchaninski Pere Ulok in Moscow, under Colonel Arkady Foteyev, with a staff of instructors in small arms, jiujitsu, code, wireless, driving, surveillance and photography. Special weapons and explosives are produced by a laboratory near Kuchino outside Moscow, and another laboratory develops poisons and drugs for use in 'special action tasks'."

Whether this training in the arts of sabotage and other violent activities is reserved for Soviet citizens or whether foreign agents are also eligible is not known; the two German agents who accompanied Captain Khokhlov on his Frankfurt assassination mission received their training, in judo, automobile driving and pistol firing only, at some other place on the outskirts of Moscow.[1] In any event, two things are certain:

(1) According to the Khokhlov Briefing Papers, the Second Chief Directorate, to which the 9th Section is now subordinate, "was cited as already having agents in place in the West for any operations for which Bureau No. 1 would have to procure, train and dispatch an agent." Bureau No. 1, it should be noted, was the predecessor of the 9th Section and especially charged with carrying out sabotage and other violent activities.

(2) According to Mrs. Petrova's evidence, MVD agents brought in from abroad were to organize the fifth column, which, if so ordered by Moscow, was to carry out sabotage. It is in the nature of things that fifth columnists are nationals and residents of the country of operations.

---

[1]The training of MVD agents in general is described at length by E. H. Cookridge in his book *Soviet Spy Net*, London, 1955, pp. 94 *seq*. But not all MVD agents necessarily go through these schools. While Khokhlov obtained his training there, it was dispensed with in the case of Petrov, who, it was thought, had gained sufficient experience in his former K.I. work.

During the last war the NKVD , as it then was, specialized, among other things, n teaching its pupils how to steal documents and records from German officers and soldiers. Cf. Dixon and Heilbrunn, *Communist Guerilla Warfare*, op. cit., p. 73.

Since these sabotage cells, like the factory sabotage groups, come under the jurisdiction of the MVD, it can be assumed that their tasks do not overlap. The sabotage cells might be assigned to factory sabotage missions if no factory sabotage group could be formed there, but apart from this they have their own special tasks.

The nature of these special tasks was revealed in the trial of Fritiof Enbom in Sweden in 1952. Enbom, a former railway employee, was accused of espionage and treason committed from 1941 to 1951. In 1941 he was recruited by a Communist to collect information about German military traffic through Sweden and to report on the technical equipment and morale of the German troops. He later extended his activities to reporting on Swedish military affairs, particularly Swedish defences on the Finnish frontier. He was supplied with a code name, a transmitter, a secret code and money. His contact man, according to the prosecution, was the Military Attaché at the Soviet Embassy. He instructed Enbom, the prosecution continued, to find a radio operator and to obtain contacts among the officials in the Service Ministries.[1]

Enbom pleaded guilty "to plotting to sabotage Sweden's northern defences and facilitating the capture of part of them by a Communist fifth column. He said he conspired with . . . a correspondent of the north Swedish Communist newspaper, *Norrskensflamman*, to seize the Boden fortifications.

"Enbom told the judge . . .: 'The disturbances in Czechoslovakia in 1948 and the Korea crisis in 1950 made me believe that a war was inevitable. I considered it would be criminal not to plan an active move by fifth columnists against the Swedish armed forces.' He said he and (the correspondent) planned to take the munitions and ordnance depôt in Boden by two railway trucks filled with armed Communists. He explained that the purpose of the coup would be to obtain weapons, ammunition, and explosives for sabotage.

"Enbom said he also planned to try to disorganize a general mobilization in Sweden. Communists would get possession of the loudspeaker points in the big sidings and dispatch train-loads of troops and supplies to the wrong destinations."[2]

The hearing was then continued in private. He was sentenced

[1] Cf. London *Times*, 17th June, 1952.
[2] London *Times*, 19th June, 1952.

to hard labour for life. "He had planned to recruit 200 local Communists for a fifth column to seize frontier fortifications if the Russian Army ever marched into Sweden.

"Other Communists, hiding in trees along the invasion route, were to report on the movement of the defending forces, and their information was to be passed on to the Russian command on a wireless transmitter supplied to Enbom by the Soviet Embassy. . . .

"During the trial the Soviet Ambassador called on . . . the Swedish Foreign Minister, rejected the Swedish protest against the alleged Soviet Embassy involvement in the spying and called it 'invention'."[1] Enbom did not appeal.[2]

There have been a great number of Communist spy trials in the recent past, but sabotage trials have been rare, for the simple reason that while espionage is going on at all times, the saboteurs will perform their tasks only after the outbreak of a new war. However, the Enbom case revealed a clear pattern: the sabotage cells are supposed to fulfil the tasks of partisan bands, viz. to lay mines, blow up bridges, derail trains, seize or blow up ammunition dumps, sabotage shipping, disorganize the mobilization, and carry out the intelligence missions in which the Soviet partisans became so proficient during the last war.

These sabotage cells, it can be assumed, are considered specially important by the Soviets as substitutes for partisan bands in those Western countries in which the Communist Party cannot organize partisan warfare. As fighting units the bands are Red Army Auxiliaries deployed behind the Allies' front. But partisan or guerilla warfare can be organized only if the country's Communists are numerous enough to supply the necessary manpower. Since in wartime the Communists are called up along with everybody else, Communist partisan bands in the West have to rely exclusively on the under- and over-age groups. It is therefore hardly likely that Moscow will waste much time on organizing guerilla warfare in countries like Western Germany, where the Communist Party cannot count on more than about 4 per cent of the population. Instead Moscow will try all the more to obtain the support of sabotage cells. As East and West Germany have a long common frontier and the inhabitants of both parts speak the same language, infiltrators from the East can hardly be detected in time, and nobody can even guess how many of them come over in the guise

[1] London *Times*, 1st August, 1952.
[2] London *Times*, 18th November, 1952.

of refugees, among the many thousands who every month seek safety in the West.

In the last war the various fighting forces sent their own military personnel on special missions behind the enemy lines: the British the S.A.S., S.B.S. and L.R.D.G., the Germans the Brandenburg Regiment of the Abwehr, the Russians their cadres of intelligence scouts. Under the new Soviet conception of warfare such tasks will be allotted to Allied civilians resident in the target area and operating against their own country.

(c) *Partisan warfare.* The study of partisan warfare as practised by the Russians in the last war is, as we stressed before, important for two reasons: the Allies will be confronted with this type of warfare in the satellite countries; and, no less important, the Allies will meet it in those countries of the West in which the Soviets are able to organize it. The tactics and strategy of anti-Allied partisan forces will be modelled on the Soviet example, not only because the Russian guerilla movement of the last war stood up to the test of battle so well, but also because the rules of co-operation between the Red Army and the Red partisans were developed to perfection.

We do not intend to discuss here the tactics and strategy of the Red partisans; this has been done in *Communist Guerilla Warfare.* Instead we shall try to visualize the type of partisan warfare we are likely to meet in the event of another war.

In 1945 P. K. Ignatov, Commander of the Ignatov Brothers' Partisan Unit, published in London, New York, Melbourne and Sydney his book *Partisans of the Kuban,*[1] one of several accounts written at about that time by various Soviet partisan leaders. Ignatov's book is a rewritten and amplified version of the diary he kept during the period of operations. His account has since been considerably revised, and it was published in East Germany in 1953, in a German translation, under the title *Partisanen.*[2] It is reported to be in use as a basic handbook for the Communist Free German Youth Organization. Hence its significance.

The Ignatov Brothers' Partisan Unit has several claims to distinction. All its members received decorations for outstanding merit in battle. But that is not all. The unit consisted almost entirely of intellectuals; it was a special unit of sappers and miners; and economically it was self-sufficient.

[1] Translated from the Russian by J. Fineberg. Hutchinson & Co.
[2] Translated from the Russian by Manfred von Busch. Verlag Volk und Welt, Berlin.

A PLAN FOR SABOTAGE

In *Partisanen* Ignatov deals with the activities of his unit from its formation at the end of 1941 to the completion of its mission at the beginning of 1943. The book is little concerned with higher strategy or tactics; it vividly describes partisan life and the operations of his unit.

Long before the German occupation of Krasnodar, the Secretary of the Party City Committee had received instructions from the District Committee to make the necessary preparations for the formation of a resistance movement and a partisan unit for special tasks. The Party Secretary thereupon appointed Ignatov leader of the partisan unit; he also appointed the unit's commissar and the deputy leader, and the list of prospective partisans was submitted to him for approval.

The band consisted of fifty-eight members at the start, fifty-one men and seven women. Nine of the members spoke perfect German. Many of the partisans were engineers and technicians, others, wounded and demobilized Red Army men, were sappers, pioneers, radio operators and so on. Many of them knew more than one trade and could work as blacksmiths, cobblers, mechanics, builders and carpenters as well.

When the unit was first formed the Party decided that it should not operate in the city if it fell into German hands; in this way it was hoped to avoid German reprisals against the city population and the exposure of the Party organization. With the expected German occupation of the city the unit was to move into the Caucasian foothills and take up its activities on the Krasnodor-Novorossisk road.

But the German occupation of Krasnodar was still eight months off. The unit utilized this time well. It received small arms training in as many weapons and different models as possible, it was instructed in jiujitsu and close combat, it practised long-distance reconnoitring, it learnt how to signal in the woods, and every team member became proficient in first aid. During this time the fact that they had been selected as partisans was kept secret from the population; they let it be understood that they were to be called up for the Red Army.

The unit commanders, too, familiarized themselves with their future tasks: they studied military literature in general and the accounts of former guerilla wars in particular. They also procured, with the active support of the Party, food, clothing, equipment, arms, ammunition and explosives. When the Germans approached the city, all the supplies were loaded on to trucks, moved, and hidden away in a number of self-contained dumps dug in the ground near their future camp. Each partisan was provided with a paper identifying him as leader, chief engineer, commercial director and so on of a geological research unit engaged in preliminary work for the construction of a timber mill in the mountains. The partisans took the oath, and the unit marched to its assigned position, Point 521.

The camp site was well hidden: it consisted of a broad meadow approached by a narrow track and steep ascents. On one side it was protected by a high mountain ridge and on the opposite side by a deep precipice. The unit pitched its tents and earmarked space for kitchen, mess-room and hospital. Then the unit was divided into four sections. The first section consisted of snipers, machine-gunners and artillerymen, though without guns as yet. In the second section were the miners, sappers, signalmen and pioneers. The third was a rifle section, and the fourth comprised the administrative and hospital staff. Long-range reconnaissance was a special group; the bravest partisans were assigned to it.

Discipline was modelled on Army lines. Political lectures were held every night by the commissar.

Partisan District Headquarters assigned Ignatov his first task: to stop the German advance in the direction of Baku and Tuapse by blocking the mountain passes at the appropriate time. In preparation for this task the area was reconnoitred, intelligence agents—including children—were appointed among the population of the various villages, and contact was established with the nearest Red Division on the other side of the German line. The Army gave the partisans a further task: they were to inform the Army about major enemy troop movements, the location of heavy enemy artillery etc., and bring in an enemy prisoner. One of the partisans soon captured a German first sergeant—without trousers, according to the shortened English text of the book (p. 34) while in the German version he appears complete with this garment (p. 135).

After two engagements with the Germans of the usual partisan ambush type, the unit had to move camp—it was too close to the route of the German advance. The new camp was located in an inaccessible, remote gorge. Two of the secret stores were moved to the new site. In addition the unit had three small camps, a summer camp, one in the buildings of a former sawmill, and a hospital in a large, empty farmhouse. Weapon study was part of the daily routine. The partisans were also instructed in countering the effects of German propaganda in the villages.

The German advance in the Caucasus had in the meanwhile been halted, and the unit now received an order from the Red Army on the other side of the German front to increase its reconnaissance activities, to report every enemy troop movement, to ascertain how bridges, camps and railway stations were guarded by the enemy, and to sketch the positions of all its artillery emplacements. Special attention was to be given to whether German officers were carrying respirators.

Numerous details were soon reported back by the partisans, through runners: the newly arrived formations, the number of tanks, trucks, machine-guns, gun calibres, location of dug-outs, artillery, anti-tank gun positions, observation posts and ammunition dumps, and the density of the railway traffic; prisoners were taken and interrogated. Subsequently the unit received orders from Partisan District Headquarters to undertake specified bridge-mining operations. Seventy per cent of the partisans' time was devoted to the preparation of operations, 30 per cent to their execution.

The engineers of the unit constructed their mines themselves, and perfected them. Particular care was taken in training the sappers, and in this respect the Ignatov unit was unique: it had its own Sappers' College, in which not only the unit's own partisans but also those of neighbouring bands were trained in the theory and practice of minelaying. The curriculum consisted of sixty lectures, followed by practical instruction on the practice ground and participation in actual missions. Only students who had passed their examination in theory were permitted to take part in actions.

On the practice ground there was everything that a sapper would find in future actions, a railway track, a high road, a river with a stony bed, overhanging rocks and a large bridge over a river. The exercise took place at night and the students were divided into groups: one had to mine the railway, a second the high road, the third cross-roads, the fourth had to fix containers with explosives on to the steel supports of the bridge, and the fifth had to block a road and make a crater in the river in order to prevent cars and tanks from crossing the ford there. The following day other groups had to locate the mines, and subsequently they were exploded. Successful candidates received diplomas.

Ignatov called his unit a sappers' and miners' unit, and as such they achieved their successes, particularly during the final phase of their operations: in concert with the Red Army they tried to dislocate the German transport system when the German retreat from the Caucasus began, and inflicted heavy damage.

General Eisenhower is supposed to have said that the French partisans were worth fifteen Allied divisions. Ignatov's sappers and miners took the view that two of them were worth one SS regiment. However that may be, the partisan's job, apart from intelligence work, is sabotage, and successful saboteurs must have a sound training. This, we believe, is the moral of Ignatov's book.

The scope for partisan sabotage is wide indeed. The Field Service Regulations of the Red Army, 1944, list the following objectives:

"The basic missions of partisan actions are:

—the destruction of garrisons, staffs, establishments, troop detachments of the enemy, individual soldiers and officers moving about, the guards of depots, establishments, transports, forage, and various parties and agents engaged in collecting grain, livestock and other supplies from the population;

—the destruction of enemy supply routes (the blasting of bridges, the impairment of railways, the wrecking of trains, attacks against motor- and animal-drawn transport), the smashing of enemy echelons with their personnel, equipment, fuel and ammunition, making it impossible for the enemy to supply the front and to carry away the national property that has been seized;

—the destruction of depots and bases with armaments, ammunition, fuel, food and other materials, the destruction of garages and repair shops;

—the destruction of signal communication lines on railways, highways and dirt roads (telephone, telegraph, radio stations), the destruction of signal communication apparatus, the killing of the service personnel—signal communication troops;

—attacks against enemy aerodromes, destruction of aircraft, hangars, depots of bombs and fuel, destruction of the flying personnel and mechanics and those guarding the aerodromes;

—the killing or capture of political agents, generals and high officials of the enemy, and traitors to our fatherland who are in their service;

—the destruction or burning of electric power plants, boilers, systems of water supply, industrial enterprises and other objects of military and economic importance."[1]

This catalogue was devised before the appearance of the V 1 and V 2 weapons and the nuclear weapons, and it has probably been enlarged in the meanwhile. Furthermore, these regulations are specifically addressed to Soviet partisans fighting on Russian soil. But there cannot be much doubt that they apply equally to Communist partisans operating in other countries.

It would be fascinating precisely to assess the value of partisan forces by presenting a kind of profit and loss account. But the Russian figures are obviously inflated and few German statistics are available. However, the German Army Group North, which fought in Russia, published some material for 1943. It was marked 'Secret' and was meant for internal use only. We therefore regard it as reliable.[2]

Among its many maps there is one of particular interest. It is marked 'Security Troops and the Band Situation in December, 1943', and it shows the location of the various Russian bands, their designation and estimated strength, and the location of the security troops, mostly German but also Baltic and Russian volunteers (East troops), and their strength by battalions, companies, and 'less than companies'. There are also several inset tables and graphs on partisan actions, partisan losses, and German losses.

The map, tables and graphs illustrate only the events in the forward area of Army Group North. They do not show the situation in the rear area of this Army Group, or in the areas of the two other Army Groups in Russia, or the Soviet territory further back, and in looking at the figures below one must always bear in mind that they do not cover those areas where the partisan forces were considerably larger and the heaviest partisan fighting took place.

The following partisan bands were deployed in the forward area of Army Group North:

[1] The Chapter 'Partisan Operations' of the Field Service Regulations of the Red Army, 1944, is reprinted in full in the Appendix to this book.
[2] *Feldzug gegen die Sowjetunion der Heeresgruppe Nord, Kriegsjahr 1943.* Bearbeitet in der Fuehrungsabteilung des Oberkommandos der Heeresgruppe Nord. Published on 24 December, 1944.

1st Leningrad 'Brigade'	600 men	
2nd Leningrad 'Brigade'	1,500 "	
3rd Leningrad 'Brigade'	2,000 "	
4th Leningrad 'Brigade'	400 "	
5th Leningrad 'Brigade'	1,500 "	
6th Leningrad 'Brigade'	2,000 "	
7th Leningrad 'Brigade'	1,400 "	
8th Leningrad 'Brigade'	2,000 "	
9th Leningrad 'Brigade'	1,000 "	
10th Leningrad 'Brigade'	900 "	
12th Leningrad 'Brigade'	1,000 "	14,300 men
2nd Cavalry 'Brigade'	700 men	
4/6/8th Cavalry 'Brigade'	600 "	
8th Cavalry 'Brigade'	600 "	
9th Cavalry 'Brigade'	300 "	
10th Cavalry 'Brigade'	900 "	
12th Cavalry 'Brigade'	300 "	
13th Cavalry 'Brigade'	400 "	3,800 men
Barakin Band	300 men	
Ivanov Band	400 "	
Lutschin Band	500 "	
Grigorjev Band	800 "	
Janowski Band	1,000 "	
Varobjev Band	200 "	
Pestrikov Band	900 "	
Krassnyi Wojewod Band	500 "	
Wassijka Sascha Band	150 "	
12th Bjele 'Brigade'	200 "	4,950 men

Also shown on the map are two more 'Brigades', without any indication of their strength; and ten 'Brigades' are listed as dispersed or location unknown. The total partisan strength was therefore between 25,000 and perhaps 30,000 men.

Against this force the Germans lined up:

	German	Baltic and Finnish	East Troops	Total
Battalions	16	2	1	19
Companies	135	18	4	157
Less than Companies	70	3	14	87

No figures are available for the precise strength of these units, but if we assume that a battalion had about 400 men, and a company about 120, and that 'less than a company' stands for perhaps 50 men, the Security Forces on the German side numbered:

```
19 battalions at 400 men each        =  7,600 men
157 companies at 120 men each        = 18,840   ,,
87 less than company at 50 men each =  4,350   ,,    30,790 men
```

Bands and security forces were therefore roughly of equal strength. It might of course be objected that the Germans would have required some security troops in the area even if the country has been pacified. But these troops, usually known as the town and field commandos and alarm units, are not included in the above count. The fact therefore remains that in this area the Germans deployed one soldier for each partisan.

However, this ratio was entirely insufficient, because it did not prevent the partisans from doing their work. The following table illustrates one aspect of their activities.

The striking increase in partisan activities from August on is easily explained. The Russians attacked at the end of September in great strength, and the partisans were preparing and supporting this attack, which continued until the beginning of the following year. The Russians were out to gain possession of Nevel as a starting point for their later operations towards the Baltic. The attack began south of Veliki Luki, at the seam between Army Groups North and Centre; the Russians at once managed to break through on a small front and to extend the gap with motorized infantry and tanks. The battle was at its height in October; so were partisan activities, in co-ordination with the Red Army's requirements.

Interference with Railway Traffic during 1943

Month	Mining	Ambush	Art. fire	Damaged or destroyed Locomotives	Damaged or destroyed Wagons	Dead from 1st May	Wounded from 1st May
Jan.	33	—	20	3	57		
Feb.	10	—	9	2	46		
Mar.	16	—	49	5	43		
Apr.	25	6	45	5	11		
May	49	—	116	30	151	41	152
June	43	2	113	19	136	25	44
July	33	—	64	15	32	16	28
Aug.	1,879	4	70	19	67	29	84
Sep.	940	2	41	13	49	15	66
Oct.	3,384	11	24	71	149	42	233
Nov.	2,736	14	6	46	70	11	82
Dec.	621	12	24	65	35	29	84
Total	9,769	51	581	293	846	208	773

Other Partisan Activities during 1943

Month	Ambush	Fighting	Destruction of Bridges	Mining	Destruction of Cables	Arson, other Destr.
Jan.	10	100	20	10	8	10
Feb.	20	60	12	8	12	5
Mar.	25	50	10	0	4	8
Apr.	30	58	15	6	17	18
May	50	165	18	12	15	30
June	60	140	15	22	10	25
July	75	150	25	23	15	22
Aug.	100	155	35	30	15	42
Sep.	140	135	25	20	10	46
Oct.	180	155	130	45	35	27
Nov.	140	145	75	45	30	16
Dec.	155	150	30	25	28	38

Other partisan activities were also stepped up before and during the crucial battle, as the previous table shows.

One might reasonably assume that partisan losses were at their highest when their activities reached a climax, but in fact this was not so.

What accounts for the high partisan losses in January, February, April and May is not known. The April figure is particularly

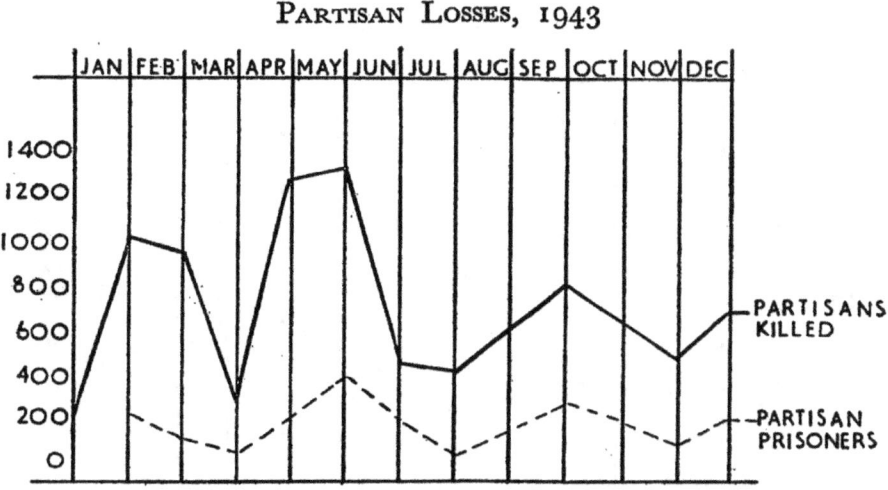

PARTISAN LOSSES, 1943

surprising since partisan activities were then at a low. It is, of course, possible that the Germans carried out some successful anti-partisan operations at that time. However this may be, in spite of the partisans' tremendous activities from August on, their losses in killed and prisoners over the following months were about average. In other words, although they greatly intensified their sabotage operations, they were not exposed to any additional risk. Their casualty rate remained almost the same, regardless of whether they mined the railway lines once a day—as they did in July—or nearly a hundred times a day—as they did in November.

How did the partisan losses compare with the German losses?

So far we have regarded the figures in the German compilation as reliable, but it is difficult to accept the last chart as accurate. For July it shows sixty-five Germans killed. According to our first table sixteen Germans were killed that month in railway accidents, leaving forty-nine killed in all other partisan operations. Yet, as our second table shows, the partisans carried out in July no less

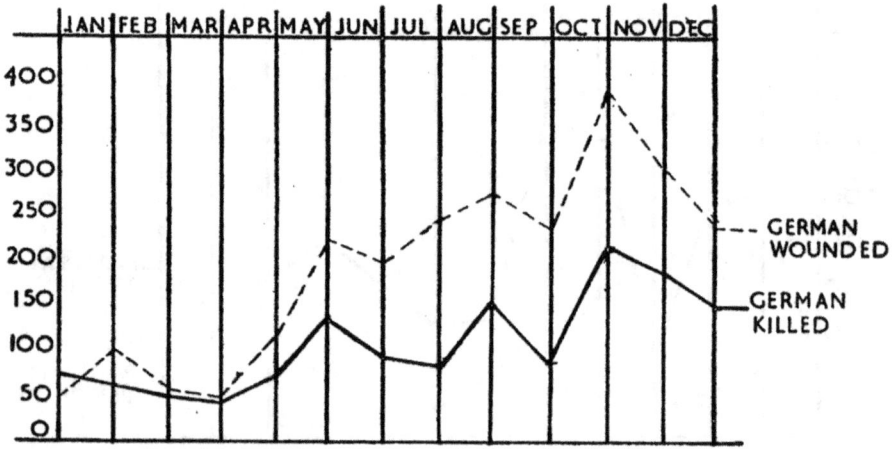

GERMAN KILLED AND WOUNDED THROUGH PARTISAN ACTIONS DURING 1943

than seventy-five ambushes, and there were also 150 other encounters; twenty-five bridges were destroyed and twenty-three mining operations were carried out. It is hardly believable that the Germans should have lost fewer than fifty killed as a result. We therefore refrain from a comparison of the German and partisan losses.

However, our tables and charts seem to support two conclusions:

(i) Partisan forces cannot be contained by an equal number of anti-partisan troops.

(ii) Partisan casualties do not necessarily increase even if the partisans greatly intensify their sabotage activities.[1]

Guerilla movements, whatever their mission or Party colours, are a menace to the occupying power. We ought carefully to consider whether West-Germans, and possibly others as well, should not receive training, as the East-Germans seem to do, similar to that described in Ignatov's book. Those who are familiar with the achievements of the Soviet partisans in the last war can have little doubt that trained pro-Allied partisans, particularly in West Germany, would be of great value to the West should the Soviets choose to attack. Under nuclear warfare conditions the value of friendly partisan forces is higher than ever before.

It has been said, though, that the Germans have neither a tradition in, nor aptitude for, irregular warfare, and Germany's vain attempts at organizing a last line of partisan resistance in the so-called Alpine Redoubt towards the end of the late war have been cited in support of this thesis. But the Germans were so tired out after almost six years of war, and further resistance seemed so senseless, that even the diehards in charge of this venture gave up the attempt as futile. We must rather look for a precedent to the aftermath of the First World War when the German Free Corps, regrettable though their activities were, fought as guerillas.

But at any rate the West must have at least a partisan organization, if not a partisan movement. Mr. Julian Amery has set out the requirements, and we cannot do better than quote him:

"Meanwhile the first task should be to train a relatively large cadre of liaison officers and technicians who would serve as the nucleus of our war-time resistance organization. These should first receive a thorough theoretical training in the strategy and tactics of resistance. This should include the study of past resistance movements and revolutions, the organization of the Communist Party, Russian security methods, and military and political intelligence. They should then be sent, like the Communist agents whose counterparts they would be, to help build up resistance movements in the countries behind the Iron Curtain, and to prepare for resistance in countries in danger of Russian occupation.

---

[1] The above conclusions may or may not be borne out by our own experience in Malaya and Kenya. However, one should not forget that the guerillas in Malaya and Kenya were the only fighting forces in the field, whereas in Russia they were auxiliaries to the regular fighting forces, the Red Army, and they had therefore different tasks. We are inclined to believe that our two conclusions are valid for any partisan movement acting as a supporting force to a regular army.

In these tasks they would require to be supported by a supply and propaganda service. This should be done now, while there is still time."[1] If the Communists withdraw their agents abroad, we can do the same.

The study of partisan warfare during the last fifteen years or so leads to one very definite conclusion:

We too must have partisans![2]

---

[1] Julian Amery, *Of Resistance, The Nineteenth Century and After*, March 1949, p. 149.
[2] Clausewitz thought so long ago. In Book vi, Chapter 26, he wrote on "Arming the Nation": "In the generality of cases, the people who make judicious use of this means will gain a proportionate superiority over those who despise its use." Cf. General Carl von Clausewitz, *On War* (translated by Colonel J. J. Graham), vol. ii, London, 1908, p. 342.

Chapter VIII

A PATTERN FOR REVOLUTION: A SATELLITE IS BORN

THE Communists have always tried to monopolize guerilla movements everywhere. When this was impossible because non-Communist partisan organizations had also taken the field, the Communist partisans never merged with them, but fought as a separate entity. During the last war Communist partisans operated in France and Italy under their own leaders, had their own chain of command, and carried on their own propaganda.

But whereas the Communist partisans in France and Italy accepted a common leadership, at top level, with the other resistance organizations, in Albania, Yugoslavia, Greece and Poland they kept their complete independence.

In the Balkan countries the Communist partisans fought not only against the Germans; they waged an even fiercer war against non-Communist rival movements. In Poland, however, the Communist partisans hardly ever engaged the Germans; all their activities were directed towards wiping out the non-Communist underground movement. In Albania, Yugoslavia and Poland it was an unequal battle, a battle from which the Communists emerged as victors, and in the wake of victory seized political power. They had turned the war of liberation into a revolutionary war and gained their aims. In each of these countries a new satellite was born.

Communist partisan movements in non-Communist countries have therefore, in addition to Intelligence and sabotage, a third function in war time: they are the Communist vanguard in the fight for Communist control of the country. For this purpose they have to remove all rival contenders, especially non-Communist guerillas, even though these may be fighting, as they were in the last war, against Russia's enemies.

The Communist partisans were set this task at the Congress of the Communist International in Moscow in August 1928. Especially in the event of war against the Soviet Union, it was laid down, Communists should form national-revolutionary guerilla units, if the situation permitted it.

During the last war the situation did permit it in a number of countries. The pattern is clearly discernible, and so are the methods applied. The International's instructions and past performance make it clear that we shall be confronted with this type of revolutionary warfare in our midst in any future war. We do not therefore apologize for dealing with this subject at some length.

In the last war the Communist partisans mainly resorted to three devices to wipe out rival movements:

(1) Open battle. In this way they eliminated, or tried to eliminate, the non-Communist partisans in Albania, Yugoslavia and Greece.

(2) Accusing the non-Communist partisans of collaboration with the enemy, thus depriving them of outside support, as they did in Albania and Yugoslavia.

(3) Collaborating with the enemy themselves, as they did in Poland, thus letting the Gestapo eliminate the non-Communist partisans.

The last two devices could of course be brought into play only because Russia then fought on our side, but the first is always applicable.

In Albania, occupied by Italy, there existed, from some time after Russia's entry into the war, a number of separate guerilla movements, some of which entered into a loose affiliation with the Communists.[1] By the end of 1942 there were two main distinct movements, the Communist-controlled and the conservative partisans. Their total strength was then only about 6,000 men. In July 1943, Italy was about to collapse, and both movements came to an agreement to work together until Albania was free. Their operations were highly successful, until Italy capitulated and the Germans occupied the country. In view of their limited forces the Germans decided to secure for themselves only the towns and the lines of communication, and the partisans remained undisturbed in the mountains. Hardly had the Communists become aware of the German occupation policy, when they decided, in October 1943, not to ratify their previous agreement with the rival movement, but to liquidate it instead in the mountains, even if they would have to curtail their own operations against the Germans. In the ensuing civil war the Communists proved superior:

---

[1] For the following description of partisan fighting in Albania we lean heavily on Julian Amery's excellent account, *Sons of the Eagle, A Study in Guerilla War*, London, 1948.

they were stronger in numbers and better equipped, and they were under a unified command, whereas their opponents, fighting under a number of independent chieftains, were divided among themselves; the only addition to their ranks came subsequently from the Royalist partisans, who ended their affiliation with the Communists when the latter broke the agreement.

The British had made it clear that they would support with arms and equipment only those who were fighting the Germans. Their inferiority made it impossible for the non-Communists to defend themselves against the Communists and fight the Germans at the same time, whereas the Communists could always spare some forces for the latter purpose. British assistance was thus denied to the non-Communists, while the Communists became even stronger. The Communists, by attacking their rivals in these circumstances, intended to drive them into the arms of the Germans and discredit them even more before the Allies.[1] In this policy they succeeded to some extent. The conservatives were short of arms and had to appeal for help to their Quisling compatriots in the Albanian Government. The Germans in turn, glad to divert the partisan war against them into a civil war among the partisans themselves, obliged with arms. Hence the Communists branded all their rivals as collaborators,[2] even though the Royalists never were.

The rest of the story is quickly told. In May 1944, the Communist partisan commanders proclaimed themselves the future leaders of Albania, and the C-in-C appointed himself head of the Provisional Government. At the end of June, 1944, the Communists started their first campaign against their rivals, and others followed. In August the 'collaborationists' joined forces with the Royalists and prepared to turn against the Germans as well. Indeed, the fiercest attacks against the Germans were not made by the Communists but by the non-Communist partisan leader Gani Kryeziu and his brother.[3]

In spite of the non-Communists' good work against the enemy of Russia the attacks of the Communists against them continued; in one instance the Communists attacked their rivals while they were ambushing the Germans.[4] As the situation became increasingly hopeless for the non-Communist partisans, they left

[1] Julian Amery, op. cit., p. 172.
[2] Julian Amery, op. cit., p. 66.
[3] Cf. Julian Amery, op. cit., p. 263.
[4] Cf. Julian Amery, op. cit., p. 295.

their units or were sent home by their leaders. The Communist partisans were in control of the country and the government. They had won their revolutionary war.

The story of the partisan war in Yugoslavia is the story of Tito, the leader of the Communist partisans, and of Mihailovitch, the leader of the Royalist partisans. As long as the Yugoslavian guerilla war is remembered, people will ask the question about Mihailovitch: Was he a hero or a traitor? In 1942 the most prominent Western war leaders praised him as a gallant warrior and sent him their telegrams of appreciation. Four years later he was condemned to death by the Supreme Court of the Federative Peoples' Republic of Yugoslavia.

Prompted by patriotism, he took up the fight against the Germans as a guerilla when no other partisan leader had as yet arisen in Europe. He did not form his movement in order to fight the Communists: when he first organized his forces, there were no Communist partisans in the field; Russia, after all, had not yet been attacked by Germany.

These facts have become blurred, and even Brigadier MacLean in his fascinating *Eastern Approaches* seems to share the view that Tito had prepared for resistance against the invader before the fateful 22nd June, 1941.[1] But this is not quite so.

"On 22nd June, 1941, Germany attacked Russia. The Politburo of the Central Committee of the Communist Party of Yugoslavia had a meeting in Belgrade on that day. . . . There it drew up the proclamation calling the people to arms. The fact is," this official version goes on, "that the call to arms *coincided* with the date of the German attack on the Soviet Union."[2]

Some coincidence, considering that the Germans had attacked Yugoslavia no less than two and a half months before, yet Russia was attacked that very same day! But any remaining doubts as to whether Tito rose in defence of Yugoslavia or the Soviet cause are removed by the signals exchanged between him and Moscow; some of them were published in Yugoslavia after Tito's break with Stalin. When Tito, in March 1942, wanted to issue a proclamation, he first duly submitted the draft to Moscow for approval. Tito's intended proclamation concluded with the slogans: "Long live the heroic Red Army! Long live Comrade Stalin!

---

[1] Fitzroy MacLean, *Eastern Approaches*, London, 1949, p. 311.
[2] Nikola Kapetanovic, *Tito and his Partisans*, Yugoslovenska Knjiga, Belgrade, 1950 (?), p. 19. The italics above are ours.

Long live the Soviet Union!" Moscow directed that these slogans be deleted in the proclamation "since as they stand they lend it a Party character."[1]

On 27th March, 1941, the Yugoslav Government which had signed the pact with Germany was overthrown and the pact declared void. Thereupon the Germans attacked Yugoslavia. The Yugoslav Army did not hold out for long; within ten days it was decisively beaten. Draja Mihailovitch, then a Colonel on the General Staff, did not give up the fight. He collected two dozen of his officers around him in the Serbian mountains and organized his resistance movement against the invaders. Soon a great number of Chetniks, a pre-war organization of veterans of the First World War, joined his bands. In his initial operations he was highly successful.

In the meanwhile Tito's partisans had come into existence, and an understanding between the two movements seemed desirable. The first meeting between Mihailovitch and Tito appears to have taken place at Struganik on 19th September, 1941, when both sides agreed on military and political collaboration in fighting the Germans. The harmony did not last long. In October Mihailovitch and Tito met again, accusing each other of not complying with the terms of the previous agreement. Their differences were patched up, but once again mutual recriminations were voiced. In November 1941 both leaders met again. The atmosphere could not have been pleasant: they quarrelled over the possession of a town taken from the Germans in joint operations; Mihailovitch accused Tito's men of plundering the population, and Tito was incensed because fighting between the two movements had broken out in the process and a number of his men had been killed. From the end of the year both movements went their separate ways and fought each other bitterly whenever they met.

Many accusations have been levelled against Mihailovitch; the mildest was that he regarded the Communists as his foremost enemies. This accusation is entirely unfounded, and the evidence comes from the Tito camp. Tito, as we have seen, was in wireless communication with Moscow. In March 1942, he received the following signal from Moscow:

[1] Cf. Mosha Piyade, *About the Legend that the Yugoslav Uprising owed its Existence to Soviet Russia*, London, 1950, p. 11, written to refute Moscow's claim after the break that without Soviet help the Tito partisans would have been annihilated.

"Unfortunately, you misunderstood our telegram. We made you no reproaches. . . . *It is not opportune . . . to emphasize that the struggle is* mainly *against the Chetniks.* World opinion must first and foremost be mobilized against the invaders; mentioning or unmasking of the Chetniks is secondary."[1]

Nothing could be clearer than that. Tito, it appears, could not so easily adapt himself to the Moscow technique of window dressing, and he seems to have told Moscow so, because Moscow replied to him in April, 1942, that "it is certainly necessary to unmask the Chetniks to the people, concretely, with documentary proof, convincingly. . . ."[2] This task was duly executed and the documentary proof was used against Mihailovitch in his trial. Long before the West denied the authenticity of some of the evidence produced in the trial, Moscow had voiced its doubts. In September 1942, Tito received from Moscow the following signal:

"Urgent. Communicate in brief contents of documents which you possess concerning role of Draja Mihailovitch. Take care to check their authenticity well. It is possible that the invaders are particularly interested in stirring up an internecine struggle between the Partisans and the Chetniks. It is not out of the question that some of these documents have been deliberately faked by the invaders themselves."[3]

Indeed, to stir up trouble between the two guerilla movements was the avowed aim of German policy right from the start, as the following German Corps directive of 28th August, 1941, shows:

"LXV Higher (Corps) Command orders: Bands known to be Chetniks should not be attacked. Distribution of pamphlets originating from Chetniks should not be prevented. Communism is to be fought with the help of the national Chetniks."[4]

The Chetniks, however, did not oblige: they fought side by side with the Communists instead. The following German reports bear this out:

[1] Mosha Piyade, op. cit., p. 12. Our italics.
[2] Mosha Piyade, op. cit., p. 14.
[3] Mosha Piyade, op. cit., p. 17.
[4] *Trials of the War Criminals before the Nuremberg Military Tribunals,* vol. xi, *The Hostages Case,* Washington, 1950, p. 945.

"Commander Serbia HQ Staff Section Ia/F.
           Belgrade, 18th September, 1941
     Very Urgent
     Important Enemy Report.
  According to a report on hand Chetniks and Communists intend to avenge their comrades who died on the Cer Mountains, in Sabac and in Obrenovac. They intend to carry out an attack on Dedinje, dressed in German officers' and soldiers' uniforms. These uniforms are those of captured soldiers. By this disguise the insurrectionists intend to deceive the German guards and murder them. The intended time of the plan's execution could not so far be ascertained."[1]

At about the same time the Senior Quartermaster in Serbia sent the following signal to the Wehrmacht High Command:

"To OKW/Operations Group   14th September, 1941.
     same text to:
        High Command of the Army,
           Army General Staff.
  Threatening development of the overall situation in Serbia demands energetic measures. . . . The (Quisling) gendarmerie is unreliable on an increasing scale. Association between the insurgents—in my opinion not aptly described as Communists by the Commander in Serbia—and the Chetniks has been confirmed."[2]

It is quite evident from these reports that nothing would have been easier for Mihailovitch than to side with the Germans against the Communists, and that he decided to fight with the Communists against the Germans instead. These reports make clear one more fact: in Mihailovitch's opinion his enemy No. 1 was not the Communists, even if Tito, as we have seen, regarded the Chetniks as *his* main adversaries.

Mihailovitch persisted in fighting the Germans. His main strength was centred on Serbia. On 2nd November, 1941, the German Armed Forces Commandant South-East reported that "the rebellion now extends over almost the entire Serbian State."[3]

[1] *Trials of the War Criminals*, op. cit., p. 962.
[2] *Trials of the War Criminals*, op. cit., p. 967.
[3] *Trials of the War Criminals*, op. cit., p. 985.

In the following months Mihailovitch greatly extended his field of operations:

"Commanding General and Commander in Serbia.
HQ, 1st July, 1942.
I. Enemy Situation.
... At present it cannot be seen to what extent the revolt in Croatia will affect Serbia and especially the Draja Mihailovitch movement, since the insurgent organization of Draja Mihailovitch is no longer limited solely to the area of old Serbia. Activity of the Draja Mihailovitch organization extends to the territory of Southern Serbia and Albania, as far as Skoplje-Prilep, Eastern Hercegovina, as well as Eastern Bosnia."[1]

And a few weeks later, the Commanding General and Commander in Serbia reports, under the 20th July, on Mihailovitch's activities in Serbia.
"It is certainly necessary to unmask the Chetniks to the people, concretely, with documentary proof, convincingly," was, as we have seen, the advice sent by Moscow to Tito in April 1942. None of the above-mentioned German documents, it appears, fulfilled this purpose, and, as we may add, not one of them was introduced during Mihailovitch's trial. Instead, on 24th May, 1942, Tito reported to Moscow:
"The whole people curse the Yugoslav Government in London which, through Draja Mihailovitch, is aiding the invader."[2]

The documentary proof adduced here shows that he did nothing of the kind. Equally untrue was the assertion that the whole people cursed the Yugoslav Government for aiding the invader. The German General, Gehlen, who has recently come into the public eye on account of Soviet attacks against him as Chief of West German Military Intelligence, was then in the Department Foreign Armies East, the Intelligence Section of the High Command of the Army. On 9th February, 1943, he signed a General Staff report on the Draja Mihailovitch movement as per 1st February, 1943. The report contains the following sentence:
"The followers of Draja Mihailovitch come from all classes of the population, and at present comprise about 80 per cent of the Serbian people. Hoping for liberation from the 'alien yoke' and for

[1] *Trials of the War Criminals*, op. cit., p. 1010.
[2] Mosha Piyade, op. cit., p. 15.

a better new order and a new economic and social balance, their number is continuously increasing."[1]

Needless to say, the Staff Report was for internal consumption; it contained no added colouring, but described the situation as the German units on the spot experienced it.

Tito did not restrict himself to communicating his opinion to Moscow. "Draja Mihailovitch is aiding the invader," became the theme song of his persistent propaganda campaign. This campaign seems to have started early in 1942.

In the Belgrade version, "at the end of 1941, it was obvious that Mihailovitch was not only passive but that he was collaborating with the Germans."[2] That this astute observation was at once communicated to the West is clear from a British war time publication: "This finally confirmed the statements that the (Tito) Partisans had been making *ever since the beginning of 1942*. They said that Mihailovitch and his officers ... had long ago (sic!) given up any pretence of fighting the Germans, and had become little more than Quisling troops. . . ."[3] At about the same time the 'Free Yugoslavia' broadcasting station in Tiflis (U.S.S.R.) began to accuse Mihailovitch of collaboration with the Germans. Exactly when this radio campaign started is a matter of some doubt. According to Mr. Branko Lazitch it began in February, 1942,[4] but Mr. David Martin fixes the beginning at July of that year.[5] It matters little. Mr. Martin quotes in his book a B.B.C. Monitoring Report of 22nd July, 1942, in which the Free Yugoslavia station alleged that all the fighting during the previous year had been done by the (Tito) Partisans, while the Chetniks had not been fighting against the Axis at all; that Mihailovitch had committed treason, and that documentary evidence had been found.

This fiction was maintained to the end. When Mihailovitch faced his judges in Belgrade in 1946, he was accused of having

"in the period from July to the end of November, 1941, organized in occupied Yugoslavia a Cetnik organization . . . and as soon as the struggle for liberation of the peoples of Yugoslavia against the

[1] *Trials of the War Criminals,* op. cit., p. 1015, Nuremberg Doc. No. NOKW-1806.
[2] Nikola Kapetanovic, op. cit., p. 26.
[3] *The Story of the Partisans of Free Yugoslavia,* Yugoslavia Emergency Committee (British), to organize and provide help to the Army of Liberation led by Marshal Tito, 1944 (?), p. 13.
[4] *The Tragedy of General Mihailovitch,* London, 1946, p. 56.
[5] *Ally Betrayed,* New York, 1946, p. 27.

invaders began, he entered into collaboration with the Germans and Italians and their servants and used his organization to suppress the struggle for liberation of the peoples of Yugoslavia and to commit countless war crimes of all kinds,"

and his judges found him guilty because, among other things,

"beginning in the second half of 1941, throughout the war and enemy occupation he organized and led the armed Cetnik formations ... whose aim was, through armed action and a campaign of terror, *in collaboration with the enemy, to maintain the occupation*. ...

"he established contact with the invaders' commanders and authorities in order to suppress the National Liberation struggle of the peoples of Yugoslavia and *to maintain the occupation*, from the very beginning of his anti-national activity; he carried on *throughout the duration of the war*. . . ."[1]

"To maintain that his collaboration dated from 1941, when the Government of General Simovich, in the words of Mr. Churchill, 'saved the soul of Yugoslavia', merely raises fresh doubts as to whether it existed in 1944 and 1945", was the *Daily Telegraph*'s pertinent comment.[2]

We are not here concerned with Mihailovitch's trial but with the Communist propaganda efforts to stamp him a traitor. To make their propaganda more convincing, they resorted to an ingenious device: they identified the Mihailovitch movement with the Chetniks, and even today most people refer to the former as the Chetniks. Mihailovitch had no influence or control over this veterans' organization and it was at no time incorporated into his own movement; many Chetniks went with Mihailovitch into the mountains and fought with him to the end, but others offered their services to the Germans. It was easy to produce any number of compromising documents against this latter group and charge Mihailovitch with their misdeeds. The Germans soon recognized that the Mihailovitch movement was not identical with the Chetnik organization of the collaborators, as the following Intelligence Report of 342nd Infantry Division of 1st November, 1941, shows:

[1] Cf. *The Trial of Mihailovic*, Stenographic Record and Documents, Belgrade, 1946.
[2] *Daily Telegraph* (London), 16th July, 1946.

"Valid passes green in colour which are certified by the German military offices by means of a stamp are only at the disposal of a part of the Chetnik group Valievo. The remaining Chetniks who are loyal to the Government have in their possession passes issued by Pecanac."

Underneath this report comes the telling handwritten remark of the German recipient: "Probably dating from the period *before the split of the Chetnik units*."[1]

Soon afterwards the Germans issued a directive according to which the Mihailovitch forces were not to be referred to as Chetniks, but as the Draja Mihailovitch organization.

In the second place, Communist propaganda charged Mihailovitch with collaboration with the Yugoslav 'servants' of the Germans and Italians. Mihailovitch has never denied his contacts. At his trial he explained that he had made them in order to infiltrate collaborating organizations and win them over to his side for the decisive blow against the invaders. Nobody believed him then and he had no evidence to offer as proof. He did not know that somewhere, in some German document collecting centre in Nuremberg, or Paris, or Alexandria (Virginia), there was hidden among stacks of files a silent witness to corroborate his evidence, a German Intelligence report, which says:

"Croatia—Serbia.
The Draja Mihailovitch movement as per 1st. February, 1943.
A. General Information.
(1) Development: Among the various insurgent movements which increasingly cause trouble in the area of the former Yugoslav State, the movement of Draja Mihailovitch stands in first place with regard to leadership, armament, organization, and activity.
It is composed of the following groups:

(*a*) 'Chetnik units';
(*b*) 'Followers of D.M.'
... Immediately after the capitulation of the Yugoslav Army most of these Chetniks grouped together in Greater Serbia Combat Units under the leadership of their officers, thus forming the foundation of the D.M. movement.

[1] *Trials of the War Criminals*, op. cit., p. 984.

In order to be able to work unmolestedly within the scope of their overall organization, *they camouflage themselves* in *Serbia* under the cover of 'Chetnik units loyal to the Government', in *Montenegro* as 'National Militia', in *Dalmatia* as 'anti-Communists' and in *Bosnia* as 'Loyal Chetnik Units'."[1]

One more sentence from this report should be quoted because it reveals Mihailovitch's state of mind: "In order to avoid measures of reprisal against the Serbian population, however, Draja Mihailovitch always warns against premature single operations."

This was a point on which Communist propaganda could thrive, and in the process build up the legend that "during the entire war . . . the Chetniks did not enter the struggle against the invader."[2] The reader will at once see the reason for Mihailovitch's caution from the following contemporaneous German reports picked at random:

"15th December, 1942: Five Draja Mihailovitch followers shot in retaliation for the German sergeant shot to death near Zlotov."[3]

"27th June, 1943: Fifteen Communists and fifteen Draja Mihailovitch hostages are to be shot to death in reprisal for the attack and destruction of mines near Aleksinac on 8th June, 1943."[4]

"13th August, 1943: In retaliation for the murder of two, and the wounding of two, German soldiers by insurgents on the highway at Pozarevac on 9th August, 1943, 150 reprisal prisoners are to be shot.

"Since the political origin of the perpetrators cannot be definitely established, seventy-five Draja Mihailovitch and seventy-five Communist reprisal prisoners are to be executed."[5]

"28th May, 1943: A total of 100 Draja Mihailovitch hostages are to be shot to death. . . ."[6]

[1] *Trials of the War Criminals*, op. cit., p. 1015. Italics supplied, underlined in the original.
[2] Nikola Kapetanovic, op. cit., p. 28.
[3] *Trials of the War Criminals*, op. cit., p. 812.
[4] German document, Nuremberg Identification No. NOKW-374.
[5] German document, Nuremberg Identification No. NOKW-148.
[6] German document, Nuremberg Identification No. NOKW-341.

The reader may wonder about the system used by the Germans for selecting Draja Mihailovitch hostages or Communist hostages for execution. It was all laid down in German orders:

"Ic Counter-Intelligence Officer, Führer HQ, 28th September, 1941. Supreme Command of the Armed Forces.
 Subject: Taking of hostages.
 To: High Command of the Army, Quartermaster-General, Armed Forces Command, South East.
 "Because of the attacks on members of the armed forces which have taken place lately in occupied territories, it is pointed out that it is opportune for the military commanders always to have at their disposal a number of hostages of the different political persuasions, i.e.:

1. Nationalists;
2. Democratic middle-class, and;
3. Communists.

"In the event of an attack, hostages of the group corresponding to that to which the culprit belongs are to be shot."[1]

For two German soldiers killed and two wounded, the Germans, according to the above report of 13th August, 1943, executed 150 reprisal prisoners. Even this ratio had been fixed by German orders: for one German killed, fifty Yugoslavs were to die; for one German wounded, twenty-five Yugoslavs had to die. No wonder that Mihailovitch warned against premature single operations. Nor was this all. Mihailovitch's followers came to a large extent from the middle-class and the Germans did enormous damage to their property by way of reprisals. The Communists were in a different position altogether, and what Mr. Julian Amery stated with respect to the Albanian Communist Partisans applies equally to the Yugoslavs:

"With no resources of their own, the (Communist) partisans had to fight if they would eat, and thus were driven from one raid to another by sheer necessity. Nor was their zeal for war and plunder restrained by fear of reprisals against property; for they were, by definition, of the dispossessed. Indeed they

[1] *Trials of the War Criminals*, op. cit., p. 973.

might even welcome reprisals; for, by adding to the number of the dispossessed, reprisals added to the number of their potential supporters; while the destruction of property which they involved weakened the economic foundations of a hostile social order. The operations of the (Communist) partisans, therefore, took the form of sustained guerilla raids; and their movement fed on the devastation which it caused and grew, Phoenix-like, from the ashes of its own defeats."[1]

But Mihailovitch laboured under another disadvantage: Serbia, his main theatre of operations, was German-occupied, and he was therefore exposed at all times to their cruel reprisal measures. Tito's partisans had for many months the advantage of operating in territory not under German control; their opponents—Italians and Bulgarians—offered less resistance than the Germans, and for this reason, too, Tito could well be more active than Mihailovitch.

And, finally, Mihailovitch "had also received over the wireless messages from the Royal Yugoslav Government in exile and from the Allied High Command telling (him) to hold (his) hand."[2]

Still, in spite of all these handicaps and his own official orders, he continued to harass the Germans. On 19th January, 1943, General Bader, the Commander of the German Forces in Yugoslavia, issued the following proclamation:

"A group of rebels, under the leadership of the former Colonel Draja Mihailovitch, is continuing to fight. These rebels give themselves out to be the regular Yugoslav Army. They are endeavouring to prolong the war, which was brought to a conclusion by the armistice...."[3]

The report by General Gehlen of 9th February, 1943, to which we have already referred, says this about the Draja Mihailovitch movement:

"Germany is considered to be the main adversary. Her occupation troops must, as the 'occupiers', be destroyed."

[1] Julian Amery, *Sons of the Eagle*, op. cit., p. 168.
[2] Fitzroy MacLean, *Eastern Approaches*, op. cit., p. 336.
[3] Cf. *General Mihailovitch, The World's Verdict*, Gloucester, 1947, p. 11.

We have now followed the course of events on the German front until 1943. One year earlier, as the reader will remember, Communist propaganda had accused Mihailovitch of not fighting the Germans, of never having fought against them, and of collaborating with them and committing treason. The evidence shows that each one of these accusations was entirely unfounded. That they were repeated at the 1946 trial explains to some extent why Mihailovitch put up so weak a defence: if he was not believed where his innocence was obvious, he had no chance where the evidence was contradictory. This leads us to the final war-time accusation against him: Did he collaborate with the Italians with a view to "maintaining the occupation"?

It is certain that a number of his commanders co-operated to a greater or lesser degree with the Italians in the fight against the Communist partisans. The Gehlen report states that

"The Italian forces of occupation tolerate the D.M. movement or even support it. Often Chetnik units are employed for combating the Communists."

Hitler found this state of affairs so disturbing that he personally wrote to Mussolini about it. After warning Mussolini against supplying the Chetniks with arms and equipment, Hitler continued:

"I foresee a danger of especial nature, Duce, in the development of the Mihailovitch movement. . . . Taking account therefore, as I do, of the danger which the Mihailovitch movement presents, I have straightaway given orders for the complete annihilation by my troops of all his adherents in the territory which they hold."[1]

To which Mussolini replied:

"Minister Ribbentrop has probably informed you, Führer, of our discussions on the question of the (Tito) Partisans and Chetniks. We are entirely agreed on the fact that the Partisans and Chetniks are the enemies of the Axis and are prepared, especially in the event of an Allied landing, to make common cause

---

[1]Letter dated 16th February, 1943, quoted from Branko Lazitch, *The Tragedy of General Mihailovitch*, op. cit., p. 17.

with the enemy, thus placing us in a very difficult position.

"Several thousand Chetniks have received arms, by local arrangements, from the Italian unit commanders in order to wage guerilla war. . . . Although Mihailovitch is denounced by the Partisan radio as a traitor, he is no less our enemy, being the Minister for War of the Yugoslav Government in London."[1]

For once Mussolini's views were shared by Sir Winston Churchill, who wrote to General Ismay as follows:

"I believe that, in spite of his present naturally foxy attitude, Mihailovitch will throw his whole weight against the Italians the moment we are able to give him any effective help. Evidently great possibilities are open in this theatre."[2]

Now we must remember that Mihailovitch, a Serb himself, first founded his movement in German-occupied Serbia. There the rebellion started and, as we have shown, by November 1941 it had spread over almost the whole of Serbia. Fired by his example, others rose in various parts of Yugoslavia, especially in the Italian zone of occupation, and declared themselves for Mihailovitch. But these movements owed their loyalty in the first place to their local chieftains, who in turn retained a large measure of independence. It is for this reason that, as Mussolini stresses in his letter, the Italians never made more than local arrangements with the 'Chetniks'. They had no commander-in-chief in the Italian zone.

As a result the chain of command was by necessity a loose one, and Mihailovitch's knowledge of the events in this part of the country depended on what the local commanders told him, or what he and his staff noticed on their inspection tours. When Mihailovitch was confronted during his trial with the evidence on his commanders' collaboration with the Italians, he always stated that he had not been informed about this, that he did not know, or that this was the situation as he found it, which, in other words, he was powerless to change.

A regular officer, commanding regular troops, can be charged with the crimes of his subordinates if he had knowledge of their actions and failed to restrain them. But it is entirely different with

[1] Letter dated 9th March, 1943, quoted from Evgueniye Yourichitch, *Le procès Tito–Mihailovitch*, Paris, 1950, p. 176.
[2] Letter dated 2nd April, 1943, quoted from *The Second World War*, vol. iv., London, 1951, p. 839.

a commander of irregulars: here it must also be shown that he had the *power* to restrain them, or, alternatively, that he actually committed the crimes himself.

In the entire trial records of 550 printed pages only four instances are mentioned which could possibly support this charge.

The first is a report sent by Major Petar Bacovich to Mihailovitch on 16th July, 1942. It reads:

"All the Cetnik detachments on the territory of Hercegovina are legalized by the Italians, and receive food, arms and ammunition. They receive no salary but they are sometimes allotted small sums of money."[1]

But on three occasions during the trial Mihailovitch pointed out that he approved of legalization as the best means for infiltration;[2] and we have already seen that the Germans regarded his 'Chetnik Units loyal to the Government', his 'National Militia' his 'Anti-Communists' and his 'Loyal Chetnik Units' as camouflage for their real activities. The Bacovich report is therefore innocuous.

The other three documents all seem to relate to the fourth offensive against the Tito partisans early in 1943—with one exception the trial records omit to give the year. There is in the first place Mihailovitch's signal, found in his telegram book. It is dated 1st January, 1943, and reads:

"Bajo has already gathered 1,200 men, Pavle has already gathered 3,000 men (for the fourth offensive against Tito). Bajo's men are at Ostrog, and Pavle's at Kolasin. *The Italians say that the decision will be taken on 2nd January.* So far they allow movement to Niksic only. Pavle would not bother as to what movements they allow if the question of food, one million and a half rounds, footwear and arms was not *still under discussion*. There is a particularly great shortage of footwear. . . . Today Rakocevic guaranteed that he would get food and shoes. . . . Whether he gets them or not, Pavle will set out, but it is better to be shod than to go barefoot. . . ."[3]

[1] *The Trial of Mihailovic*, op. cit., p. 441.
[2] *The Trial of Mihailovic*, op. cit., pp. 132, 135 and 147.
[3] *The Trial of Mihailovic*, op. cit., text p. 434 f., facsimile, p. 246, *Examination of Mihailovitch*, pp. 191 f. The italics are ours.

In the second place, according to the trial records, Mihailovitch instructed one of his commanders to see to it that if Tito's partisans appeared on the cliffs, they should be strongly engaged by the twenty-two. Twenty-two, it should be noted, was the code word for the Italians.

Finally, a document was introduced in which Mihailovitch asked for the help of an Italian company in his fight against Tito. The Italians obligingly sent a battalion. Mihailovitch admitted the authenticity of the message.[1]

To complete the picture, we quote from the trial records:

"Prosecutor: Did you ever give orders to any of your commanders to attack the Italians and to wage an open armed struggle against them?

Defendant (shaking his head): There were some fake attacks. After the attacks the Cetniks came to free the Italians, and they took their arms.

Prosecutor: Was there any open fighting . . . ?

Defendant: I can't answer straight off, it is too difficult, I have no material at my disposal."[2]

These few lines easily qualify as the most phantastic trial examination of any war crimes trial. That the defendant had no material at his disposal may be noted in parenthesis. The main point is: Mihailovitch tells us that his units staged sham attacks against the Italians, who, by agreement reached beforehand, it appears, had to play the part of the losers, be taken prisoners and be disarmed; and when the show was over, they were freed, collected their belongings and walked home again. Why, and for whose benefit, these shows were produced is unfortunately not explained in the trial records, and we cannot think of any valid reason. But this much is certain: proceedings of this kind raise doubts as to the weight which an outside observer can attach to the evidence.[3] We shall, however, regard it as genuine in the following discussion.

---

[1] *The Trial of Mihailovic*, op. cit., pp. 197 and 447.
[2] *The Trial of Mihailovic*, op. cit., p. 163.
[3] For a charge-by-charge analysis of the trial cf. Evgueniye Yourichitch, *Le procès Tito–Mihailovitch*, op. cit. We are not directly concerned with the trial here, but three incidents involving British and American officers should be mentioned.

(a) According to the judgement, the British were responsible for the break between Mihailovitch and Tito and the ensuing civil war: "Having made all the necessary preparations for a general attack on the (Tito) Partisans, and in accordance with the

To make it quite clear, we repeat that we are not here concerned with the question of whether or not Mihailovitch was justly condemned to death because he killed Partisans, or had some accommodation with the Italians. Nor are we interested in showing whether or not this accommodation was justified. The sole object of our investigation is to ascertain whether he was rightly branded as a Quisling by the rival Partisan movement because he had Italian support in fighting it. The answer is in the negative.

---

message that Captain Hudson had transmitted to him from his superiors and which read: 'Yugoslavs must fight for Yugoslavia and the struggle must not be transformed into a Communist rebellion for Soviet Russia', the Accused, Mihailovitch, broke the agreement regarding the joint struggle of the Cetniks and Partisans against the invaders and their hirelings...." (p. 511 of *The Trial of Mihailovic*). For the genuine text of the letter cf. Col. Hudson, *News Chronicle*, 14th June, 1946.

(b) " 'Annihilate the Partisans'. Message of Colonel Bailey, the Chief of the British Mission, to Mihailovitch" is the headline on p. 191 of the Trial records. The text goes on:

"Prosecutor: When did Colonel Bailey come to you?
Defendant: In December, 1942.
Prosecutor: From whom did you learn that the Allies would land?
Defendant: When Bailey came, I learned about it....
Prosecutor: Did he ask you to discontinue your attack against the (Tito) Partisans and to co-operate with them in an attack against the invader in order to make the landing safer?
Defendant: Here I must be definite and ask not to be objected to for something which looks improbable. I intended to establish contact in some way, and went to the terrain to try to find some means of contact. This may seem unbelievable to you, but I told him: 'I shall go and try'; but I could not, because the fighting was very bitter. He advised me differently. As the indictment has already stated, he advised liquidation or annihilation of the Communists.
Counsel for
Defence: The Communists or Communism?
Defendant: The Communists or Communism, I do not quite know. I ask the President, should not this be answered in secret session?
President: In the Federative People's Republic of Yugoslavia you can speak freely before the Court.
Defendant: He said: 'Annihilate the Partisans.'
Prosecutor: Annihilate the Partisans? Is that so?
Defendant: Yes."

On 12th June, 1946, the British Government sent a Note to the Yugoslav Government asking, among other things, for documentary evidence and adding that on information at present available the Yugoslav allegations seemed baseless, also that Colonel Bailey and Captain Hudson had denied the statements attributed to them. Cf. London *Times*, 14th June, 1946. It is impossible to understand why Mihailovitch admitted that he received such messages from the two officers concerned (pp. 124 and 192 of the Trial records). No reply to the British representations has apparently been received.

(c) Again according to the Trial records, Colonel McDowell came to Mihailovitch in July 1944 and told him: "Your present situation is difficult, but the future is yours." (p. 305) "Your fight against the Germans does not interest us, you have to keep your position among the people—I have come to help you." (p. 307.)

For a final piece of Belgrade fabrication the reader is refered to p. 465 of the Trial records.

He knew, approved, and himself made use, of Italian cooperation in 1943. One year earlier—one year before he committed it—Communist propaganda had accused him of this crime. Merged with the preposterous charge of having collaborated with the Germans ever since July, 1941, it could not but have its effect. It was aggravated by the fact that we in the West understood the term 'collaboration' as equivalent to 'giving aid and comfort to the enemy'; but at no time was Mihailovitch motivated by such thoughts.

In any event, in 1943 the British Government had doubts whether Mihailovitch was doing his utmost to defeat the Germans and whether the Partisans were not doing at least as much. In May of that year a British Mission was therefore sent to Tito in order to form an estimate of the relative value of the Partisans and to determine the best means of helping them.[1]

Mihailovitch's 'collaboration' with the Italians did not last long; in the summer of 1943, they capitulated. Mihailovitch's position became precarious. For many months now the Partisans had been operating in Italian country, and arms could be picked up there more easily than in Mihailovitch's German-occupied Serbia. When the Italians capitulated, Tito's units reaped the harvest and collected great quantities of war material. Mihailovitch had acquired little: not much had reached him from British sources, and in the words of a German report, dated 30th December, 1942:

"According to the documentary material in our hands the number of arms is frequently in striking disproportion to the number of organized Draja Mihailovic men.

"Thus it appears from prisoner interrogations that the Rosina Brigade with 6,000 men has only 300 rifles and 5,000 rounds of ammunition. . . ."[2]

The author of this report goes on to state that this estimate takes into account only the rifles stored by the staff and not those stored by individual members of the brigade; however, this cannot change the picture very much, if such private stores existed at all.

---

[1] Fitzroy MacLean, op. cit., p. 279.
[2] The document, issued by the Commanding General and Commander in Serbia, has the Nuremberg Document Identification No. NOKW-1248.

Still, even after the Italian capitulation Mihailovitch did not turn to the Germans. A number of his operations against the Germans during the period August to October 1943 have been recorded by Captain Walter R. Mansfield, of the U.S.M.C.[1] At the end of 1943, Tito's National Liberation Movement set up their government of Yugoslavia. Following the Teheran Conference Allied support was withdrawn from Mihailovitch, and Tito was liberally supplied with arms. The Yugoslav Government in exile withdrew its support from Mihailovitch, whose Minister for War he had been, and many of his supporters joined the other side. Mihailovitch was isolated.

"With the help of our own propaganda," says Brigadier MacLean, "we had in our own imagination built up Mihailovitch into something that he never seriously claimed to be. Now we were dropping him because he had failed to fulfil our own expectations."[2] "While we were exhorting the underground movements of France, the Low Countries, Poland and Norway to lie doggo until the decisive moment came," notes Mr. Jaspar Rootham, "we enjoined a contrary policy in the Balkans, and criticized Mihailovitch for taking the very line which, in other parts of Europe, we said was the right one."[3] The reason for the Western policy is, of course, clear: whereas in Western Europe risings long in advance of the Allied landing would do more harm to the population than good to the war effort, it was different in the Balkans; as long as the fighting in Africa lasted, the German supply lines went through these countries, and when Italy was invaded it became the Balkan's task to pin down the German occupation forces which would otherwise have gone to Italy. Mihailovitch's record shows that within the limits of the possible he was prepared to shoulder this burden.

In the course of his trial Mihailovitch admitted that in November 1943, in what has been called the sixth offensive against the Partisans, his units took joint action with the Germans. But the Germans knew that Mihailovitch had no intention of giving aid and comfort to them. A German witness in the U.S. War Crimes Case against Field Marshal List et al. summed up the position in these words:

[1] In *Marine with the Chetniks*, The Marine Corps Gazette, January 1946, pp. 3 f., February 1946, pp. 15 f.
[2] *Eastern Approaches*, loc. cit., p. 438.
[3] Jasper Rootham, *Miss Fire*, London, 1946, p. 103. Cp. Also Branko Lazitch, op. cit., p. 53.

"This desire on the part of the Chetnik leaders to enter into negotiations with German authorities was certainly not based on any special love for the Germans, but rather on an emergency situation in which the Chetniks found themselves because they were simultaneously fighting the Communists, and in order not to have to fight on two fronts they often tried to arrive at a compromise, a healthy compromise with the Germans. . . . All these negotiations with the Chetniks did by no means represent a guarantee for the German armed forces that after a few weeks the negotiator of today would not be an opponent of tomorrow."[1]

Whether Mihailovitch approved even at this stage of parleying with the Germans, we do not know. All that could be shown in his trial was that he had had two meetings with the Germans. One took place in November 1941; what it was all about, the trial did not reveal, but he fought fiercely afterwards—as before—against the Germans. The second meeting in 1944 was authorized by the U.S. High Command: as Colonel McDowell has made clear, it was held to accept the surrender of the Germans.[2]

On 1st September, 1944, Mihailovitch issued his orders for a general uprising, as he had always promised he would.

In Yugoslavia, as in Albania, the Liberation Movement had persistently accused their non-Communist rivals of collaboration until, deprived of outside support, they succumbed.

We now turn to Greece.[3]

By 1942 several resistance movements had come into existence. The strongest had been formed by the Communist-controlled National Liberation Front; its People's Liberation Army has become known by its initials ELAS. Non-Communist movements were the EDES, under General Zervas, and EKKA, under Colonel Psaros. Both ELAS and EDES had British support.

ELAS was more concerned with suppressing their rivals than with fighting the Germans. In spite of their promise to the British, ELAS attacked the EDES movement in October 1943. British supplies alone would not have saved General Zervas. He had to safeguard his rear against a simultaneous German attack. The Communists, as was to be expected, had already accused him of collaboration with the Prime Minister and the Minister of the

[1] *Trials of the War Criminals*, op. cit., p. 1074.
[2] Cf. Colonel McDowell's account in the *Times*, 12th June, 1946.
[3] Cf. Especially the authoritative book by Colonel C. M. Woodhouse, *Apple of Discord*, London, 1948. Also Sir Reginald Leeper, *When Greek meets Greek*, London, 1950.

Interior in the Quisling Government, and through them with the Gestapo. His temporary 'agreement' was in fact with the Wehrmacht.

It is easy, of course, to censure him on this account. But General Zervas had seen how the Communists had previously attacked one resistance movement after another, including the EKKA, whose leader, along with hosts of others, they executed.[1] The Communists were superior in numbers and equipment. In any event, Zervas could not continue to fight the Germans while he had to defend himself against the Communists, and by stipulating in his agreement with the Germans that neither side should resume hostilities against the other,[2] he gained respite without giving anything away. That he, too, had no intention of giving aid and comfort to the enemy is clear from his subsequent action. In March 1944, thanks to the efforts of the British and American liaison officers, a truce was announced between the Communists and EDES, and by June EDES had once more turned their activities against the Germans "in the form of bloody raids."[2]

On the same day as that on which the truce between the Communists and EDES was made known, the Communists announced that a Political Committee of National Liberation had been formed, whose main purpose was to provide a government.[3] In the spring a Communist-inspired revolt engulfed Greece; it was suppressed, and the Communists decided to go slow. In May 1944, representatives of all political parties, including the Communists, agreed to form a government.

This did not stop them from trying to secure for their ELAS partisan organization control of the country by dubious means. They had accused their rivals of collaboration yet, on 1st September, 1944, one of the Communist leaders signed an agreement with a German major at Livadi by which the Partisans undertook not to harass the Germans on condition that the latter handed over authority to him in the evacuated region.[4]

In October 1944, the German troops evacuated Greece and the Government of National Unity entered the country. Most of

[1] A. A. Pallis, *Problems of Resistance in the Occupied Countries*. London, 1947, p. 10.
[2] Affidavit by Claus Goernant, introduced as evidence in the Hostages Case, *Trials of the War Criminals*, op. cit., p. 1049.
[3] Dimitrios G. Kousoulas, *The Price of Freedom*, Syracuse University Press, 1953, p. 106.
[4] A. A. Pallis, op. cit., p. 10. Ibidem also references to *The Nineteenth Century and After* of May 1947, for the original text of the agreement, and *Time and Tide* of 15th March, 1947, for the translation.

Greece was in Communist hands. The Government decided to demobilize all guerilla formations and establish a regular army. When the Communists refused to disband their Partisans, fighting broke out again, regular British troops intervened, and peace and order were restored. In the agreement of 12th February, 1945, the Communists undertook to disarm. "This was a defeat for the Greek Communists, and it was not due to factors within Greece but to British intervention: without British action Greece would have had the same regime as Yugoslavia."[1]

The pattern, at any rate, was the same.

In Poland, however, different tactics had to be employed. The Communist partisan movement was a negligible force and open battle with its rivals was therefore out of the question. Nor would the usual accusation of collaboration be of any use: the Polish underground movement had no outside support of which it could be deprived. Other means had therefore to be devised to remove the rivals.

The brunt of the guerilla fighting in war-time Poland was borne by the Home Army, and during the last war few people in the West were aware that there also existed a separate Communist movement, the so-called People's Army. When the Red Army stood at the gates of Warsaw in 1944, the Home Army rose in its epic fight in the city. Although it was evident that it could not hold out for long without outside support, the Red Army made no attempt to relieve it. When the Western Allies wanted to help and asked for permission to land planes on Soviet-controlled airfields, permission was refused. The Home Army, exhausted, surrounded, and without ammunition, was left to its fate. The People's Army did not then lift a finger to fight the common enemy, Germany. The People's Army was not supposed to: the main enemy was the Home Army.

In 1941 Russia's fate hung in the balance. One would have thought that in the circumstances every ally who was willing to fight the Germans would have been more than welcome. But, again, the Russians felt otherwise. At the end of 1941, they dispatched an agent to Poland with instructions to discover the network of the Polish underground and liquidate it. The details of this mission and the subsequent developments have been revealed by

---

[1] Hugh Seton-Watson, *The Pattern of Communist Revolution, A Historical Analysis*, London, 1953, p. 217.

Lt.-Colonel Jozef Swiatlo, formerly of the Polish Political Police, who fled to the West in December, 1953.

According to Swiatlo[1] the fight against the Home Army was carried on not only by the People's Army, but also by the Polish Workers' Party and Soviet Intelligence. All collaborated with the Gestapo to achieve their aims. 'Rola', who subsequently became the commander of the People's Army, C-in-C of the Polish Army, Marshal of Poland (and a prisoner of the regime), was the first to establish contact with the Gestapo, betraying, as Swiatlo tells us, the secret quarters of the underground organizations. An agent from Moscow supplied the Gestapo with data about the activities of the Home Army and names and addresses of its members, adding that they were all Communists. Another Communist underground organization, called 'Sword and Plough' and working under Soviet Intelligence, sent some of their men and a People's Army Intelligence officer, all dressed in Gestapo uniforms, to the Home Army's Central Archives, sequestrated the files, and passed on those on the Home Army itself to the Gestapo. Among the rivals to be liquidated, Swiatlo states, were the members of the London Government Delegate's Office.

While the Communists tried and succeeded in Albania, Yugoslavia and Poland, and tried but failed in Greece, they did not try very hard in France and Italy. That they failed there was due, in France, to the efforts of General de Gaulle and his administrators. "The second reason for the failure was"—and this applies to Italy as well—"that the war was still on, and Allied military commanders had to be obeyed. This was as important for Moscow as for Washington or London, and the leaders of the French Communists were obliged to order their followers to give wholehearted support to the war effort. Thus the course of the war in 1944 prevented the French Communists from using the strength that they had gained through resistance as a means of seizing power. The state machine was rebuilt by de Gaulle's men, and the forces in French society—very different from Balkan—which opposed Communism were able to reassert themselves. After the autumn of 1944 the Communists' only remaining hope was to obtain power by constitutional means."[2]

---

[1] *The Swiatlo Story* was published in "News from behind the Iron Curtain", vol. iv, No. 3, March 1955, pp. 3 *seq.* "News" is published by the Free Europe Press of the Free Europe Committee, Inc., New York.

[2] Hugh Seton-Watson, *The Pattern of Communist Revolution*, op. cit., pp. 222 and 225.

If Russia goes to war against the West, the restraint on the Communist partisans in France and Italy will no longer be applied. They will be under orders from Moscow to remove any opposition to Communist domination of the country.

We may well ponder what this implies.

Chapter IX

THE NEW WARFARE ORGANIZATION

THE Soviet organization which directs the new warfare is complicated and confusing. In the first place, some of the agencies concerned frequently alter their initials: the Secret Police, once the Cheka, changed its title several times before it became the NKVD; and it subsequently called itself the MVD. To make things more difficult, the Intelligence Service of the State Security Committee was at one time or another merged with the NKVD and the MVD and adopted their initials, whereas during other periods it led an independent life and was known under its own initials as MGB—though true to form it subsequently made another switch and became part of the KGB.

But this is not all. The functions of the top agencies overlap. Until Stalin's death both the MVD and the G.R.U. (Chief Intelligence Directorate of the Red Army) carried out military and political intelligence abroad, but since the MVD is responsible for State Security its officers are not confined to work within their own organization, but crop up as well in other organizations which they supervise, for example the G.R.U.

And finally, at the bottom of the structure, there is more than one body which can carry out a specific assignment. While the Party is responsible for propaganda and agitation, and some secret sections of the Party deal with sabotage and others with intelligence, the partisans, in addition to their operational duties, take care of all these functions as well.

There was, of course, a lot of overlapping of this sort in Nazi Germany as well, for which there were two reasons: the bosses were fond of private empire building; and Hitler liked it because he could play one against the other. The result was mutual jealousy and inefficiency. The glaring example is the Cicero affair, in which Himmler's Political Secret Service and the Wehrmacht's Intelligence Service fought it out between themselves, and the winner in the contest declared the loser's prize collection of the most secret Allied war plans to be forgeries; they were assigned to the waste-paper basket.

It is difficult to say whether the overlap in the Soviet structure is due to similar reasons. No doubt Beria was as much a private empire builder as Himmler, and Stalin, like Hitler, kept the control of State and Party exclusively to himself. However this may be, the Soviet Sixth Column does not show any signs of inefficiency, whether it is in the field of atom espionage, subversive propaganda or guerilla warfare.

In peace time the Sixth Column has the following functions:

(a) Propaganda and Agitation.
(b) Sabotage and Terror (assassinations, kidnappings).
(c) Intelligence.
(d) Preparation of Partisan Work.

In war these activities are supplemented by:

(e) Partisan Warfare.

We shall deal with the functions in that order.

(a) *Propaganda and Agitation.* These are the normal functions of the Communist Parties of all countries where they are not in control of the Government. It was formerly the Comintern which laid down the general rules and supervised their execution. The Comintern was the organization of the Communist Parties in the various countries moulded into a single World Communist Party. It had a special Section for Agitation and Propaganda. In order to soothe Allied ill-feelings the Comintern was allegedly disbanded in 1943. Whether this really took place is a matter of doubt. The Royal Commission in Canada which in 1946 investigated the facts relating to the Communication of Secret Information to the Soviets has adduced evidence to the contrary.[1] It may not be mere coincidence that soon after the publication of this Report, in 1947, the foundation of the Cominform was announced, which for all practical purposes seems to carry on the Comintern's functions.

The type and form of the propaganda and agitation have been dealt with at length in Chapter V and they require no further elaboration.

---

[1] Cf. *The Report of the Royal Commission to Investigate the Facts relating to . . . the Communication of Secret and Confidential Information to Agents of a Foreign Power,* 27th June, 1946, Ottawa, 1946, p. 37. Subsequently quoted as Royal Commission, Canada.

(b) *Sabotage and Terror*. Terror and diversion abroad are regarded by the Soviets as part of their Foreign Intelligence and are instruments for the safeguard of their own State security. The main source of information on the present organization and functions are the Khokhlov disclosures, which were made public at the offices of the United States High Commission in Germany on 22nd April, 1954. The following account is based on the briefing papers issued by the U.S. authorities at the time.

The direction of terror and diversion is in the hands of officers of the Ministry for Internal Affairs. The life of its officers is a varied one. Captain Khohklov was trained during the war to engage in partisan activities in German uniform behind the German lines, and as Herr Oberleutnant Wittgenstein of the Geheime Feldpolizei he played a leading part in the elimination of the German Gauleiter in Minsk.[1] He then worked as a partisan in the Minsk area, in eastern Poland, and in Lithuania. In 1945 he went to Rumania, so that he and others in East European satellite countries could organize partisan and para-military activities should the territories be overrun by enemy forces.[2] Subsequently he acquired a Polish passport, Rumanian citizenship, and Austrian papers; in 1952 he refused to carry out an assassination mission in France, for which he would have been supplied with Swiss papers. At the end of 1953 he was given the task of murdering a prominent Russian *émigré* in Frankfurt, West Germany. However, he told his intended victim the entire story and asked the U.S. authorities in Frankfurt for political asylum.

These activities were organized by what is now the 9th Section for Terror and Diversion, a fitting though rather unusual designation for a Government department. It is subordinate to the MVD Second Chief Directorate, Foreign Intelligence—the First Chief Directorate being responsible for counter-espionage. In 1952 a task of a different nature was handled by the Section: an agent was dispatched to Denmark with the mission of inducing the Danish Communist Party to take action against the imminent conversion of Denmark into an Anglo-American base.

The 9th Section is located in Moscow. It had its advanced operation bases in Austria and East Germany; the Austrian base was in Baden near Vienna and the German base is in Karlshorst. A

[1] Khokhlov's story also appeared under the title *I Would Not Murder for the Soviets* by Nicolai E. Khokhlov, as told to Milton Lehman, in the *Saturday Evening Post* of 20th, 27th November, 4th and 11th December, 1954.
[2] For the factory sabotage groups and sabotage cells cf. Chapter vii above.

special Danish section was attached to the latter at the time of the Danish venture.

The 9th Section and the Second Chief Directorate are MVD agencies, but Captain Khohklov, who worked for them, has described himself as an MGB officer.[1] There is nothing contradictory in that; it is the direct outcome of the Russian habit of juggling with the initials of their various agencies. We have already mentioned that the Secret Police under the Ministry for Internal Affairs was originally known as Cheka. In 1922 this was changed to GPU and soon afterwards to OGPU. After the purges, when this organization had fallen into disrepute, it adopted the initials NKVD. In 1943 another reorganization took place and it then became known as NKGB. Three years later it took the title Ministry of State Security—MGB. After Stalin's death MGB and MVD were merged. They now belong to one and the same agency, known as the MVD, the Ministry for Internal Affairs.[2]

Khokhlov had as assistants for his Frankfurt murder assignment two East Germans whom he had previously recruited. But normally there is no need to rely on outside helpers because the secret sections of the Communist Parties abroad have special panels of members available for tasks of this nature. These secret sections supply personnel for sabotage, espionage and assassinations. Their members are recruited from the Communist Party, but once they belong to these special organizations they cease to have contact with the Party.[3]

(c) *Intelligence.* A number of Soviet agencies are interested in the collection of foreign intelligence. Diplomatic intelligence concerns the Commissariat for Foreign Affairs, and Naval Intelligence is busy in its own special field. These activities are not unusual and do not require any further treatment.

Tass collects newspaper and magazine reports of interest, but its members abroad have special functions as well: Mr. Petrov revealed that the Tass representative in Australia was an MVD man. He ordinarily reported to the MVD officer at the Embassy but also acted as a contact man with the outside.[4] Petrov added

---

[1] Cf. Especially his *Saturday Evening Post* article of 20th November, 1954.
[2] Cf. Commonwealth of Australia, *Royal Commission on Espionage*, Official Transcript of Proceedings, taken at Melbourne, 6th July, 1954, pp. 151–2. These Proceedings in the Petrov case are subsequently referred to as Royal Commission, Australia.
[3] Cf. A. Rossi, *A Communist Party in Action*, New Haven, Yale University Press, 1949, p. 183.
[4] Royal Commission, Australia, Transcript 17th May, 1954, p. 9.

that the Tass man in practically every country is an MVD officer.[1]

More unusual still are the foreign intelligence missions of the Cominform, the MVD, and the G.R.U. of the Red Army. MVD and G.R.U. personnel are usually employed at the embassy. But although the G.R.U. personnel are Red Army officers of Army Intelligence, they are not necessarily employed in the Military Attaché's department; in Australia G.R.U. representatives worked as 'Repatriation officers'.[2]

Nor is there, of course, an MVD department in a Soviet embassy: any embassy official might be an MVD man, and even the other embassy officials do not know who is or is not an MVD man. They have all some other function at the embassy: Petrov for instance, an MVD officer with the rank of colonel, was in charge of the consular section. To make the camouflage even more effective, the official rank at the embassy is in no way indicative of the rank within the MVD hierarchy: Petrov, a Third Secretary, was in his MVD capacity superior to an MVD man with the rank of Second Secretary.

The MVD is chiefly interested in foreign political, economic and technical intelligence, in fact in every bit of intelligence except purely military intelligence, which is taken care of by the G.R.U. officers.[3] The Cominform concentrates on political and economic intelligence. However, the Comintern, and now probably the Cominform, fulfils a special task for all: whenever it is intended to recruit an agent for any agency, he is first vetted by the Comintern, which has for this purpose an enormous central index on individuals at its disposal all over the world.[4] It is located in Moscow. The vetting procedure has a double purpose: prospective agents who are unreliable, and agents already working for another network, are eliminated from the list.

One of the paramount tasks of the Comintern therefore is to keep up its dossiers on individual Communists everywhere. Furthermore it requires information on foreign social problems in general and on the activities of the various Communist Parties in particular in order to enable it to direct their propaganda and agitation campaigns.

[1]Royal Commission, Australia, Transcript 1st July, 1954, p. 87.
[2]Petrov evidence, Royal Commission, Australia, Transcript 2nd July, 1954, pp. 106, 107.
[3]Petrov evidence, Royal Commission, Australia, Transcript 1st July, 1954, p. 97. It appears from this source that since 1953 the MVD does not concern itself any longer with military intelligence.
[4]Cf. Royal Commission, Canada, p. 25 et passim.

Its Intelligence machine is fed through three channels. The various Communist Parties abroad constitute one obvious channel. The second is the Central Committee of the Communist Party of the Soviet Union, which gets its information from the Political Section of the various Soviet embassies.[1] Thirdly there are the individual agents abroad specially appointed for this task; Sorge the master spy was once one of them.

The G.R.U., Chief Intelligence Directorate of the Red Army, specializes in collecting Intelligence of a military as well as political nature. In addition to information useful in assessing a foreign country's economic and military potential, and on the location of its defence industry, it seeks to obtain all data which reveal the political plans of the country. But it is not only after top level Intelligence; it also concerns itself with variegated tasks of a very specialized nature, such as information on telephone tapping devices, or on how agents could enter the country illegally.[2]

The four sources of its information are the Military Attachés, the spy rings, the partisans, and the secret intelligence groups.[3]

During the last war at least three spy rings worked for the Soviets: the Red Orchestra in Western Europe, the Sofia network covering South-East Europe, and the Sorge spy ring covering Japan. We have dealt with the Red Orchestra at length. The Sofia network was directed by the Soviet mission there. Herr von Papen has described it in his Memoirs as quite the best information-gathering centre of the Moscow system,[4] but nothing is known about its operations. The work of the Sorge spy ring has already been mentioned in Chapter III.

The Intelligence tasks of the partisans have also been discussed earlier, in Chapter IV.

The secret Intelligence groups in Canada were mainly made up of Canadians recruited principally from the Communist Party,[5] and it may be assumed that more or less everywhere the secret sections consist mainly of nationals of the country concerned.

These secret groups operate under a very ingenious system. Naturally, those working for the Red Army do not work for any other agency. But, and this is the unusual feature, the various

[1] Royal Commission, Canada, p. 12.
[2] Royal Commission, Canada, p. 89.
[3] Cf. Major-General Charles A. Willoughby, op. cit., pp. 139 *seq.*, for Sorge's own story, which, by the way, omits to mention the partisans.
[4] London, 1952, p. 474.
[5] Royal Commission, Canada, p. 25.

groups employed by Military Intelligence do not work under the same Russian boss; the Soviets maintain instead several distinct networks working under different Soviet Chiefs.[1]

This parallel undercover system affords special security to the Soviet networks: neither the members nor the bosses can reveal too much if they choose to confess, and if the country's counter-intelligence uncovers one group, the others can still continue their clandestine work. Only the top agencies in Moscow know the full extent of their networks.

As the Royal Commission in Canada revealed, the NKVD, as it was then called, works parallel to, but quite distinct from, the Red Army's network;[2] and these findings have since been confirmed in the hearings of the Royal Commission in Australia: there as well as in Sweden the respective agents worked separately and did not exchange their information.[3] But both use the same system, and, as a Moscow directive stresses, one of the means for obtaining secret information is through "agent penetrations of government institutions and leading circles."[4] The training of the MVD and G.R.U. representatives also seems to be along identical lines.[5]

The tasks of an MVD representative abroad were described before the Royal Commission on Russian Espionage in Melbourne on 6th July, 1954, as follows:

"A letter dated 6th June, 1952, from Moscow instructed (Petrov) to establish an organization of illegal agents in Australia to work in the event of war, but not to frighten them by saying that war was likely in the near future. The letter said that intelligence work in Australia in 1951–2 was actually at a standstill and had produced no discernible results. It spoke of the necessity of a radical reorganization of all intelligence work for exposing the designs of the enemy and urged the creation of illegal operators in Australia as a first priority task.

"Mr. Petrov was to recruit agents who had access to intelligence and counter-intelligence work and could possibly supply information about the plans of the Anglo-American bloc to

[1] Royal Commission, Canada, p. 19.
[2] Royal Commission, Canada, p. 23.
[3] Royal Commission, Australia, Transcript 30th June, 1954, p. 74 and July 2nd, 1954, p. 106.
[4] Royal Commission, Australia, Transcript 18th May, 1954, p. 32.
[5] E. H. Cookridge, *Soviet Spy Net*, London, 1955, p. 100.

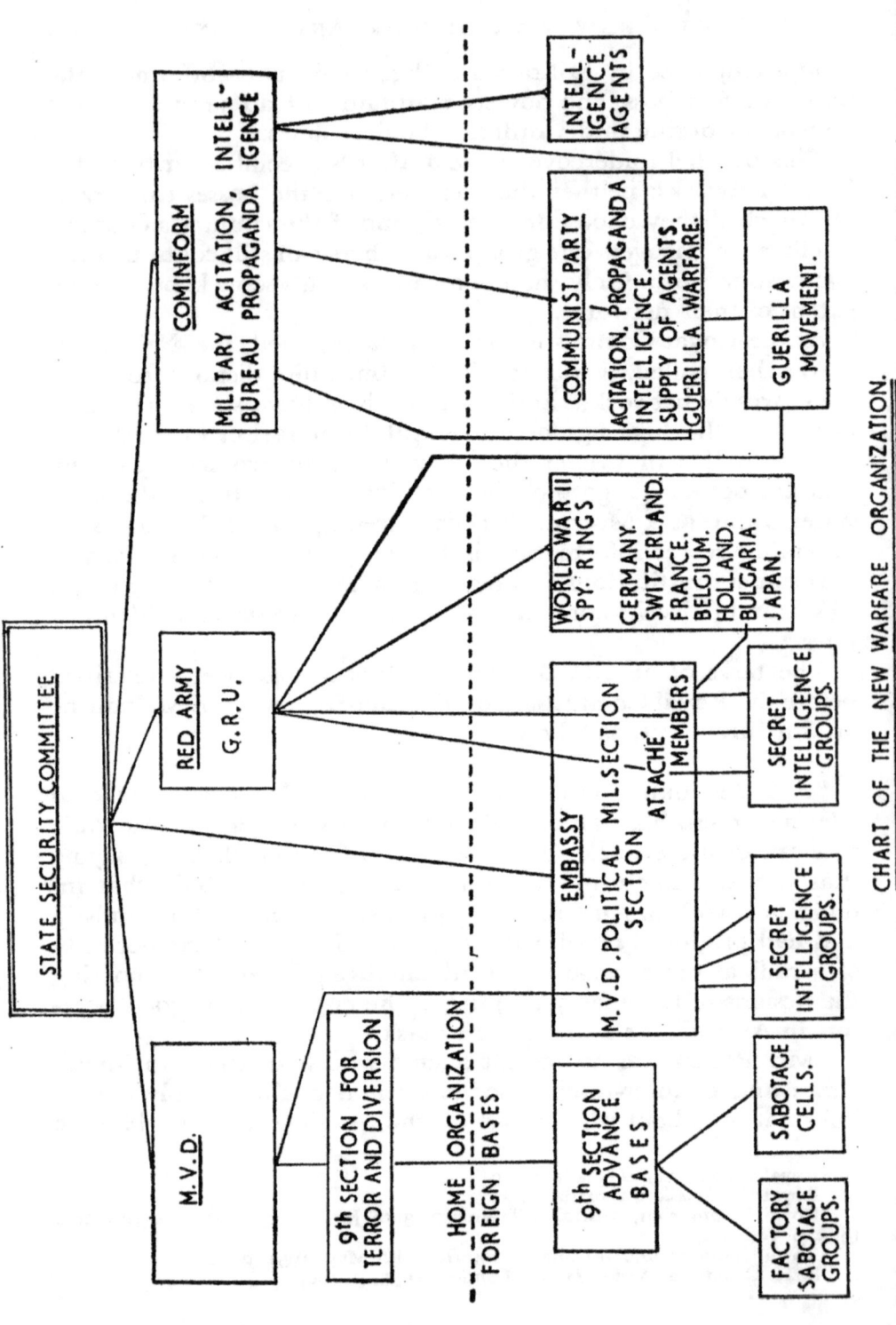

CHART OF THE NEW WARFARE ORGANIZATION.

sabotage Soviet and Communist countries. Agents were to have concrete tasks alloted to them in advance, because there were signs that war was inevitable in the near future; they were not to be recruited from persons known to counter-intelligence.

"Interception and unmasking of enemy agents in the Soviet Union was sought. Mr. Petrov was to concentrate on people engaged in secret Government work capable of supplying valuable information. The plan was to be carried out boldly, accurately, aggressively, and with inventiveness; there was to be no indecision, negligence or cowardice. Mr. Victor Antonov, the new Tass representative, would help with this work."[1]

These instructions reveal one further item of interest: they stress the necessity for developing counter-intelligence work, adding that this is a new (sic!) but extremely important line. This admission allows of only one conclusion: at this time the European Defence Community seemed to become a reality, and the Soviets began to realize that the free world was determined to defend itself against aggression.

We might pause here for a moment to review the allocation of intelligence and counter-intelligence work within the MVD. It seems quite clear from the above instructions that Petrov was to deal with both types of work. It may indeed be assumed that all MVD residents abroad engage in both activities: an MVD circular letter to its residents abroad stressed that they should make separate reports for each line of work, intelligence to be marked 'O' and counter-intelligence 'K'.[2]

All reports are sent to MVD Headquarters and not to a particular Directorate, and it is not at present clear which Directorate deals with Intelligence and which with counter-intelligence. According to the Khokhlov Briefing Papers counter-intelligence is the responsibility of the First Chief Directorate and Foreign Intelligence that of the Second Chief Directorate, but Mr. Cookridge asserts that the First Directorate deals with both Intelligence and counter-intelligence, while the Second Directorate looks after positive State security.[3] To make things even more involved, Petrov stated that Panyushkin is Head of the First Chief Directorate,[4] while in Mr. Cookridge's and Captain Khohklov's view Panyush-

[1] London *Times*, 7th July, 1954.
[2] Royal Commission, Australia, Transcript 1st September, 1954, p. 670.
[3] Op. cit., pp. 45 and 50.
[4] Royal Commission, Australia, Transcript 1st July, 1954, p. 97

kin is the Chief of the Second Directorate.[1] And finally, Messrs. Cookridge and Khokhlov disagree again over the question of who heads the First Directorate.[2]

So much for the Intelligence work of the three main agencies named above. In April, 1954, however, a fourth agency came into being, the State Security Committee attached to the U.S.S.R. Council of Ministers. "The functions of the new Committee are likely to include the co-ordination of intelligence and counter-intelligence activities."[3] It thus takes over the job formerly handled by the K.I. or Information Committee, a branch of the Central Committee of the Communist Party.[4] That the new Committee, like the old, maintains a direct link with the embassies can be assumed but not ascertained.

This, then, is the new warfare organization, which we have tried to outline on our chart.[5]

(d) *Preparation of Partisan Work* was formerly in the hands of Bureau No. 1 of the MVD. In 1953 it was renamed 9th Section for Terror and Diversion, some of whose activities we have already discussed. In the following account we quote from the Khohklov Briefing Papers.

Bureau No. 1 was formed in 1945, and it was staffed with high-ranking MVD officers and agents who had had experience of partisan work behind the German lines during the war. "The

[1] E. H. Cookridge, op. cit., p. 50, and Chart in the Khokhlov Briefing Papers. Mr. Panyushkin's career illustrates the versatility of a top MVD official. He had received a military education and served in the Red Army. He now holds the rank of Lieutenant-General, probably his MVD rank. He was formerly an officer of the K.I., the Party Central Committee for the co-ordination of all Intelligence-gathering activities. From 1939 to 1944 he was Ambassador to China; in 1947 he became Ambassador to the United States, where he remained in this capacity until 1952, when he was appointed Ambassador to Red China for a year. Khokhlov discussed the Frankfurt assassination mission with Panyushkin in detail, "including the weapons", according to the Khokhlov Briefing Papers.

[2] This last disagreement might of course be due to the fact that there had been a change during 1954.

[3] London *Times*, 28th April, 1954.

[4] The K.I. was dissolved at the end of 1951. Cf. Royal Commission, Australia, Transcript 6th July, 1954, pp. 153 and 157. Mrs. Petrova, secretary to the Ambassador and book-keeper to the Embassy, had also acted for the K.I.

[5] In his diagram of an "Avanpost" opposite p. 128 of his book, Mr. Cookridge shows the Military Attachés as being in direct contact with the MVD Directorates. We believe that this direct connexion was severed when G.R.U. was retransferred in 1948 from the MGB to the Red Army. The diagram also shows the Military Attaché as sharing his network with the embassy, but it seems to appear from our evidence that they have separate and distinct networks. Furthermore it is not indicated on the diagram that the MVD HQ has its officers at the embassies and maintains direct contact with them. Nor do we agree with Mr. Cookridge when he says on page 36 that the Red Orchestra worked under Beria; on p. 188 the author himself shows how the Red Three were financed by Red Army Military Intelligence.

original intention was to establish key agents in areas outside the Soviet Union who would become familiar in the course of time with the language, customs, politics, terrain, and special problems of the area. They were intended to receive and perhaps command partisan troops either infiltrated or parachuted into the area in case of war. The programme was actually launched in the satellite countries and was proposed for Western European nations.... The first residents established were in Rumania in 1945, followed by Poland, Hungary and Czechoslovakia. A group was established in Austria early in 1951, and another was created in Eastern Germany late that same year.

"The mission of Bureau No. 1 began to change in 1951 when it was desired to spread the network over Western Germany. Experience had proved that it was too difficult to use Soviet nationals for the operations, and the plan was changed to recruit and train East Germans, who could then be sent across to establish themselves in the Federal Republic. Soviet MVD officers would direct these nets from Berlin and, in the event of war, would seek to make their way illegally to Western Germany to continue the operation."

In 1952 and 1953 further changes took place. All available agents were to be used for sabotage and other violent activities, while the 'long-term prospect' was 'abandoned'. Furthermore the operations of Bureau No. 1, now known as 9th Section for Terror and Diversion, were considered wasteful duplications of other Soviet intelligence operations, especially those of the Second Chief Directorate, which, as we noted in Chapter VII, "was cited as already having agents in place in the West for any operations for which Bureau No. 1 would have to procure, train, and dispatch an agent." The 9th Section was therefore made subordinate to the Second Chief Directorate (Foreign Intelligence) of the MVD. The 9th Section was given the mission of carrying out 'special action tasks', as we have seen in Chapter VII, for the Second Chief Directorate.

Since the war each of the satellite countries has formed its own guerilla brigades, and it is therefore easy to understand why the 'long-term prospect' was abandoned in 1952 in respect to these countries. But there can hardly be any doubt that the preparation of partisan warfare in those countries of the West where the strength of the Communist Party makes it feasible is still entrusted to the Second Chief Directorate, acting through its network of "agents ... in the West for any operations".

(e) *Partisan Warfare.* The Communist Party of the country forms and organizes the guerilla movement, it appoints the leaders, and it directs operations. These are the uniform features of the guerilla movement in every country, whether it be Russia, France, Malaya, or China. But the organization itself is not rigid and varies from country to country.

Technical and practical reasons account for the organizational variations. During the last war the Russian guerillas fought as auxiliaries to their regular army, but in the case of Malaya the guerillas are the only fighting force in the field. The Communist partisans in France, the FTP (*francs-tireurs et partisans*), were fighting in the last war on the Allied side, and were loosely subordinate to Allied commanders: but partisan forces ranged against the Allies are under the command of the Fifth, or Military, Bureau of the Cominform,[1] and the Cominform will take command over French Communist guerillas, should the Allies be involved in war against Russia. And yet in Russia the Comintern did not put in an appearance at all in the last war—anyway, during half the campaign it was supposed to be in a state of dissolution—and it may be that the Russian partisan movement does not come under the Cominform's supreme command.

But one can take it for granted that in a future war the bands and their staffs will once again adopt the structure which stood up so well to the test of battle in the last war.

The Russian guerillas in the last war were commanded by Partisan General Headquarters in Moscow; all subordinate staff headquarters, and of course the partisan bands, worked on the other side of the German lines.[2] Directly subordinate to Partisan GHQ were the Partisan Commands (White Russia, Ukraine, Crimea), all purely headquarters staffs; under them were the Partisan District Headquarters, who were operational HQs for combined operations of several detachments; and at the bottom of the ladder were the Partisan Detachments or bands, the troop units. The bands varied greatly in strength: some had ten or twenty men, others had 2,000, but the norm was a few hundred or less. The bands, therefore, hardly ever reached battalion strength and higher units, such as regiments or brigades, were unknown.

[1] Lt.-Colonel John Baker White, *The Armies of Communism*, Military Digest, General Staff, Army HQ (New Delhi), No. 22, July 1954, p. 80.
[2] For further particulars cf. Dixon and Heilbrunn, *Communist Guerilla Warfare*, pp. 59 *seq.*

Operational orders were issued to the bands through their own chain of command, viz. the Party hierarchy in the guerilla movement. But if the Red Army wanted a partisan detachment to go into action it did not use the normal channels: the various bands received such orders direct, as we noted earlier, either from the Army units on the other side of the German lines or from the General Staff of the Red Army, with whom every band of some importance was in regular wireless contact.

The Party exercised its influence over the movement not only through supplying the leadership at all levels, but also through appointing commissars to each unit, even the smallest. In addition, a number of bands required their members to swear allegiance to the Party.

The NKVD was strongly represented at the various higher and lower headquarters, and a number of NKVD people fought with the bands. But they certainly did not take charge of the partisan movement, which, under their watchful eyes, was under the effective control of the Party. However, the NKVD had bands of their own, and these bands and individual NKVD emissaries carried out a number of special missions.

The FTP in France was built up on different lines. Since the Communist partisan movement was not the only one in the field and subordination to Allied commanders was necessary, a *modus vivendi* had to be found with the other groups, and this was effected through the National Council of Resistance, which exercised at top level a loose political and military control over the FTP and the other French guerilla organizations. In France the top control of the movement was thus vested outside the Party.

In France the Communist organization was less elastic than in Russia. Whereas the Russian bands had no fixed establishments, the French Communist bands adopted an almost military rigidity. The smallest unit, the combat group, consisted of a leader, a deputy leader and six men; three combat groups formed a section; three sections made up a company; and a battalion had three companies. The battalions were under the control of Party Departments; these in turn were subordinate to Groups of Departments; above them were the Party Territories; and, finally, the Zones.[1]

The French partisans did not then adopt the commissar system, nor did the NKVD enter into the picture.

[1] Cf. in particular F. O. Miksche, *Secret Forces*, London, 1951, pp. 84 and 147.

In Russian and France the bands procured their supplies themselves, and they provided their own intelligence service. In Malaya, however, there is a strict division between the fighting units, the Malayan Races Liberation Army (MRLA), and its supply and intelligence units, the Min Yuen. The Party is in exclusive control of the movement, and the commissar system is rigidly applied at all levels. The chain of command goes down from the Politbureau to the Central Executive Committee, which exercises control over the North, Central, and South Federation. Under each Federation follow, in descending order, the State Committees, the District Committees, the Branch Committees, and finally the Cells.

The fighting units are organized by regiments, companies, platoons and sections, the regiments being attached to the State Committees and the subordinate units to the subordinate Party Committees and Cells. From District Committee level downwards the Party officials are divided into two distinct groups: those responsible for MRLA leadership, and those in charge of the Min Yuen movement.[1]

As far as the organization of the Chinese guerillas is concerned, it is not possible to be very specific at the present time. In the Far-East post-war theatres the guerillas, though organized by the Chinese, were not Chinese themselves. Mao Tse-tung, it is true, drew up a number of tables for the organization of Chinese guerillas, and we find such tables in his *Aspects of China's Anti-Jap Struggle*,[2] tables for Independent Medium Units or companies, Independent Major Units or battalions, Independent Detachments or regiments, Independent Columns or divisions, and for the organizational system of a Military Area. But these schemes were not meant to be permanent. They were suitable for the special conditions of the time and the guerilla character of the Chinese Red Army at that period.

By guerilla character Mao meant the lack of fixed operational fronts and the 'fluidity' of his base areas, but as early as 1936 he made it clear that the Red Army would discard its guerilla character as soon as possible.

"Our workers' and peasants' democratic republic is a State, but today it is as yet an imperfect one. Today we are still in the phase

[1] Cf. H. Miller, *Menace in Malaya*, London, 1954, pp. 103 f.
[2] Bombay, 1948, pp. 30, 32, 34, 36 and 42. Cf. also Colonel Samuel H. Griffith's translation of the Mao booklet in the (U.S.) *Marine Corps Gazette*, 1940.

of strategic defensive in the civil war, the form of our political power is still a long way from that of a perfect State, our Army is still far inferior to the enemy both in numbers and material equipment, our territory is still very small. ... To define our policy on this basis, we must honestly admit the guerilla character of the Red Army. ... It is useless to feel ashamed on this score. On the contrary, this guerilla character is precisely our distinguishing feature, our strong point, our means for defeating the enemy. We should prepare to discard this character but we cannot yet discard it today. Some day this character will definitely become a thing to be ashamed of and therefore to be discarded, but today it is invaluable and must be firmly retained."[1]

Typical of this 'guerilla-ism' is the decentralization, non-uniformity, lack of strict discipline and simplicity of the methods of work in the Army. "All these things," Mao then explained, "have emerged in the Red Army's infancy, and some of them have answered precisely the needs of our time. But when the Red Army reaches a higher stage, we must gradually and consciously eliminate them so as to make the Red Army ... more regular in character."[2]

With this aim in mind, Mao insisted a year later, the guerilla war must "gradually develop and elevate its main forces to become regular armies, to wage a co-ordinated war with less developed guerilla forces as well as both existing and newly organized regular armies." "In this way, the combination of existing and newly organized regular armies with regular armies developed from guerilla forces, as well as broad guerilla forces which have not yet been developed into regular armies, constituting the total armed forces of the national revolutionary war, will serve final victory."[3]

It is therefore obvious that the guerilla character of the Chinese Red Army, so vital to them during the 'Second Revolutionary Civil War' (1927-38) and still necessary during the subsequent struggle against the Japanese (1938-45), would at the earliest possible moment be discarded, and with it Mao's above-mentioned organizational schemes designed for the struggle against Japan.

[1] Mao Tse-tung, *Strategic Problems in China's Revolutionary War*, in *Selected Works*, London, 1954, vol. i, p. 244.
[2] Mao Tse-tung, *Strategic Problems of China's Revolutionary War*, in *Selected Works*, op. cit., p. 246.
[3] Mao Tse-tung, *Aspects* etc., op. cit., pp. 1 and 2.

That the Chinese will also in future employ guerillas cannot be in doubt, but their new organizational pattern has not yet emerged. When the Civil War (1946–9) started, the Communist forces were too inferior to Chiang's armies in numbers and equipment to drop their guerilla character. In 1945 the Communists could muster against Chiang's two and a half million men only 300,000 regulars, supplemented by 700,000 militia and innumerable guerilla bands; and when war broke out the following year, the Nationalists had a period of successes during which the Communists were restricted to guerilla-type actions.[1] In 1947, the Communists went over to the offensive, but at first they still relied exclusively on guerilla methods—refusing battle in unfavourable country, but executing quick raids and surprise attacks on garrisons and isolated units, followed by fast retreats and dispersion.[2] They were so successful in these engagements, and reduced the disparity in material to such an extent, that from June 1947 on they could start to discard their guerilla methods and undertake instead large-scale offensive operations of a decisive nature.[3] But while the Communists gradually renounced the guerilla nature of their operations, their guerillas remained in being, engaged in their usual activities of cutting the enemy's communications, and also fighting beside the regulars or on their own. By the middle of 1948 the Communists had one and a half million regular troops and about 700,000 guerillas, against the Nationalists' 2.1 million men.[4] In 1948 the war took a disastrous turn for Chiang. On 23rd January, 1949, the Communists established themselves in Peking. Soon afterwards Mao estimated the Nationalist forces, irregulars included, at one and a half million men.[5]

It was thus only during the last year of the war that the Communists reached parity in numbers and then achieved superiority over their opponents. The Red Armies' guerilla character could be finally discarded only after Mao had established himself as the sole ruler of the Chinese mainland and had reorganized his Army on the Russian pattern. It can only be assumed that the Chinese

---

[1] Général L.-M. Chassin, *La Conquête de la Chine par Mao Tse-tung* (1945–9), Paris, 1952, pp. 47, 52, 55 and 91.
[2] Général L.-M. Chassin, op. cit., p. 107.
[3] Cf. Général L.-M. Chassin, op. cit., p. 107.
[4] Général L.-M. Chassin, op. cit., p. 172.
[5] Mao Tse-tung, *Speech at the Preparatory Committee of the Chinese People's Political Consultative Conference*, 15th June, 1949, reprinted in *Mao Tse-tung on People's Democratic Dictatorship*, Peking, 1951, p. 31.

guerillas' new organization will also not be very different from the Russian model.

Indeed, the organizational differences between the various partisan movements are more apparent than real. Most of the differences are entirely due to local circumstances. The functions were always identical: politically the Communist guerilla movements were the Party's instrument for the instigation and waging of civil war; militarily they were the Red Army's second front.

FINAL ARGUMENT AND SUMMING UP

Chapter X

A LEAF OUT OF THE GERMAN BOOK

WE have tried in the foregoing to give chapter and verse for the Soviet conception of the new warfare. Much of the case material relates to Russian operations during the last war. A brief survey of Germany's conduct of the war without battlefield against the Russians seems pertinent, however, in order to profit from her experience and learn from her mistakes.

Compared to the Soviet grand design the German approach to the new complex of agencies and methods is pedestrian. In their planning before the start of the campaign the Germans relied almost exclusively on the might of their Armed Forces, which, they thought, would assure a quick military defeat of Russia and, as a consequence, destroy Bolshevism. But they treated even some military problems with strange casualness. In July 1940, less than a year before the German attack, the German intelligence system on the Eastern Front "was not yet organized, that means we (the Germans) had no radio interception service or anything of this kind."[1] But whereas this deficiency was soon to some extent repaired, political warfare received scant attention. Propaganda, it is true, was mentioned as an important contribution to warfare in one of the High Command orders which outlined the operational aims of the campaign against Russia. But not until a month after the start of the campaign, apparently, did it dawn on Rosenberg—Commissioner for the Central Control of Questions of the East-European Region and subsequently Reichsminister of the Occupied Eastern Territories—that "there were certain independence movements in the Ukraine which deserved furtherance."[2] Himmler's Political Secret Service had as yet taken no interest at all in political warfare, and only Military Intelligence prepared for some diversionary activities. Apart from military planning the Germans, before the outbreak of hostilities, gave

[1]Testimony of Col.-General Halder in the 'Ministries Case' (No. 11) at Nuernberg, in *Trials of the War Criminals before the Nuernberg Military Tribunals*, Nuernberg, vol. xii, pp. 1306, 1309.
[2]Rosenberg at the conference with Hitler, Goering, Keitel and others of 16th July, 1941, reprinted in *Trials of the War Criminals etc.*, op. cit., vol. xii, p. 1293.

serious thought only to the spoliation and subjugation of Russia.

Even anti-Communist Russians had nothing to gain and a lot to lose from such a policy. Most of the Russians who had in the beginning welcomed the Germans as liberators soon learned their lesson. As a result the Germans could not count on the mass support of Russian malcontents for any length of time. And furthermore, the Germans had no well-wishers in high official positions who could supply them with the innermost secrets of the Soviet State Committee for Defence.

The Germans, therefore, had no 'Brown Orchestra' or 'Brown Three' at their disposal, and their subversive propaganda and political warfare had little effect on the Russian population.

German radio propaganda was not only handicapped by the short-sighted policy of the German political leadership, but it suffered also from psychological limitations of its own. Just as the Russians, in their broadcasts to Germany, took it for granted that their political system had an irresistible attraction for the German worker, so the Nazis imagined that anti-semitism was bound to appeal to the Russians and would induce them to desert. German broadcasts to the Soviet troops were therefore clumsy and ineffective.

One of the earliest examples of this type is a broadcast by the German Danube Station on 10th July, 1941:

"Men and officers of the Red Army! The Red Army received the order to march against National Socialist Germany. The Red Army must make an end of the small group of half-starving armed men hired by Capitalism, and liberate the German people from the gang of Fascist dogs, so say the Jews, the political commissars. Is it true? Do you know that the German Army is an army of the German workers and peasants? That the German Army is a Socialist army? Do you know that it is the best army in the world? Do you know that the German Army is standing behind its leader and Supreme Commander Adolf Hitler, as one man?

"Do you know who Adolf Hitler is? During the World War he was a simple soldier. Then, with the best sons of his people, he began the struggle against the domination of world Jewry. Fourteen years of keen struggles have passed. . . .

"And who is Stalin? He began with highway robbery. By treachery and numerous murders he reached supreme power and began to call himself a leader of the nations of the Soviet Union, the leader of the toilers of the entire world, the prophet of world revolution. The world revolution has not come to pass. He wanted to build Socialism on the blood of millions. What is Socialism? Is it the bloody experiment of oppression and exploitation? How many people have died of starvation or were liquidated during the twenty-four years of his People's Government? You know this well....

"The German Army is bringing liberation to you. This strong and tried army is marching now against your oppressors in the Kremlin. The victorious German troops will not tolerate the threat of the Jewish centre in Moscow....

"To resist the German Army is useless. Now you must know against whom to level your rifles, hand grenades, machine guns and guns. Down with Stalin, down with Kaganovich, down with Beria, down with all this Jewish riff-raff, down with the oppressors of your people and of the entire world....

"Men and officers of the Red Army, save your lives! Come to us! Don't throw away your equipment, and keep your military documents on you. Collective farmers and workers, guard the harvest, keep bread and other foodstuffs! Don't forget the famine!"[1]

There were also German-sponsored broadcasts from the 'Russian Freedom Station' and Russian prisoner-of-war talks in a similar vein. It is hard to believe that Russian soldiers would have risked their lives by listening to these tiresome tirades, or that Russian experts took part in composing them.

But there is a lesson to be learnt from the German radio propaganda flop: unlike the Germans we should not take it for granted that the Russians long to embrace *our* political system; all the less since they have been taught to believe that Bolshevism is the only genuine form of democracy.

German front-line propaganda was not very inspiring either. The usual technique was described in a German broadcast of 31st July, 1941:

"It is reported from the Eastern front that numerous groups of Soviet soldiers hide in woods and engage in marauding activities in the neighbourhood and sometimes try to cut German lines of communication. When they use arms in these operations they are

[1]B.B.C.'s Daily Digest of Foreign Broadcasts, No. 723, Part I.

dealt with at once by German troops and annihilated, but if they are merely hiding and German soldiers have more important things to do, they are dealt with in another way. The German propaganda service comes into action and a Russian-speaking officer sends an enormous shout over the loudspeaker saying: 'Your troops are defeated, we will treat you well and give you food and drink.' After this has been going on for some time, the distant sound of balalaikas is heard with the soft notes of Russian folk songs. The brutalized spirits of the Russian soldiers begin to be softened. Then the German propaganda officer begins again and speaks to them of their wives, their children and their harvests. Soon after, shadows begin to creep out from the hiding places, where they have only been held by fear and lying reports about the Germans."[1]

The Germans also dropped leaflets over the Russian front, and the Russian soldiers were assured that these leaflets would serve as passes for them when they surrendered. Since it was considered dangerous for Russian soldiers to carry such passes while they were still with their units, the passes were replaced by passwords such as: "We are fed up with the Jewish Commissars". Special passes were dropped over partisan areas, and practically every day German broadcasts tried to intimidate those who chose to fight on; but with little success, as a German order indicates, because "shooting in spite of the leaflet promise will soon become generally known".

However, not all German propaganda efforts were futile; though such successes as the Germans had were by far outweighed by their failures. They were able to form SS Divisions from Ukrainian, Caucasian and other volunteers; they enlisted an SS Cavalry Cossack Corps; they had some partisans fighting for them against the Russians; they obtained the support of the captured Russian General Vlassov and the East troops, an army of Soviet war prisoners in German hands; a great number of indigenous voluntary helpers served with them; the propaganda operations 'Silver-lining' (Silberstreif) and 'Winter Fairy Tale' (Wintermärchen) did induce Soviet front-line soldiers to desert; and a number of Russians, grouped into Indigenous Security Units, assisted the Germans in fighting the Soviet partisans. But the Germans themselves, by their insane policy, had roused the

[1] B.B.C.'s Daily Digest of Foreign Broadcasts, No. 749, Part I.

Soviet partisan spirit and provoked this menace throughout occupied Russia, and these partisans outnumbered, outmanœuvred and outfought any collaborators the Germans could muster to oppose them.

A survey of the activities of these various groups of collaborators is outside the scope of this book, but several German operations deserve attention, especially the espionage and sabotage of 'Action Zeppelin' and the similar war-time exploits of the Political and Military Secret Service.

Action Zeppelin was the code name for a special activity of Branch VI of Himmler's Reich Security Main Office. This Branch VI was Germany's Political Secret Service. "In Germany itself Branch VI had so-styled 'Observers' in each Secret Service Region with tasks very similar to those of the Military Intelligence Offices but on a much smaller scale to begin with. In neutral and friendly countries the organizations of the Secret Service came under the control of a 'Principal Representative, Branch VI'."[1] It was, in fact, Himmler's private Military Intelligence, and this extraordinary state of affairs lasted until 1944, when he finally managed to absorb the Military Secret Service into his own organization. In 1941 Action Zeppelin was entrusted not to the Wehrmacht but to Himmler's Secret Service. Its purpose: the use of Soviet P.O.W.s for Intelligence and sabotage behind the Russian lines. In launching Action Zeppelin the Germans copied the Soviets.

In charge of Branch VI and Action Zeppelin was SS Major-General Schellenberg. According to him

"Among the population of the Soviet Russian area occupied by us and among the millions of Russian prisoners of war taken, already after a short time in increasing measure a well-operating Russian espionage system was recognized as being in existence. The Soviet espionage system . . . worked with the aid of German prisoners of war who had been specially trained in the Soviet Union for that particular type of service. It was specifically these Germans who, after being processed from the front, had the duty mainly to transmit intelligence.

"Due to the speed with which military operations progressed, our own survey of the condition became beclouded, and the military as well as the political operational staffs very heavily

[1] Wilhelm Hoettl, *The Secret Front*, London, 1953, p. 17.

criticized why on our part the intelligence service wasn't exploiting all means. Thereupon I was issued the strict and clear order that likewise on my part I was to use Russian prisoners of war for Intelligence service on behalf of Germany in the Soviet Union."[1]

For this purpose a special office, VI-C-Z, was formed in Branch VI. Its first task was to select from the POW camps suitable Russians who could be trusted to be enemies of the Soviet system and who would volunteer as saboteurs or intelligence agents. The Germans had in fact many volunteers for the job of 'activists', as they called themselves. Unfortunately for the Germans, a good number of them were Soviet infiltrators.

Typical is the case of one Koschilev. He had been interrogated by the town mayor of Stodolischtsche, Herr Hauptmann Kranzl, whose office somehow came to the lucid conclusion, "as a result of this interrogation, that the man is actually a spy, only the question is whether in the Russian or the German service." Koschilev slightly overplayed his hand. He stated that he had worked in 1936 and 1937 as a Gestapo agent under a certain Keller in Moscow.

"He claims to have received an assignment from this man in 1936 to blow up coal station 1 at Spitzbergen. This was allegedly not successful but he blew up station 2 instead. He claims that he later carried out an assignment to blow up the radio station on Wrangel Island. He claims further that on Keller's orders he sank, with the help of two stokers, the ships *Ulitka* and *Somji*, which were carrying secret documents from Vladivostok to Murmánsk. In 1937 he claims that, acting under orders, he destroyed radio communications between 'Schmidt' island and the steamship *Sibirjak* by blowing up the electricity plant on 'Schmidt' island; in the same year he also claims to have blown up a radio station in Moscow. In 1937 he also succeeded in getting the plans for the newly constructed airplane of Professor Prokofjev by taking photographs."[2]

According to the SS Senior Colonel who interrogated Koschilev, he "makes a very convincing impression". But when the Reich

---

[1] Direct examination of the defendant Schellenberg, reprinted in *Trials of the War Criminals* etc., vol. xiii, p. 574 of the English edition.
[2] *Trials of the War Criminals* etc., op. cit., vol. xiii, pp. 564 and 565.

Security Main Office checked up on him, they found that "the above mentioned person as well as the contacts mentioned by him are absolutely unknown." One would have expected this to put an end to the career of Koschilev. But it did not. During the subsequent months he was trained in the SS Special Camp at Vissokoje—one wonders what the SS could still teach the hero of so many exploits—and, as the SS reports, this training "and his collected impressions on this trip to Germany (24th June to 1st July, 1942) have without a doubt convinced K. that Bolshevism must be destroyed." The SS report concludes: "K. seems best suited for sabotage acts within the sphere of Action Zeppelin." But then events took a sudden turn. A few months later Koschilev, "as a result of various things which happened in the meantime", as the report from the SS Special Camp at Vissokoje put it, was shot by the Germans. Another report from the same camp tells us of several activists who "left furtively and without reason."

In one case at least the NKVD not only infiltrated one of the groups but also made short work of the activists:

"The NKVD had been successful in having the Drushina unit ... infiltrated by spies of their own, and they exercised extensive courier contacts right into Germany. One day it happened that all German soldiers active in this unit, SS men and SS fuehrers, were mutilated and killed in an atrocious manner, as well as, at the same time, all of those Russian activists who were willing to work for Germany against Russia. All this was done by a small group of the NKVD who were then able to escape to Moscow by airplane."[1]

While the Russians tried to kill the activists, the Germans shot the suspected spies among them: in Auschwitz alone it appears that 200 suspects were executed. But the Germans were unable to weed out the infiltrators. Shortly after fifty activists had been transferred to a Drushina unit it happened that its German liaison officer was killed. Thereupon the entire unit went over to the partisans, whom they were supposed to be fighting.

Action Zeppelin was not confined to sending agents behind the Russian front: it also collected information from the various

[1] Schellenberg, Testimony, in *Trials of the War Criminals* op. cit., vol. xiii, p. 580, English edition.

Police attachés, the infamous Einsatzgruppen, and from prisoners of war in the camps. Among the P.O.W.s the Germans sought out the intelligentsia; it was the task of the interrogators "to collect, besides factual information of general importance, information about the political, economic and cultural conditions in the Russian areas not yet occupied, by means of questioning and interrogating." The interrogation of these prisoners, as well as those who volunteered as activists, was carried out in the P.O.W. and transit camps. Those found suitable as activists were transferred to an SS Special Camp, where they received political schooling; it culminated in a week's trip to Germany, where they stayed on farms and visited factories and were probably impressed by the German standard of living. They also received the special training usual for Intelligence agents and saboteurs. An evaluation report was then made on the trainee. One report reads as follows:

"As an officer K. displays a particular consciousness of his social standing. By the schooling in camp Vissokoje, K. has obtained a clear political attitude. For him the annihilation of Bolshevism means the liberty of the Russian people. He is energetic and methodical."

At least, so it appeared to the SS instructor, until K. too "left furtively and without reason."

When the training was completed, the agent was given a cover name and assigned to an area of operations behind the Russian lines.

Altogether thousands of agents were trained, on the assumption that mass assignments produce maximum Intelligence results. Working at ground level, as it were, the Germans probably had no other choice, but nothing can reveal the crudeness of this method more clearly than a comparison with the Soviet system of penetrating the German top agencies with a handful of infiltrators.

Office VI-C-Z gave the orders and assignments to the various agents. Its Central Directing Staff was in Berlin, and it had at first two, and later a few more, Main Intelligence Centres (Meldekampfkommandos), located near the Army Group Headquarters. The agents were sent on their way to unoccupied Russia either by being taken through the front line or by being dropped from an aircraft, usually in groups. It was also planned to land them in the Black Sea area by speedboats. It appears that on some occasions at least Action Zeppelin was severely handicapped by the lack of aircraft; during the period December 1942 to March 1943, none at all seems to have been available.

Action Zeppelin's information requirements were rather peculiar. Here are two examples. At one time, for planning purposes, it urgently requested details about the location of, and the conditions in, the concentration camps in unoccupied Russia. It wanted in particular an analysis of their inmates, how many of them were political and criminal internees, their sex, age, nationality, their state of health, their present output in and outside the camp, the location of the camps and the transport facilities, and the number of camp guards, their arms and equipment.

At another time prisoners of war were to be interrogated, under the direction of VI-C-Z, on the current political views and sentiments of the population of the five Turkestani Republics of the Soviet Union; on whether they wanted to remain within the Soviet Union or aspired to independence, and also on the economic and food situation and on distribution. In addition they were to be interrogated about "the military situation, troop concentrations, the morale of garrison troops and the NKVD militia", the activities of the NKVD and the attitude of the population towards them, travel regulations and conditions, and so on.

The information thus gathered from the Einsatzgruppen, the P.O.W.s and the activists was then put to good use: reports were made by Office VI-C-Z. The following quotation from "Report No. 2 from the Occupied Eastern Territories" by the Chief of the Security Police and SD, dated 8th May, 1942, is presumably based on information supplied by Operation Zeppelin:

"It appears from interrogations of Soviet agents that the situation in Moscow until about March, 1942, was as follows: During the critical October days of 1941 the population was infuriated on account of the let-down by the Soviet authorities, who saved themselves and left the population to its fate. However, the Soviet propaganda machine is once more fully in control of the situation, because Stalin returned to Moscow at the beginning of November and newspapers and radio continuously report victories. Generally speaking it is no longer thought that Moscow could fall."

Then follows a paragraph about life in Moscow: about transport, schools, newspapers, food rationing, propaganda, and the changing attitude towards the Church.

This information was compiled for the benefit of some top Nazis who were on the distribution list for the SD Reports. In addition, there was a mutual exchange of incoming reports between Operation Zeppelin and the Army Section Foreign Armies East.

If Branch VI considered this type of information as particularly useful, they were soon to receive a severe shock. The activists felt considerably less energetic from January 1943 on, when the tide turned. "After Stalingrad and the general retreat in Russia it became increasingly more difficult to influence the Russian prisoners of war", stated SS Major-General Schellenberg when he was interrogated in 1945. "It became necessary therefore to discontinue the mass deployment of Russian prisoners, for instance in parachute operations, and to use instead only a few highly skilled and intelligent Russians who served with us out of conviction."

Action Zeppelin had thus been short-lived. Started only at the end of 1941, it could hardly have selected, schooled and trained its first action groups before the spring of 1942; in December of the same year operations came to a standstill for lack of aircraft, and it had practically closed down two months later for lack of volunteers. Branch VI is known to have organized parachute operations against the Persian oilfields. "Other far-reaching plans, the undertaking 'Ulm', paralysing the armament centres behind the Ural mountains with the help of Russian anti-Bolshevist parachutists, never got beyond the planning stage, because suitable aerodromes for dispatching them were lost."[1] Also the information collected does not seem to have had any immediate value. Compared with the highly efficient Soviet Intelligence system, it was amateurish in its conception and execution.

German Military Intelligence, however, tackled the job with more thoroughness, through its special Intelligence staff, known by the code name Walli, which was formed in May 1941, before the attack. Germans still travelling in Russia on various missions were used as Intelligence agents. Other Intelligence agents were

---

[1] Walter Goerlitz, *Der Zweite Weltkrieg*, Stuttgart, vol. ii, 1952, p. 76.

deployed behind the Russian frontier.[1] And special attention was given to the conduct of subversive activities. The former Deputy Chief of Section II of German Military Intelligence, Colonel Erwin Stolze, gave the following information to the Russians in 1945:

"I received instructions . . . to organize and lead a special group under the code name 'A' which had to engage in the preparation of diversionary acts and in the work of disintegration of the Soviet rear in connection with the intended attack on the U.S.S.R. At the same time . . . (I was given) an order which came from the Operational Staff of the Armed Forces and which contained basic directives for the conduct of subversive activities in the territory of the U.S.S.R. after Germany's attack on the Soviet Union. . . .

"It was pointed out (in this order) that for the purpose of delivering a lightning blow against the Soviet Union, Abwehr II, in conducting subversive work against Russia, with the help of a net of V-men (i.e., confidential agents), must use its agents for kindling national antagonism among the people of the Soviet Union.

"In carrying out the above-mentioned instructions . . . I contacted Ukrainian National Socialists who were in the German Intelligence Service and other members of the nationalist fascist groups, whom I roped in to carry out the tasks as set out above.

"In particular, instructions were given by me personally to the leaders of the Ukrainian Nationalists, Melnik (code name 'Consul I') and Bandera, to organize immediately upon Germany's attack on the Soviet Union, and to provoke demonstrations in the Ukraine in order to disrupt the immediate rear of the Soviet armies, and also to convince international public opinion of alleged disintegration of the Soviet rear."[2]

The German's choice of Melnik and Bandera was not a lucky one. After the Germans had occupied the Ukraine, "Bandera openly opposed them", as the Chief of the Security Police and SD pointed out in his Report on Events in the U.S.S.R., dated 2nd February, 1942. Bandera, a revolutionary if there ever was one,

[1] Interrogation of Lt.-Gen. Hans Piekenbrock, Document No. U.S.S.R.–228, *Trial of the Major War Criminals* at Nuremberg.
[2] Cf. *Trial of the Major War Criminals*, Nuremberg, 1947, U.S. edition, vol. vii, pp. 272 and 273.

proved as unwilling a tool in the hands of the Wehrmacht as he had been of the Soviets. He soon fell out with the more conservative Melnik, the leader of the Organization of Ukrainian Nationalists, and, as subsequent SD reports show, caused the Germans a lot of trouble. The Germans also tried in June 1941 to encourage and prepare a revolt of natives in the Georgian Republic (code name 'Tamara'), but it does not seem to have been successful.

"Apart from this," Colonel Stolze told his interrogator, "a special military unit was trained for subversive activities on Soviet territory, a special duty regiment for special tasks, Brandenburg 800, under the immediate command of the head of Abwehr II, Lahousen. Among the objects of this special unit, created in 1940, was to seize operationally important points, such as bridges, tunnels, and important military installations, and hold them till the arrival of the advance unit of the German Army.

". . . The personnel of this regiment, mainly composed of Germans from beyond the border, made extensive use of enemy uniforms and equipment in order to camouflage their operations."

Brandenburg 800 was in fact first raised in 1939 as a company, and did some damage behind the Polish lines for a few hours before the start of the attack. Sabotage was also carried out there by a unit of about 500 or 1,000 Ukrainian immigrants from Galicia, who received some para-military training under the direction of German Military Intelligence, and were then assigned to specific sabotage tasks—the wrecking of bridges and the destruction of other objectives of military importance—set by the Wehrmacht Operational Staff in accordance with the requirements of the German Army. This Ukrainian unit seems to have been active throughout the campaign.[1] Such foreign contingents were subsequently incorporated into Brandenburg 800: a battalion of former Polish soldiers was attached to it, and a battalion recruited from Caucasians distinguished itself by fighting for some months in partisan operations in the Caucasus Mountains, where it had been dropped by parachute behind the Russian lines.[2] "Turki volunteers landed by parachute in the area of Lake Aral in order to sabotage the oil installations. Similar undertakings were carried out several times in the enormous Soviet assembly area between

---

[1] Testimony of the former Head of Abwehr II, General Lahousen, *Trial of the Major War Criminals*, vol. ii, pp. 470 and 478.
[2] Cf. Leverkuehn, op. cit., pp. 164 and 166.

the Volga and the Urals."[1] In the meanwhile Brandenburg 800 had been considerably enlarged: in 1940 it grew to battalion and then regimental strength, and in 1942 it became a division.

In addition to sabotage missions the Brandenburg Regiment also carried out occasional political warfare operations, and while their successes were not lasting, they seem to have performed their task pretty efficiently, staying behind the Russian lines for some length of time and spreading unrest among the population.

Brandenburg 800 was at the disposal of Section II of Military Intelligence, but its formations were also attached to the individual Army Groups. It suffered severely under this split-up, particularly as it was frequently used at the front simply as an ordinary fighting unit. It had its heyday during the German advance, when its long-range reconnaissance penetrated far behind the Russian lines, in Red Army lorries; holding a bridge here or destroying a railway line there, and creating confusion in the enemy's rear, it carried out the small raids which produce the big results. In 1943 the bulk of the division was deployed in the Balkans, as ordinary infantry, in anti-partisan warfare; one coastal commando unit landed, together with other troops, on Leros to take over from the Italians after the Badoglio armistice; and only one battalion remained in Russia. The division had become a unit without a purpose, and eventually part of it was swallowed by Skorzeny's Special Troops and the rest was re-formed as an ordinary Panzer-grenadier division.

As saboteurs, and particularly as Intelligence agents, German Military Intelligence mostly used Russian P.O.W.s, just as the Political Secret Service did; but we need not go into any details since the successes were limited:

"That these operations," states Dr. Leverkuehn in his book,[2] "were not expanded into acts of sabotage of tactical and strategic significance, or even into a nuisance value on a big scale, is attributable partly to professional shortcomings in the Abwehr, but principally to the unhappy policy pursued by Germany in the Eastern territories and the treatment meted out to minorities within the Soviet Union."

[1] Walter Goerlitz, op. cit., p. 76. Brandenburg also maintained contact with Arabian, Iranian and Indian Nationalists. Cf. Goerlitz, ibid.
[2] Op. cit., p. 163.

The instructors of the selected prisoners of war were just as untrained for their task as their opposite numbers of the Political Secret Service, and Germany's 'unhappy policy' in the East has become too well known to require any amplification here. But further reasons ought to be adduced for the Abwehr's failure. In the first place, it was never in control of its own house; it had constantly to guard against trespass by the Political Secret Service, and the selection of P.O.W.s by rival teams for rival purposes could only be detrimental. But that was not all: the assignment of some Brandenburg troops to Army Groups and their subordination to front-line commanders severely reduced the strategic potential of this task force. Above all, however, Military Intelligence—and German Military Intelligence was no exception—is not an Operational Staff, and it should not therefore be charged with carrying out para-military operations.

Let us take stock at this point. The first question surely is whether or not we should have strategic assault troops. Those familiar with Charles Foley's penetrating study *Commando Extraordinary* can have no doubts in their minds that the answer must be in the affirmative,[1] and in reviving the incomparable S.A.S. the War Office has endorsed it. As Major-General Sir Robert Laycock points out in his Foreword to Mr. Foley's work, "the logic of this book is that another step forward in the realm of *strategic* shock attack is now due and the reader, after considering the evidence arrayed, may well feel that it should not be postponed."

But if so, and if war were to come, should we, too, use Russian prisoners of war as saboteurs and Intelligence agents? As we have seen, although they achieved no outstanding results, the German Political and Military Secret Service relied heavily on them.

That the Russians have given serious thought to the whole complex cannot be in doubt. How much of the German Secret Service Archives they captured is not known, but the Pentagon collection is certainly not complete. They took prisoner the former Chief of Section I of the Military Intelligence, Lt.-General Piekenbrock, the Deputy Chief of Section II, Colonel Stolze, and, to complete the catch, the Chief of Section III, Lt.-General Bentivengi. As Mr. Foley points out in his book, after the war Soviet agents made two attempts to kidnap Skorzeny and whisk him off to Moscow.

---

[1] Charles Foley, *Commando Extraordinary*. With a Foreword by Major-General Sir Robert Laycock. London, New York, Toronto, 1954.

Prisoners of war will be used by the Russians for any purpose they deem desirable; they have done so already, during the last war. If Russia were to attack us, our war aim would be the liberation of the subjugated peoples of the East. There is no moral objection to helping them to liberate themselves. And this much is certain: we would in a future war take an active interest in any resistance movement, just as the Russians did in the last war.

If we were, then, to enrol P.O.W.s, it might not be wise to lean too heavily on them, as the Germans did. In the first place, the first weeks or even days of a future war might be decisive, and no trained P.O.W.s are then at hand. In the second place, many of the activists are shifty, and they might turn out, in the changing fortunes of war, to be a liability rather than an asset. But a great number of them would no doubt be useful: they might not be able to undertake precision work like the immobilization of an airfield, but they could easily be trained to do the normal partisan jobs and act as agents.

German experience proves what is in any case obvious; a negative policy, or no policy at all, will alienate the willing elements. What they expect is a positive policy which assures them of a decent future.

But here the Allies face a dilemma: which Russian policy should they sponsor, that of the Unionists, or the Federalists, or the Separatists? Of the Democrats, or neo-Democrats; or of which of the various groups of *émigrés* who all pretend to represent the majority opinion? Whatever policy is decided on, it will not only create friends but also enemies.

Yet the purely political questions are probably the least important. The Russians have never known freedom of speech; political discussion as we understand it has never been allowed;[1] and their views on the Western political systems are distorted. We need not decide whether the Russian is politically inert, as is often asserted, or much more politically-minded than the citizens of the West, as others hold. The Russians attribute little importance to abstract politics and to the merits and mechanics of

---

[1] Vice-Admiral Leslie C. Stevens relates a typical incident in his *Life in Russia*, London, New York, Toronto, 1954, p. 71. A student of Moscow University insisted in a conversation with the Admiral that they had freedom of speech in Moscow, that once a week they held a debate in the University and everybody could speak his mind freely. He added that specially trained people answered all criticism of the Government. The student "must agree with them, because they are right. And before the debate is over, he must admit in public that they are right"—or he cannot stay in the University.

a system of government. What they are concerned with is its effect: it is good or bad?[1]

A new political order can only be evolved by the Russians themselves. If war were to come, Allied propaganda should concentrate on three questions:

(1) Restitution of private property, and this means in Russia mainly the dissolution of the Kolchos. A Memorandum drawn up in 1942 by Dr. Braeutigam, a senior official in the Main Department for Politics of the German Ministry for the Occupied Eastern Territories, has this to say on the subject:

"Considering the exceptionally great significance of the agrarian question in the Soviet Union, the Main Department for Politics was demanding even before the beginning of the Eastern campaign, that the Kolchos be dissolved and private property be introduced again. This proposal was turned down by the (German Office of the) Four Year Plan with the remark that organic changes were not to be considered during the war. . . .

"A form of government which was not intent only on plundering and exploitation, and which put aside the Bolshevist methods, would have kindled the greatest enthusiasm and put at our disposal a mass of millions. And the enthusiasm in the occupied Eastern territories would have had its repercussions on the strength of resistance of the Red Army. It would have been easily attainable to have the Red Army man say to himself: 'I fight for a system that is throughout worse than that which awaits me in case of defeat. I will be better off in every respect among the Germans than I have been until now'."[2]

(2) Restoration of religious freedom. The Bolshevist attitude towards the Church has changed during the last fifteen years. In the late war the Soviets had to tune down their militant atheism and reopen the churches in order to forestall such a move by the Germans. Today church-going is discouraged by continuous references in the Party Press to the fact that it is inconsistent with Party membership. But there cannot be any doubt about the deep religious feelings of the Russian people; many German Army reports of the last war bear witness to that.

[1] Cf. Oleg Anisimov, *The German Occupation in Northern Russia during World War II*, op. cit., Research Program on the U.S.S.R., New York City, 1954, p. 7.
[2] A fuller version of the above Memorandum is reproduced in the Appendix to this book.

Religion is the only antidote to the immorality of Marxism.

(3) But it is not enough to assure the Russians of their economic and spiritual well-being. They, like any other people, regard self-government as the only good government. Let us again quote from the Braeutigam Memorandum:

"The Main Department for Politics has always emphasized that the Eastern people must be informed in concrete terms about their future. ... It has accordingly often directed the attention of the Wehrmacht units to the expediency of having the Slavic Eastern peoples receive calming assurances about their future from the German authorities. As the best means, the establishment of a sort of counter-regime to Stalin with a captured Red general was indicated; or, if the word government should be avoided, just a rebellious general somewhat after the model of de Gaulle. ... The correctness of this conception has been confirmed ... by countless statements by prisoners of war, who have all said independently that the worst might be feared if Germany remained silent on the future of Russia. Many would like to desert, but they did not know to whom to turn."

This failure to provide a rallying point was directly responsible for one of the strangest incidents of the last war, when two Russian armed units, both anti-Bolshevist, fought each other in a pitched battle. Both wanted an independent Russia, free from German and Soviet control, but the one had chosen the Wehrmacht and the other the Red Army as its temporary ally for achieving this aim.[1]

A figurehead, if not a rallying point, was however soon found by the Germans in the person of Red Army Lt.-General Vlassov. General Vlassov had made a name for himself in the defence of Moscow. In the summer of 1942 he became a German prisoner, and in December 1942 he was placed at the head of the German-sponsored Russian National Committee.[2] In 1945 he and his followers, the Russian Army of Liberation recruited from P.O.W.s in German hands, paid the price for collaboration with the enemy;

---

[1] Cf. Vladimir D. Samarin, *Civilian Life under the German Occupation, 1942–4*, Research Program on the U.S.S.R., New York City, 1954, Mimeographed Series No. 58.

[2] For literature on the Vlassov Movement cf. George Fischer, *Soviet Opposition to Stalin*, Cambridge, Mass., 1952. W. Anders, *Hitler's Defeat in Russia*, Chicago, 1953. Jürgen Thorwald, *Wen sie verderben wollen*, Stuttgart, 1952, and Edwin Erich Dwinger, *General Wlassow, Eine Tragödie unserer Zeit*, Frankfurt, 1951.

they were handed over by the Western Allies to the Soviets, who promptly executed the leaders. During his two and a half years with the Germans Vlassov was used as a propaganda exhibit; against the advice of a number of German officers with a clearer perception of the needs of the hour, he was not allowed to assume any political significance, and even his military command was never more than nominal.

Vlassov and his subordinates, being soldiers, wanted to fight against Bolshevism as a military formation, side by side with the Germans. But Hitler had decreed that only Germans were allowed to bear arms. However, some of these East troops did actually take part in front line combat, although most of them were employed in duties in the rear, either as police units or in the fight against partisans in Russia, Poland, Italy and France. Others again worked simply as labour units. By the time of the Normandy landing most of the East troops had already been withdrawn from Russia and sent to other theatres of war.

What made these men fight against Bolshevism is a matter for speculation. A number of them, no doubt, merely wanted to escape from the intolerable conditions in the German P.O.W. camps, and, influenced by the German propaganda, considered the Vlassov Movement as good a means as any. But many must have been motivated by the wish to destroy Bolshevism. They may not all have been sincere in this desire; to be on the winning side may have tempted quite a few. But much of the prisoners' support for the Vlassov Movement must have been as genuine as that of the civilian population in German-occupied Russia: not only did the Soviet-appointed Russian Orthodox Metropolitan Bishop of the Baltic States agree to assist Vlassov, but the majority of the people, too, approved of the Vlassov Movement; and if the approval was mixed with scepticism, it was due to justified doubts about German intentions.[1]

But if the civilian population was uncertain whether the Vlassov Movement was really meant as a liberation movement, the soldiers, especially after their withdrawal from the Russian front, could even less be expected to know what they were fighting for. In spite of his continuous demands Vlassov was not permitted to assume command over the Army of Liberation until 28th January, 1945, when Germany had already lost the war and the Vlassov Movement was only kept going by fear of Soviet reprisals.

[1] Cf. Oleg Anisimov, op. cit., p. 13, ftn. 4, and p. 36.

But even then the Germans refused to vest Vlassov with any political power. He published, it is true, an open letter; he was allowed to make two political propaganda tours through German-occupied Russia; and in the autumn of 1944 Himmler authorized him to proclaim his political aims in what has become known as the Prague Manifesto of the Committee for the Liberation of the Peoples of Russia; it was made public on 14th November, 1944.[1] While Vlassov and his followers were thus allowed by the Germans to form a political committee, they were never recognized as a sort of counter-regime to Stalin, as Dr. Braeutigam and others had demanded. Any influence beyond the German-occupied areas of Russia—as General de Gaulle had in France—was thus denied to them.

But the Prague Manifesto still commands a certain interest because it was generally recognized by the various Russian factions as providing the most acceptable common basis for a non-Communist government in Russia. Many of the Committee's aspirations were only vaguely defined, such as the strengthening of family and marriage, the guarantee of social justice, providing the intellectuals with the opportunity to create freely, and so on. But the Manifesto, as to some extent did the Braeutigam Memorandum two years earlier, held out the prospect of the liquidation of the kolchos, the establishment of private property earned by work, the abolition of forced deliveries, the inviolability of persons, property and homes, and last but not least the introduction of freedom of religion. Any excursion into forms of government, it should be noted, was carefully avoided.

We do not intend to enlarge on these points. Let us note in conclusion what a competent observer, Mr. Oleg Anisimov, who travelled widely in German-occupied Russia during the last war, notes as the main elements of a 'good' policy as understood by the Russians to whom he talked: freedom, justice, prosperity, security, better housing, more and cheaper food and better clothes.[2] And among the freedoms, we would add, freedom from world revolution ranks high in the hearts of many peoples everywhere.

The subject needs serious study. It is not a matter which can be decided by one NATO member country for all, or in which various member countries could come to different conclusions.

[1] Cf. For the text of the Prague Manifesto George Fischer, op. cit., pp. 194 *seq*. This author is also our source for the assertion that the Manifesto was widely accepted as common ground among the Russian factions.
[2] Cf. Oleg Anisimov, op. cit., p. 8, footnote.

There must be one over-all policy shaped and accepted by all, well in advance of hostilities.

Our next step is clear. If we decide to use Soviet prisoners of war as agents, some organization must be formed in peace time to select, train, equip, and dispatch the agents in the event of war. It must be one organization and not two, as the Germans set up. It must have a highly qualified staff, preferably Russian-speaking, to fulfil its difficult task. An *ad hoc* structure such as the Germans used in both their Political and Military Secret Service will not do.

The Soviets take a pride in their subversive skill. When Stalin delivered his Report to Communist Party Officials in 1925, he threatened to open in the event of war the floodgates of revolution throughout the world, adding that the leading personalities in capitalist countries could not deny that the Soviets had some experience in this domain.

We consider this sort of warfare rather distasteful. But just as the choice between peace and war will not be ours but the Soviets', so too will be the choice of weapons in the war without battlefield.

We must therefore be prepared to make use of the entire arsenal, because the Soviets will do likewise.

Chapter XI

ON A POINT OF LAW

THOSE who still cling to the idea of conventional war and reject irregular warfare in all its forms ought to realize that they are more conventional than the International Conventions themselves. These Conventions do not, repeat not, outlaw irregular warfare.

Guerilla warfare in particular is permissible under the Hague Convention concerning the Rules and Usages of Land Warfare, which sets out the relevant rules in its Article 1. And the Hague Convention and the Geneva Convention for the Treatment of Prisoners of War do not prohibit the recruiting of P.O.W. volunteers by their captors.

International law, to be sure, has not caught up with the modern 'refinements' of warfare. It protects the population of occupied territories against the occupant, it protects the P.O.W. and the wounded against the captor, and it protects the fighting soldier against the use of certain weapons. But it does not protect the one belligerent against the villainy of the other if he tries to enlist traitors—military or civilian—in his ranks. Domestic laws are supposed to take care of these traitors, and in past wars the loyalty of the population to their own country proved as a rule stronger than any inducements which the enemy was able or willing to offer. We shall deal with these issues at once.

The modern weapons of war play havoc with the protective devices of international law.

As far as the protection of civilians by international law is concerned, two examples may illustrate the point.

In one of the so-called Subsequent Proceedings against the War Criminals before the U.S. Military Tribunals at Nuremberg there was a long legal argument about whether a German General had acted unlawfully by forcefully preventing the starving Russian civilian population of Leningrad from leaving the besieged city.[1] If he had then possessed, and showered, innumerable V weapons on the city, no legal questions would have been asked

---

[1] We refer here to the *U.S. War Crimes Trial against F. M. von Leeb et al.*, High Command Case, No. 12.

afterwards, but the civilian population would have suffered worse. And the second illustration: It was held by an American Tribunal[1] "that under certain very restrictive conditions, and subject to certain rather extensive safeguards, hostages may be taken, and after a judicial finding of strict compliance with all pre-conditions and as a last desperate remedy hostages may even be sentenced to death. . . . Killings without full compliance with such pre-conditions are merely terror murders."[2] But it is still an open question whether the killing of hostages is at all permissible: in the British view it is not. When the Judge Advocate, Mr. Justice Collingwood, summed up the evidence in the case against the former Field Marshal von Manstein, he advised the British Military Judges that the weight of authority is heavily in favour of the view that the killing of hostages or reprisal prisoners is a violation of the rules and usages of war and is murder.[3] What it all amounts to is this: even under extreme provocation an occupant acts unlawfully if he has a single hostage executed with a view to stamping out the guerilla menace in the area. The civilian is protected. But the occupant can use his atomic guns against the guerilas freely, without having to answer for the number of innocent civilians killed in the process; the civilian then enjoys no protection.

The soldier in the field, too, enjoys some protection against inhuman warfare in as much as the use of poison gas is prohibited. But there is, of course, no limitation in respect to nuclear weapons, which may be used against the civilian population as well.

It may be argued that if only the use of nuclear weapons were prohibited, the laws and customs of war would once again be in harmony with the old conceptions of international morality which the Conventions are meant to codify. But we find that this is not quite so, if we turn from the physical weapons to the psychological weapons of war.

With the advent of psychological warfare as we now know it, it has become permissible to induce enemy soldiers to lay down their arms while they are still able to hold out, about the worst crime a soldier can commit. No holds are barred either when it comes to undermining the morale of the enemy civilian population, and if as a result it revolts against its government, committing treason into the bargain, Action Propaganda is considered a

[1] In the *U.S. War Crimes Trial against F. M. List et al.*, South-East Case, No. 7.
[2] *U.S. War Crimes Trial against F. M. von Leeb et al.*, p. 92 of the judgement.
[3] *British War Crimes Trial against the former Field Marshal von Manstein*, in Hamburg, p. 3305 of the Transcript.

brilliant success. Nobody has as yet advocated that psychological warfare be abolished, and as long as it serves its purpose it probably never will be.

Clearly, as far as psychological warfare is concerned, the basic conception of the usages of war amounts to this: Let the enemy worry about the disloyalty of his subjects, civilian and military, and let us try to profit by it, as long as we can find volunteers. Yet if it is considered legitimate to incite the enemy population to take up arms against their government, it is difficult to see why the same rule should not apply to captured enemy soldiers.

The position, simply, is this: After the Hague Convention was signed, and even before the Germans and Russians used their P.O.W.s and civilians for all types of missions, the principle had already been established; Allenby and Lawrence turned "the oppressed in Turkey" against the Turks in World War I. Psychological warfare as conducted by all belligerents during both World Wars recognized the seduction of enemy nationals as lawful. When in 1946 the eminent judges of the International Military Tribunal at Nuremberg laid down in their judgement that by 1939 the rules of the Hague Convention had been recognized by all civilized nations,[1] the Russian judge signified by his assent that in the Russian view the laws and customs of war permit a belligerent to use P.O.W.s as volunteers in any capacity against their own country. And in the Russian view the same obviously applies to all the other actions taken by enemy nationals on Russia's behalf in World War II.

The Russian view, it should be noted, is correct: nothing in the International Conventions forbids a belligerent to use enemy nationals for any purpose for which they volunteer; only compulsion is prohibited.

For civilians the Hague Convention lays down:

Art. 23: "A belligerent is ... forbidden to *compel* subjects of the hostile power to take part in the operations of war against their own country."

Art. 45: "It is forbidden to *force* the inhabitants of occupied territory to swear allegiance to the hostile power."

[1] *Trial of the Major War Criminals before the International Military Tribunal* at Nuremberg, p. 253 of the judgement.

Art 52: "Requisitions in kind and services shall not be *demanded* from the local authorities or inhabitants, except for the needs of the army of occupation. They shall be . . . of such a nature as not to involve the inhabitants in the *obligation* of taking part in military operations against their country."

For soldiers the Geneva Convention relative to the Treatment of Prisoners of War, of 12th August, 1949, states:

Art. 50: ". . . Prisoners of war may be *compelled* to do only such work as is included in the following classes. . . ."

The operative words, in regard to soldiers and civilians, are 'compel', 'force', 'demand' and 'obligation', but it is lawful for the enemy to obtain any such services from volunteers.

This is the accepted German view, and it was frequently expressed in various war crimes trials.[1] It is also the American understanding of the law, which was stated in regard to 'Action Zeppelin' as follows:

"The counsel for the prosecution contend that the use of prisoners of war for espionage and other like purposes against their own nation, even if voluntary, is a violation of International Law and of the Hague Convention respecting the Rules and Customs of War (Article 6 of Chapter II, and Article 31 of Chapter VI of the Geneva Convention). No other authority than the articles themselves have been cited to us, and we have been unable to find any. Ordinarily a national of a country, whether or not he is in military service, who gives aid or comfort to the enemy, is a traitor to his country. But we have never before heard it suggested that the enemy who takes advantage of his treason is guilty of a breach of International Law. We hold that the cited prohibitions of the Hague Convention prohibit the use of prisoners of war in connection with war operations, and apply only when such use is brought about by force, threats, or duress, and not when the person renders the services voluntarily."[2]

The same applies, for the same reason, to civilians, and this is the International Law as it stands.

[1] Cf. For instance *Trial of the Major War Criminals*, vol. xxi, p. 398.
[2] *U.S. War Crimes Trial against von Weizsaecker et. al.*, Ministries Case, No. 11, Judgement on p. 28564 of the Transcript.

Perhaps more important than the merely legal issue is the factual one: the practice of psychological warfare has established a new usage of war. To put it no higher than that, the enemy nationals may be incited to passive resistance, which may develop into active resistance and collaboration.

While psychological war, as we know it in the West, tries to promote resistance within the enemy camp and possibly collaboration *after* the start of a war, the new warfare has already firmly organized and established resistance and collaboration *before* the outbreak of war.

Once we recognize the facts, we may deplore the development; but we have no justification, on legalistic or other grounds, for disregarding the weapons of the war without battlefield.

Chapter XII

THE SOVIET SIXTH COLUMN

ESPIONAGE, subversion, infiltration and sabotage: are they specifically designed by the Soviets as instruments of war? And if so, can they, wielded as they are by civilians, change the pattern of conventional warfare? The answers to these questions are rather obvious.

Our classic in espionage dealt, in fact, with Soviet espionage in war time. Its success, as we have shown, was due to infiltration, just as Russia's other spy network, under the German Dr. Sorge, in Japan, achieved its war-time triumph in espionage in no small measure through infiltration.

Infiltration, in Soviet eyes, is therefore a weapon forged with the specific purpose of giving assistance to the Red Army in war. The function of the infiltrators is to obtain, in peace and war, secret official information calculated to be directly or indirectly useful to an enemy, and to communicate it to an enemy.

The infiltrators then working for Soviet Russia against their own country were Germans and Japanese.

Again, our case material for subversion dates from the last war, when subversion was practised by the Soviets in favour of their then 'ally' Germany. The Soviet proxies in this case were Frenchmen who helped to defeat their own country. It would be utter hypocrisy to pretend that the Soviets, while prepared to assist their erstwhile friend Hitler in this way, would refuse to use this weapon in war time for their own purpose.

Nor can it be doubted that sabotage—by civilians—will be used by the Soviets as a weapon of war. Since much of what we unfolded in Chapter VII consisted of Soviet plan and not practice we have to fall back on pronouncements by the Soviet leaders to show its purpose. These pronouncements are unequivocal and plentiful.

The general concept was outlined by Stalin in 1927:

"A revolutionary is he who without arguments, unconditionally, openly and honestly . . . is ready to *defend and strengthen the*

U.S.S.R., since the U.S.S.R. is the first proletarian, revolutionary state in the world. . . . An internationalist is he who, unreservedly, without hesitation, without condition, is ready to *defend* the U.S.S.R., because the U.S.S.R. is the base of the world revolutionary movement, and to defend, to advance this revolutionary movement is impossible without defending the U.S.S.R."[1]

Indeed, as Stalin stated in the following year,

"there is no doubt that the revolution in the U.S.S.R. not only has obligations with respect to the proletarians of all lands and is fulfilling them, but that *the proletarians of all lands have some sufficiently serious obligations with respect to the proletarian dictatorship of the U.S.S.R.*"[2]

These obligations of the proletarians of all lands to defend and strengthen the U.S.S.R. consist in the following:

(*a*) "In preaching that the armies of imperialism should go over directly to the side of the proletarian dictatorship of the U.S.S.R., *in case of an attack on the U.S.S.R.*"[3]

(*b*) "*At the time of declaration of war* (especially in case of war against the Soviet Union), *or during it*, the situation permitting, Communists should proclaim slogans of national-revolutionary uprisings against imperialists and of immediate formation of national-revolutionary guerilla units."[4] (International, 1928).

(*c*) "Such a *war*," Stalin elucidated in 1934, "will be waged not only at the fronts but also in the rear of the enemy. The bourgeoisie need have no doubt that the numerous friends of the working class

---

[1] Stalin, *The International Situation and Defence of the U.S.S.R.*, (1st August, 1927), Sochineniya (Gospolitizdat, Moscow, 1949), vol. x, p. 61. Quoted from *Soviet World Outlook, A Handbook of Communist Statements*, prepared by the Division of Research for U.S.S.R. and Eastern Europe, Office of Intelligence Research, Department of State, for the Co-ordinator of Psychological Intelligence, U.S. Information Agency (subsequently quoted as "*U.S. Handbook*"), 1954, p. 156. The italics in the above and subsequent quotations are ours.
[2] Stalin, *On the Programme of the Comintern*, Speech made 5th July, 1928, Sochineniya (Gospolitizdat, Moscow, 1952), vol. ii, p. 152, *U.S. Handbook*, p. 156.
[3] Stalin, *On the Programme of the Comintern*, loc. cit.
[4] Cf. T. A. Taracouzio, *The Soviet Union and International Law*, 1935, p. 441. Quoted by permission of the Macmillan Company.

of the U.S.S.R. in Europe and Asia will be sure to strike a blow in the rear of their oppressors."[1]

(d) "The Communist Parties (abroad)," Lenin proclaimed in 1920, "must carry on persistent propaganda urging the workers to refuse to transport *war materials* for the enemies of the Soviet Republics."[2]

The Communists abroad are therefore directed by the Soviets in case of war to undermine morale in their national armies, to wage guerilla warfare against them, to promote civil war, and to sabotage the delivery of war materials. It would be tedious to give further quotations in a similar vein. That other holds are by no means barred is shown by this final all-embracing exhortation:

(e) "A real internationalist," Vyshinsky declared in 1948, "is one who brings his sympathy and recognition up to the point of practical and maximal help to the U.S.S.R. in support and defence of the U.S.S.R. *by every means and in every possible form*. Actual co-operation with the U.S.S.R., the readiness of the workers of any country to subject all their aims to the basic problem of strengthening the U.S.S.R. in its struggle, that is the manifestation of revolutionary proletarian internationalism on the part of workmen in foreign countries.... The defence of the U.S.S.R., as the socialist motherland of the world proletariat, is the holy duty of every honest man everywhere...."[3]

In order that "every honest man everywhere" can be persuaded to regard the impairing of the military power of his own country not as a crime but as an honourable duty, he must be shown that his country's army is nothing but a willing tool in the hands of the

[1] Stalin, *Report of the Central Committee of the Communist Party of the Soviet Union*, delivered at the 17th Congress, 1934. In *Socialism Victorious*, London, undated, p. 15.
[2] Lenin, *Conditions of Affiliation to Communist International* (1920), Selected Works, London, 1943, vol. x, p. 205.
[3] P. Vyshinsky, *Communism and the Motherland*, Voprosi Filosofii (Problems of Philosophy), No. 2, 1948. *U.S. Handbook*, p. 158. The frequent use of the word 'defence' in all these statements must not mislead the reader into thinking that they are meant to apply only if the U.S.S.R. were the victim of imperialist aggression. This is not so. As the "Theses of the 6th World Congress of the Communist International" (1928) make clear "there is no contradiction between the Soviet Government's preparations for defence *and* for revolutionary war *and* a consistent peace policy. Revolutionary war of the proletarian dictatorship is but a continuation of revolutionary peace policy 'by other means' ". (International Press Correspondence, No. 84, 28th November, 1928, p. 1590, *U.S. Handbook*, p. 360.)

capitalists and imperialists for the suppression of the worker. Since even Communists cannot demonstrate that the Western armies are trained to shoot down their own people, the thought-cleansing treatment must be applied in a more subtle way in order to foster hatred against these armies. While the Red Army, they say, is identical with the people, the Western armies are divorced from the people.

"The first and basic peculiarity of our Red Army," Stalin expounded, "lies in that it is the army of liberated workers and peasants. . . .

"All the armies that have existed up to this time under capitalism . . . are armies fostering the power of capital."[1]

Indeed, Communist leaders everywhere propagate this conception:

"The Communists, whether in Russia or China or Indo-China, have never hidden the fact that they regard their armies and the totality of their military science as something wholly different from that of the capitalists. The army, said Lenin long ago, is for Communists the self-conscious marching proletarian. The army, said Mao, ever since the Long March, is the peasant on the march. The army to Nam Il in Korea is the marching people, and to Ho it is the marching nationalist. When the marching ceases, all these leaders have said, the army ceases to be the army and becomes the peasant or the proletarian or the people or the nationalist. It has also been claimed by all these leaders that because they march they do not cease to be what they are. . . . On the other hand the traditions of capitalist warfare insist that there is a watertight separation between the army and the people. This difference springs from the difference of the army and the people. This difference springs from the difference of the economics and social philosophies of the two systems and is inevitable."[2]

Here Stalin chimes in again: the armies under capitalism

"were and remain the armies of the domination of capital. . . . In all the capitalist countries the army has been drawn in and is

---

[1] Stalin, *On the Three Special Qualities of the Red Army*, Sochineniya (Gospolitizdat, Moscow, 1952), vol. ii, pp. 22–4, *U.S. Handbook*, p. 304.
[2] From a review in *Shankar's Weekly*, Delhi, 16th May, 1954.

being drawn into the political struggle, serving as a weapon to suppress the workers. Is it not true that there the army suppresses the workers, that there it serves as the stronghold of the masters?"[1]

Once this difference has been rammed home, it is clear where the Communist's supra-national duty lies in a conflict between the Red Army and the West. And in a wider field, while under the Soviet Constitution of 1936 "treason to the country, violation of the oath of allegiance, desertion to the enemy, impairing of the military power of the State, espionage—is punishable with all the severity of the law as the most heinous of crimes", it is, to quote Vyshinsky again, "the holy duty of every honest man everywhere" to commit these very crimes against his own country in the defence of the U.S.S.R.

While wars of the past have been fought by soldiers identifiable as friend or foe by their uniforms, the war without battlefield is waged by *francs-tireurs* who, in civilian clothes, escape detection. Furthermore, while most countries normally employ their own nationals in sabotage and subversive activities, the Communists will try to commit nationals of the West to the fight against their own countries on a big scale. Above all, in Western countries with a sizeable Communist Party organization the State, in the event of war, is no longer up against individual traitors but against an organized body of them, the Communist Sixth Column.

How effective the Soviet call to treason will be in case of war it is impossible to say. But it should be remembered that, at Moscow's order, as we have tried to show in Chapter V, the French Communists assisted Hitler's armies in their march into France; and we know how quickly these same Frenchmen became the backbone of the Resistance against Hitler when he invaded Russia.

We are often told that enemy agitators and partisans will have little chance in the West because they can operate successfully only where the populace supports their cause. But the about turn of the French Communists knocks the bottom out of this argument. After all, though the Communists changed sides overnight, the sentiments of the French people as a whole remained as they were. And yet the Communists were successful in both of their operations.

Indeed, while it is no doubt of tremendous help to the partisans to operate in a friendly country, they can also maintain themselves

[1] Stalin, *On the Three Special Qualities of the Red Army*, loc. cit.

by terror if need be. This was frequently shown during the late war by Soviet partisans in Russia. Numerous accounts tell of the partisans attacking in strength and raiding villages for food, sheep, cattle and equipment, deposing the local burgomaster and taking hostages along with them—unmistakeable signs that the populace was not at all well-disposed towards the partisans, who nevertheless managed to carry on.

"If war breaks out," stated Sig. Terracini, Communist member of the Italian Senate in 1951, "the *peace partisans, who are also partisans of war* in defence of freedom, know what their duty is."[1] And it has been said "that it is as good as certain that in countries like Italy and France Communist partisans will emerge in considerable numbers."[2] The only question is whether the Russians can arrange partisan warfare on a menacing scale. That they will try to cannot be in doubt. This proposition has been expounded in *Communist Guerilla Warfare* and was accepted by all reviewers, military and civilian. But even if the Soviets were unable to form organized bands, it is certain that their agents and saboteurs will act individually, though not less dangerously to us. One saboteur using—or destroying—nuclear weapons can do unimaginable harm, and agents and saboteurs can certainly operate even among a hostile population.

Subversion will no doubt be practised by the Soviets where it has once before been used with success. It is also more than likely that West-German troops will be considered an attractive target. In all discussion of the pros and cons of West-German rearmament the most pertinent question has remained unasked and unanswered: In a conflict between East and West will the West-Germans regard the East-Germans as enemies or as Germans? In the exploitation of this divided loyalty subversion might find a fertile breeding ground; all the more so since the unification of Germany, the idea of One Germany, has been, is, and will remain the dominant issue in West-German politics.

It may of course be said that the Russians face the same problem in rearming East-Germany, but this is not quite so. Soviet superiority in manpower allows them to employ only specially selected East-German fanatics in the front line, and their 'reliability' will be guaranteed by the ubiquitous commissars. The West cannot adopt a similar solution.

[1] London *Observer*, Sunday, 1st April, 1951, p. 5, "Sayings of the Week."
[2] Helmut Bohn in *Ost-Probleme*, Bad Nauheim, 23rd October, 1954.

It might be thought a mistake therefore to rearm West-Germany at all, especially since a West-German defence contribution would be almost matched in numbers by an East-German contribution. Such a deduction would be entirely wrong, for two reasons: the Russians, for all we know, will employ East-German troops in any case; and secondly, while the West values the fighting quality of an East-German contingent at par and no more, the Red Army, it should be remembered, attacked German troops in the last war only if it had at least a fourfold superiority. As a deterrent, therefore, twelve German divisions represent a contribution to the defence of the West greatly in excess of their numbers, and the West gains very considerably more than the East from a rearming of the respective parts of Germany.

The fighting qualities of German soldiers are beyond doubt. With the memories of the late campaign against Russia still vivid in their minds, few of them in the West relish the thought of fighting against the Red Army, but they would no doubt give an excellent account of themselves if required to do so. Yet, we repeat, can we be equally confident if West-Germans had to fight against East-Germans? It is a long time since German soldiers engaged in civil war, and their reaction to such a prospect is untested and unknown. This problem ought to receive serious and immediate consideration in the West.

If there were war, and if the Soviets could organize guerilla warfare behind our lines, the results would be obvious: the pattern of conventional warfare would be fundamentally changed. We need look no further than to the lessons of Soviet partisan warfare against the Germans in the last war.

In 1944 the German Army Group Centre found itself in a precarious position: it was entirely dependent for its transport on one solitary railway line which ran through partisan territory. For months on end the partisans had attacked the railway line, on an average about forty times a day. Suddenly, at the orders of the Soviet High Command, these attacks stopped, and at this moment the Red Army made a feint attack against the southern part of the German Army Group's front line. Army Group Centre therefore at once dispatched all available reserves by rail to the southern front. This troop movement encountered no partisan interference whatsoever. "Hardly had the German reinforcements arrived in the south, when, surprisingly, the Red Army attacked with full force in the north, and when the Germans wanted to send the badly needed reinforcements back by rail to the north in order to prop up the tottering northern front, the partisans, again on Red Army orders, in an unprecedented demonstration of mass destruction, brought the rail traffic to an almost complete standstill. Army Group Centre, denuded of troops and cut off from reinforcements, collapsed."[1]

This battle in the region of Orscha, Minsk and Brest is a classic in combined Army-partisan operations, in which the paralysing stroke is delivered from the rear by immobilizing the entire reserves, far away from the endangered front line. The battle was already decided behind the line by the partisans before the Red Army attacked.

Not only the partisans' operational activities but also their intelligence work leaves its imprint on the pattern of conventional warfare. As we have seen in Chapter IV, the German dispositions were frequently known to the Russians; so were German troop movements and intentions. Under such conditions the Germans could no longer utilize the element of surprise; but it was all the more effectively monopolized by the Russians.

In the last war the Russians employed only two of the instruments of the new warfare against the Germans: espionage through infiltration and partisan warfare. Subversion and widespread sabotage on the German home front could not be brought into play because Communism, after a decade of National Socialist rule, had ceased in Germany to be an organized movement, open or clandestine. And again, only subversion was practised against France. In the absence of experience it is therefore pointless to theorize on the interplay or combined impact of these weapons of the new warfare. But the Soviet stratagem is clearly discernible, and this allows the West to determine its own policy.

Its first aim is obvious: we must eliminate our 'security risks' and check up on our suspects; and, needless to say, this work is being carried out. But there is one aspect to which we might devote a little more attention, and that is Soviet propaganda, if, against present expectations, the cold war were to continue.

It must be realized that the aim of this propaganda is not only to win new recruits for the Communist Party. It has at the same time a more subtle purpose: by constantly sponsoring peace, disarmament, and other good causes the Soviets try to create the

---

[1] Dixon and Heilbrunn, *Communist Guerilla Warfare*, p. 91, and Hermann Teske, *Die silbernen Spiegel*, Heidelberg, 1952, pp. 192 *seq.*, 210 *seq.*

impression that they are not the worst of nations; if they have defects, they also have virtues, and in his choice between two evils the individual might as well choose the Soviet evil as the lesser one.

It was in all probability this sort of reasoning which made some Germans side with the Soviets against Nazism during the last war, and the same argument has been heard since. People who are not Communists, but who are afraid of a revival in Germany of reactionary nationalism and National Socialism, have thrown in their lot with Russia. Dr. John is a case in question, and Roessler might well be another example. But the effects of the Russian propaganda are not restricted to a few Germans.

The West has repeatedly stated that in the event of war it will use nuclear weapons. The Russians have never made a similar announcement; far from it, they apparently advocate that the manufacture and use of these weapons be prohibited, as they did again in the Eastern Security Pact of 14th May, 1955. By frequently reiterating this demand, they try to convince people everywhere that the atom bomb is safer with Russia than the West, and that the same goes for peace. And here again, Soviet propaganda does not seem to have been unsuccessful.

The reader will remember the case we discussed in Chapter II in which there had been serious leakages of information from meetings of the French National Defence Council in 1954. The officials allegedly responsible for these leakages were apparently no Communists; they were described as having acted from ideological motives which could be classified as crypto-Communist. One of their alleged motives was that they were opposed to any possibility of an atomic war. The result: highly secret defence documents are supposed to have passed into Communist hands.

There is no need to give further examples. Suffice it to say that for protection against Communist subversion we ought not to rely on security measures alone. We should also try to safeguard ourselves against this virus by preventive measures. We in the West restrict our counter-propaganda to the various broadcasting services for overseas listeners. We might also do a little for the benefit of people at home. Nobody wants a Goebbels-for-enlightenment Ministry in our midst, but the Press and Radio in the West could give a little more space and time to publicizing *our* viewpoints.

It may be said that there is no need to contradict Soviet propaganda because only high-ranking traitors could become dangerous to the security of the West, and that such people cannot be won over by Soviet propaganda. It may be difficult sometimes to say why a particular individual allowed himself to be recruited by the Soviets. At any rate, we should not so underestimate the effect of insistent Soviet propaganda, which, after all, seems to have convinced some members of the 'Red Three's' German cell. If we let Soviet propaganda go unchallenged, the Russians will continue to snatch from us, if not fervent believers in Communism, at least well-conditioned followers who are no less of a risk to the security of the West.

The second aim of our policy should also be obvious: we must be able to retaliate in the war without battlefield. Only by achieving and maintaining equal strength with the Communists can we hope to avoid the outbreak of World War III.

This being so, we must include, and correctly weigh, the new warfare potential in *both* scales.

This means that since we cannot completely eradicate the Soviet potential in this field, we must have the same weapons of the new warfare that the Soviets possess, and we must also see to it that ours are no less effective than theirs.

Hence our three-point programme:

(1) We must assess the Soviet clandestine war potential.
(2) We must be able to deal with this menace.
(3) WE TOO MUST BE ABLE TO WAGE A WAR WITHOUT BATTLEFIELD.

APPENDIX

Appendix I

FIELD SERVICE REGULATIONS OF THE RED ARMY, 1944, MOSCOW[1]

Branches of the Service and their tactical purpose
Combat and March Formations
Control of Troops
Political Work in tactical situations
Combat Security of Troops
Offensive Battle
Pursuit
Meeting Engagements
Defensive
Retreat and Withdrawal from battle
Combat to break an encirclement
Employment of large units of combat aviation
Movement of Troops
Disposition for Rest and its security
Organization of the Rear and supplying it with *matériel*
Partisan Operations

CHAPTER XVII. PARTISAN OPERATIONS

1. General Regulations

851. The partisan movement is an armed struggle of the popular masses of the territory occupied temporarily by the enemy against the foreign invaders, in defence of their fatherland and its independence.

852. The strength of the partisan movement consists in the deep, popular, patriotic character of the movement, in the striving

[1] These Field Service Regulations are referred to in Chapters iv and vii of the book.

of the people of the occupied territory to throw off the yoke of the hated invaders.

The general character of the partisan movement gives rise to numerous forms of partisan struggle in the towns and villages. One of the chief forms of the partisan movement is the armed struggle of partisan detachments, for the purpose of joint action with the Red Army, to crush the enemy and drive him from our Soviet land.

853. The basic missions of partisan actions are:

――the destruction of garrisons, staffs, establishments, troop detachments of the enemy, individual soldiers and officers moving about, the guards of depots, establishments, transports, forage, and various parties and agents engaged in collecting grain, livestock and other supplies from the population;

――the destruction of enemy supply routes (the blasting of bridges, the impairment of railways, the wrecking of trains, attacks against motor and animal-drawn transports), the smashing of enemy echelons with their personnel, equipment, fuel and ammunition, making it impossible for the enemy to supply the front and to carry away the national property that has been seized;

――the destruction of depots and bases with armament, ammunition, fuel, food and other materials, the destruction of garages and repair shops;

――the destruction of signal communication lines on railways, highways and dirt roads (telephone, telegraph, radio stations), the destruction of signal communication apparatus, the killing of the service personnel—signal communication troops;

――attacks against enemy aerodromes, destruction of aircraft, hangars, depots of bombs and fuel, destruction of the flying personnel and mechanics and those guarding the aerodromes;

――the killing or capture of political agents, generals, and high officials of the enemy and traitors to our fatherland who are in their service;

――the destruction or burning of electric power plants, boilers, systems of water supply, industrial enterprises and other objects of military and economic importance;

――informing the units of the Red Army concerning the dispositions, numerical strength and movements of the enemy.

854. The basic organization and combat unit is the independent partisan detachment.

The detachments are organized in the rear of the enemy from

the men and women of the population capable of bearing arms and ready to carry on a fight against the enslavers to the bitter end.

Each person joining the detachment takes the partisan oath of devotion to the fatherland.

855. The numerical strength of the detachments may differ, depending on the conditions and the locality. It should not be so large that the detachment will be difficult to manœuvre, easy to discover and hard to control. In the event of a large influx of partisans, it is necessary to create new detachments.

856. The internal organization of the partisan detachment depends upon the size of the detachment and the type of its activities.

The detachment is headed by a commander, a political deputy of the commander, and a chief of staff.

857. The general leadership of the partisan detachment is exercised by the staffs of the partisan movement.

858. The partisan detachments are armed and supplied chiefly with weapons and ammunition captured from the enemy. If necessary they are supplied with weapons, ammunition and explosives by units of the Red Army.

Food supplies are secured from local resources. The depots and supply bases are organized in advance in well-concealed places, strictly guarded.

The depots are replenished in the main from captured supplies. The detachments must have reserve bases.

859. The partisan detachments operate independently. In special cases, depending on the situation, they may be operationally subordinate to the commander of the large division or regiment operating in the rear of the enemy in the immediate proximity of the area of action of the partisan detachment.

2. Tactical Operations

860. The distinguishing characteristics of the combat actions of the partisan detachment are:

——secrecy in appearance, and surprise attacks on the enemy's most vulnerable spots;

——knowledge concerning the intentions of the enemy, his dispositions and movements, based on reconnaissance data and on extensive contacts with the local population;

——extensive use of ambush, military ruse, military cunning and camouflage;

——conduct of battle by brief destructive blows from short ranges, without ever repeating the attack in the same place;

——extensive conduct of actions at night;

——rapid withdrawal, after attack, to specified places of assembly over routes selected beforehand.

861. Co-operation of partisan detachments with units of the Red Army includes:

——observation and reconnaissance of the numerical strength of the enemy forces, disposition of his defensive installations and mine fields;

——target designation to combat aviation and long-range artillery;

——destruction of enemy communications, destruction of his rear works and control of troops, in connection with the operations carried out by our troops;

——reporting to the command of the units of the Red Army concerning the results of bombardments of important objectives (bridges, aerodromes, stations, depots, railway junctions) by our aviation; concerning routes inaccessible or dangerous for tanks; places suitable for landing aircraft and for dropping landing parties.

862. The commander of the detachment must have a plan of action for any situation that might develop.

863. Partisan detachments operating in the rear of the enemy organize and conduct continuous reconnaissance in the interest of the Red Army and of the partisan movement.

Partisan detachments must be constantly on the alert in carrying out their own reconnaissance, employing for the execution of this task both partisans and the population.

Along with the carrying out of strategic, tactical and combat reconnaissance, the partisan detachments organize and conduct reconnaissance through secret agents, constantly improving their methods of secret action, liaison and direction of the agent network.

864. In all forms of partisan reconnaissance one should:

——exercise continuous surveillance of the disposition and movement of troops and supplies along railway lines and main roads, determine the numerical strength of the enemy, the type of his weapons, direction of his movement and time of movement;

determine the formation and strength of the security troops of enemy echelons and transports;

———determine the precise location of the troops and staffs, the name and the numbering of the establishments and agencies of the occupying forces;

———reconnoitre the aerodromes of the enemy, determine their location, number and types of planes, whether they are based on the given aerodrome permanently or temporarily, the aerodrome equipment, auxiliary and special motor vehicles, fuel supplies and oil, and also the guards over the aerodromes, on the ground and in the air;

———organize reconnaissance of the towns and large inhabited localties for the purpose of determining: the number of troops in the garrisons (the numerical strength branch by branch of the army, the name, the numbering, the command); the anti-aircraft defences; the army depots and the workshops for military industry; the location of the higher military and civilian administrations;

———find out where and what defence lines have already been constructed, their organization from an engineering standpoint, armament, arrangement of signal communications, and whether or not they have garrisons at the place;

———watch over the results of bombardment by the aviation of the Red Army and ascertain precisely what they accomplished;

———on all possible occasions, capture orders, reports, operational maps and other documents of the enemy;

———find out and uncover agent-diversionary activity of the enemy on Soviet territory and in the partisan detachments.

The command of the partisan detachment transmits the results of its reconnaissance work to the directing agencies of the partisan movement without delay.

865. The partisan detachments establish and maintain continuous liaison (signal communications):

———between the small units of the detachment;

———between the adjacent detachments;

———with the staff of the partisan movement;

———with the military staffs in the zone in which they operate.

For the establishment of signal communications, use is made of all available means: foot messengers, carrier pigeons, dogs, radio, aircraft.

The reports are transmitted in cipher.

866. The location of the base of the partisan detachment and dispositions for rest are selected in localities difficult of access and well concealed from ground and air observation.

The detachment must change its location and base as often as possible.

The radius of action of the partisan detachments depends upon the character of the locality.

867. In order to give warning of sudden enemy attacks and in order to make possible timely preparation for battle, the detachment organizes all-round security and reconnaissance.

868. The combat formations of the partisan detachments should assure concealed movement of the detachment over any locality, and convenience of control in battle.

869. In movement of the detachment, the roads should be carefully reconnoitred by observation. The detachment crosses open localities by bounds, from cover to cover.

Upon the appearance of enemy aviation, the troops camouflage themselves, and, upon the order of the commander of the detachment, either stop moving or move in dispersed formation.

870. Ambushes are prepared in places offering good opportunities for concealment and for firing upon the enemy from short ranges. The location of the ambush should also have cover from fire and covered routes of withdrawal. The numerical strength and armament of the ambush will depend upon the strength of the enemy and the mission assigned.

The force in ambush allows the enemy to approach within close range and then opens fire point blank, distributing its fire against all the column.

An attack against moving enemy tanks is carried out from ambush in places where it is difficult for the tanks to deploy to the side of the road.

The ambush allows the column of tanks to come up within close range and then attacks them with concentrated charges and bottles with fuel mixtures, and also bombards them with anti-tank rifles. The road should be mined in advance.

The ambush destroys advancing motor-cycles without making any noise by stretching wire across the road, or by a sudden attack against the motor-cycles or the motor-cycle riders.

If the enemy pursues the ambushing force, the latter withdraws in a direction away from its base, to a previously specified point of assembly.

871. An attack against enemy communications requires thorough preparation. The attack should be preceded by careful reconnaissance of the object of attack, its location, covered approaches to it, and means of signal communications at the disposal of the enemy. The attack should be carried out in a ruthless, resolute manner and by surprise.

872. The main attacks against railways are made against the track at various places: in deep cuts, on slopes, curves, and high embankments. One should try to damage the track in such a way as to cause a train wreck.

One may also interrupt railway traffic by damaging or destroying various objects on the railway line: bridges, culverts, block signals, switches, frogs, water hydrants, and water reservoirs, water towers, houses and station installations.

873. In attacks against railway installations one first seizes and destroys the centres of communication.

For attack, the detachment is broken up into three main groups: a combat group, which noiselessly removes the guards and destroys the centres of communication; a demolition group, which carries out the direct destruction of the given object; and a reserve group.

Each soldier should clearly understand his role and duties in the approaching action.

874. In attacks against railway trains containing enemy personnel, the groups place themselves in ambush. The main group of the detachment should plan its position in such a way that at the moment when the train is wrecked, it will be opposite the middle of the train. The group with machine-guns and submachine-guns places itself at the tail of the train, on both sides of the permanent way, selecting a position such that fire can conveniently be directed along the railway cars. Fire is opened and interrupted upon the command or signal of the commander of the detachment.

875. The destruction of a station should be planned in advance, for which purpose the commander of the detachment must point out:

———the sectors of the station against which he plans to make the attack;

———the composition of the demolition parties for the operations against the sectors, and the objects to be blown up;

———the location of the blasting materials and the accessories for blasting;

——the amount of blasting material and the place where it is to be laid on each of the objects; the sequence of the actions or the signal for detonating the explosives;

——the time for completing the work, the position of the command when the blasting is done, the time and place of assembly.

When the station is captured one sends out on both sides of it, to a distance of three kilometres, parties whose mission it is to destroy the road and signal communication lines.

876. When attacks are made against staffs, it is necessary first of all to make a careful reconnaissance, determine the precise location of the staff, fire points, guard houses, officers' quarters, fuel base or motor vehicle base of the enemy. One should ascertain the location of the outposts, guards, listening posts, march routes of the patrols, and find out the enemy passwords.

When staffs are captured, all their papers are seized; any property which cannot be used by the detachment should be destroyed.

877. In attacks against an inhabited locality, the commander of the detachment, after learning the location of the inhabited locality and the approaches to it, works out a detailed plan of action in which:

——he details soldiers for the noiseless destruction of the outposts at the places where the detachment infiltrates;

——he specifies precisely the beginning of the action, usually carried out at night, so as to be able to move off into a forest (unless the mission is to hold the inhabited locality);

——he determines the signals for the beginning and ending of the action, the place of assembly after the action and the place of assembly of the separated men in case of failure; he assigns soldiers for carrying away the wounded;

——he determines the method of signal communications, designates their location, and appoints a deputy.

878. In attacks against an enemy aerodrome or landing strip one determines the precise location of the aircraft, the approaches to the machine and to the fuel and ammunition depots. In working out a plan of attack, special attention should be given to the destruction of the guards located in barracks or tents. The covering groups carrying out the destruction of the aircraft and fuel should be reinforced. The cover should draw to itself all the fire of the guards in the guard-house or in the barracks.

One may also set fire to and destroy hangars, machines, bomb depots and fuel dumps by the fire of anti-tank rifles, rifles, armour-piercing incendiary bullets, grenades, mines, incendiary mixtures, and thermite compositions.

879. The destruction of enemy depots and bases is carried out chiefly by setting fire to them.

In setting fire to depots we should first of all destroy or damage the fire-fighting equipment.

Artillery depots are destroyed by exploding boxes of shells or explosive substances found in them with a supplementary charge and an incendiary fuse, or by firing upon these boxes with anti-tank rifles and armour-piercing incendiary bullets.

880. The destruction of the enemy's means of signal communications should be carried out systematically, by cutting out sections of the field conductors and destroying them. One should not destroy the telegraph and telephone poles, but the wires, and inflict other damage.

It is particularly important to knock out radio stations, telegraph-telephone stations and commutators, using any means available.

In the Field Service Regulations, this chapter on Partisan Operations is followed by Chapters on:

Joint Actions of Troops with the Navy.

Joint Actions of Troops with River Flotillas.

Appendix II
PROTOCOL 'M'[1]

THE coming winter will see the decisive epoch in the history of the German working class. In conjunction with the entire working class in all European countries it will gain power through an energetic campaign for the key positions in production. This is not a manœuvre for obtaining ministerial appointments but for the starting positions in the final battle for the liberation of the world proletariat. Discipline of the comrades and ruthless activity of every functionary are the prerequisites for the final victory, so soon to come, of the working class. There must not be any doubt that for the sake of this final victory all the paraphernalia of the proletarian battle will be put into operation. The motherland of socialism, the Soviet Union, can and will support the fight against the powers of monopoly-capitalism with all and every means.

The Communist Information Centre (Cominform) will co-ordinate the common fight of all the socialist movements in Europe. Although the German Party is not yet a member of this Centre, the Party holds a key position in the coming campaign. It has to conduct the battle for the European centre of production in the Ruhr area. The entire working class of all nations will furnish the necessary means. The German Party has the task of using these means ruthlessly wherever it can be done to the greatest advantage.

The object of the winter campaign is to repel the monopolistic-capitalistic attack of the so-called Marshall Plan.

After extensive discussions the comrade functionaries have come to the following decisions:

Part I

The centres of the battle of the masses are:

(i) The Ruhr area and its production, and
(ii) The means of transport in West and North Germany.

[1] The text of Protocol 'M' (cf. Chapter vii of the book) was reprinted in full in the Berlin newspaper *Der Kurier* of 15th January, 1948, and elsewhere.

For tactical reasons it is necessary that the comrade functionaries are not in the front line when the strikes break out. But in accordance with Plan R experienced functionaries in the strike cadres are required to ensure, with even more care than hitherto, that the workers' risings occur simultaneously in transport and production. The trade unions of the transport and iron and steel workers will carry out a succession of strikes. The Party must in all circumstances refrain from any operations. It will have to reckon with its prohibition by the military authorities. The plan for the new organization must therefore be carried out with the utmost speed.

From past experience it must be expected that the Ruhr workers will be given substantial preferential treatment, with the result that the strike idea may be rejected for opportunist reasons. In this respect it is up to the transport worker to perform his task. Special importance is to be attached to the railway lines from Bremen to Dusseldorf and from Hamburg to Bielefeld. Key point of the transport workers' strike is Dortmund. Essen must not be permitted to gain preponderance through wild strikes; this would jeopardize the entire plan. It appears from previous communications that the military authorities are already organizing lorry transport which could take over soon after the railways and private lorry transport have come to a standstill. It is therefore necessary to find out the likely routes (earmarked by the military) and to sabotage the supply lines. Foodstuffs should not thereby be destroyed; the aim is only to prevent their punctual arrival. The co-ordination in time of delays in the arrival of food transports and the organization of wild strikes, leading to a loss of production, is an essential feature of the operation. Comrades . . . (here follow their names) will be at their posts from the middle of November on, as previously announced. Security measures for these posts have been taken by the cadres and the funds for strike pay are available. The leading principle for strikers in other parts of the West remains as hitherto: their aim must be the unity of the working class.

Part 2

As far as organization is concerned, it is based on the iron and steel workers' union. But it must not be neglected to obtain or control if possible the position of treasurer in every union.

Up to now all attempts in this direction have failed. Should it not be possible to win over a sufficient number of agents before the appointed day, it must be ensured that the task can be fulfilled under the leadership of social-democratic comrades. In this event the Party must, by agitation, see to it that the R-men, from below, succeed in getting the time-table adopted, and thereby restrict the liberty of action of the Schumacher people (viz. the Social-democrats). The unity of the working class must at this moment become a reality, even if this involves renunciation of complete control.

The cadres have the special task of ascertaining the weaknesses in the mass organization of the Social-democratic Party. Subsequently they will be ruthlessly exploited.

Internal trade union negotiations must be initiated forthwith. It must be attempted to obtain organizational control of the iron and steel workers' union by yielding other positions.

All appointments have already been made. Comrades ... (here follow the names) have been approved as members of the executive committee for Operation Ruhr. They can be reached at any time under the known code names.

Part 3

Agitation will be uniformly directed by the central executive committee. Propaganda targets are:

(i) The Marshall Plan, as a plan by the monopoly-capitalists in the U.S.A. for enslavement.

(ii) The strikes in countries dominated by the monopoly-capitalists, as an indication of the quickening dissolution of capitalistic society.

(iii) The serene and progressive development of the east-European economy under the protection of the Soviet Union.

Press polemics have principally to concern themselves with the protests by non-Communists against the dismantling in the West. They are an attempt to protect future capitalist markets. Since a complete prohibition of all Party Papers has to be reckoned with, stationary transmitters and the established courier network will continuously provide agitation and information material. It must be ensured that the receiving sets which have been provided are installed in time and safe against sequestration.

It is the task of agitation cadres 7, 11 and 14 to popularize the plebiscite and the socialization of the Ruhr industry. It is necessary to conduct, together with the Social Democrats, a campaign at public meetings on this common basis. The unity of the working class must be promoted by means of this joint propaganda for a plebiscite. It is quite agreeable to the central executive committee that the Social Democrats should, at first, hold the important positions in the joint action committees.

Part 4

Time-table:

(a) Until the end of December: Arranging a common basis between the Social Democrats and the Communist Party for a plebiscite.

(b) Until the end of February: Organization of strike cadres.

(c) From the beginning of March on: Organization of the general strike.

If necessary, the time-table may be changed. The central executive committee is in permanent session and at all times prepared to make amendments or issue directives if required.

Part 5

The MA cadres are entrusted with supervision. Ando 47 105 and 47 109 are applicable. Punctual execution of the cadres' directives by the comrade functionaries must be ensured.

V. I. Lenin: "He who puts first in his programme, tactics and organizational work, the political mass agitation which reaches the entire population, runs the least risk of failure in the revolution."

Appendix III

THE COMINTERN APPEAL OF THE 1st MAY, 1940[1]

WORKERS and labourers of the entire world!

In the sinister atmosphere of a new imperialist war, the workers celebrate the 1st May, the day of international proletarian solidarity. Never before was the idea of international proletarian solidarity of such vital importance to the workers of all countries as in these times of conflagration by war, which sets Europe and Asia on fire.

The war in Europe has now been on for eight months, and the end is not in sight. The theatre of operations becomes more and more extended. The imperialist powers forcibly drag the colonial peoples under their domination into this war. The longer the war lasts, the more it becomes evident that the neutral countries are regarded merely as pawns in the hands of the imperialists. In reply to the brutal violation—by Great Britain and France—of the neutrality of the Scandinavian countries, Germany has marched into Denmark and occupied strategic positions in Norway.

Once again the capitalist scoundrels send the people to the world-wide imperialist slaughter.

The great country of Socialism stands up against the capitalist world caught by the war fever. The Anglo-French war-mongers and their social-democratic lackeys are furious because the Soviet Union remains neutral in their imperialist war. Furious because they see the U.S.S.R. progress and continuously gain strength while they themselves struggle in the grip of imperialist antagonism and war. Furious, because the U.S.S.R. has secured the benefits of peace for her people, because she lives in peace with Germany, just as the country of Socialism lives in peace with those other countries which do not infringe on her rights. Furious, because the U.S.S.R., thanks to her policy of loyal neutrality, opposes the extension of the war to other countries.

The war-mongers rage because their provocations were foiled in Finland, because the glorious Red Army has wiped out this base of operations which were long ago prepared against the U.S.S.R.

[1] This Appeal is referred to in Chapter v of the book.

They are angry because the Soviet Union, by signing the peace treaty with Finland, has exposed the Anglo-French war-mongers, she has made them show their hand, she has revealed their designs to the peoples. . . .

Workers of the capitalist countries!

The war has already caused you unheard-of misery and privations. There have not yet been any major battles but the soil is already red from the blood of the victims. Thousands and thousands of sailors have perished on the high seas. In Europe alone 20 million people are under arms, people taken on from their production work and their homes. Hunger and misery threaten these homes, whose providers have been thrown into the trenches by the bourgeoisie: wives, mothers and children of those called-up are left to their fate.

The bourgeoisie robs the hungry and poor by raising the prices of the most necessary commodities. It rations the people by introducing ration cards, while the rich, whose larders and cellars are well-stocked, are feasting. The bourgeoisie chains the workers like convicts and binds them to the factories like slaves. It makes them toil by indefinitely extending working hours, by scandalously reducing wages, by exploiting them to the utmost. It ruins the villages by sending the sons of the farmers to the war, by requisitioning horses, cattle, foodstuffs and fodder. The bourgeoisie takes away the fruits from those who have worked the land by the sweat of their brow. The young generation is sacrificed, condemned to perish so that (the bourgeoisie) can fill its strong-boxes. Sombre thoughts beset the soldiers in the trenches; they anxiously ask themselves what the next day has in store for them, what will become of their families.

In the rear, there is the odious orgy of the war profiteers and speculators, who enrich themselves at the expense of the people. For them the war is a bonanza. They convert the human blood and tears into shares, dividends and fabulous profits.

But the bourgeoisie attacks furiously not only the workers, by making use of the servility of the Blums, Jouhaux, Attlees and Citrines; it also installs in every capitalist country a system of reaction, of obscurantism, despotism, terror, a régime for the enslavement of the workers. It uses the war to deprive the workers in town and country of their last rights, where they still had any. The bourgeoisie replies to the desire of the masses for peace with war councils, with heavy prison sentences and executions. It outlaws those who fight in the front rank for the liberty and welfare of the people: the Communists. It throws hundreds of thousands of Communists, Spanish refugees and political immigrants into prisons and concentration camps.

This is the true picture of the war and the bourgeois régime.

But, workers, what has the bourgeoisie in store for you if you do not end the war, and the capitalists maintain their hold over you?

Europe and Asia and perhaps other continents as well will see a massacre such as the history of mankind has never witnessed before: millions of dead and wounded, millions of widows and orphans, a crushing burden of new contributions and annexations, a destruction of worldly goods, disaster for the people even more terrible than that which followed the war of 1914–18. That is what the war will bring us.

Workers and labourers!

Who has supported, and continues to support, the bourgeoisie so that it can extract the last piece of bread from you and your children and choke you in the terror of bourgeois dictatorship? Who has prepared the present bloody crime in complicity with the bourgeoisie?

The leaders of the Social-democrats and of the reformed trade unions did it!

If they had not helped the bourgeoisie to suppress the movement of the workers against capitalism after the World War 1914–18, would the world be what it is now?

Like watch dogs did they defend, and they are still defending, the capitalist régime. Their Noskes have shot down the workers, their Bauers have deceived the workers with the phantom of the 'bourgeois democracy'. Their MacDonalds have strangled the general strikes. Their Blums, in co-operation with the world reactionaries, have called and are still openly calling for a crusade against the country of Socialism. By their policy of co-operation, of the working classes with the bourgeoisie, they have paved the ground for the capitalist tyranny.

The workers more and more realize that there is no other way of escape from the catastrophe initiated by the bourgeoisie than the resolute fight against, and the clear rejection of, the imperialist war, reaction and capitalism. They know that this demands sacrifices. But those imposed by the bourgeoisie to maintain its domination are a hundred times heavier.

Millions of people at the front and in the rear repeat at the moment in a subdued voice what the Communists loudly proclaim. Today it is not just an isolated hero who turns against the imperialist war: ten thousands of proletarians in the vanguard all over the world raise the sacred banner of proletarian internationalism, the banner which the French Communist deputies courageously raised in the precincts of the War Council. This is the banner under which hundreds of thousands of workers fight in obscurity in France.

1st May, 1940

Appendix IV

MEMORANDUM ON THE GERMAN POLITICAL AIMS
IN SOVIET RUSSIA[1]

IN the East, Germany is carrying on a threefold war: a war for the destruction of Bolshevism, a war for the destruction of the greater Russian Empire, and finally a war for the acquisition of colonial territory for colonizing purposes and economic exploitation.

The populace has more of an understanding of the measures and duties necessitated by war than the conquered peoples of the West. But the labourer and peasant, who were educated to the highest degree of self-consciousness by Bolshevism, soon perceived that Germany did not regard them as partners with equal rights, but considered them only as objects of her political and economic aims. This disillusioned them unspeakably, all the more since they had placed colossal hopes on Germany.

The Main Department for Politics of the Reich Ministry for the Occupied Eastern Territories claims that it has been quite aware of this situation from the beginning. It was soon apparent that the war could not be decided in a short time by arms alone, because of the vast areas and the enemy's inexhaustible reserves of manpower and material, but that as in all great wars of recent times a spiritual disintegration would have to come, and the war would have to be changed at the final conclusion to a civil war, all the more since the Wehrmacht does not intend to occupy completely the territory of the Soviet Union. The Russian collapse of 1917 and the German breakdown of 1918 were actually not brought about by weapons alone, but primarily by political disintegration. What Lenin achieved in Russia, the fourteen points of Wilson and the undermining effect of Marxism accomplished in

[1] This Memorandum, which is referred to in Chapter x of this book, was written on 25th October, 1942, by Dr. Braeutigam, who was at that time a senior official in the Main Department for Politics of the Reichsministry for the Occupied Eastern Territories, and previously, until the outbreak of war, German Consul General in Baku. The Memorandum, which was introduced by the prosecution during the Trial of the Major War Criminals at Nuremberg, is reprinted in *Nazi Conspiracy and Aggression*, vol. iii, Office of United States Chief of Counsel for Prosecution of Axis Criminality, United States Government Printing Office, Washington, 1946, pp. 242 *seq.*

Germany. In the Soviet Union we found on our arrival a population weary of Bolshevism, which waited longingly for new slogans, holding out the prospect of a better future for them. It was Germany's duty to find such slogans, but they remained unuttered. The population greeted us with joy as liberators, and placed themselves at our disposal willingly and freely with body and life. Wherever Ukrainians, Russians, White Ruthenians and members of the Baltic peoples were enlisted in the German Wehrmacht or in the police they have proved themselves and fought excellently almost without exception. The Main Department for Politics tried every means of keeping this vast capital that has fallen into our lap, and of utilizing it for our purposes. For this reason it was necessary that National Socialism should separate itself from Bolshevism with a sharp line of distinction, and open to the populace prospects of a new, better life. All measures which the Main Department for Politics suggested were directed toward this one goal of preserving this capital. . . . Should this political policy succeed, the greatest repercussions on the enemy troops were to be expected. For years the masses of the Soviet Union were stirred up against the surrounding world by the most efficient propaganda machine that has ever existed. Until 1939 National Socialism had been the target of the most spiteful attacks. Day after day it was hammered into the labourers and peasants that the active masses in Germany were subjected to the most terrible exploitation. It was with extreme tension that the workers and peasants looked forward to the German administration. To be sure, they had not completely trusted the Bolshevist propaganda, but in spite of that they met the new masters with a certain feeling of doubt.

As we all know, the peoples of the Soviet Union have gone through the hardest times. Consequently, they are of a simplicity inconceivable to us, even in the political sphere. A form of government which was not intent only on plundering and exploitation, and which put aside the Bolshevist methods, would have kindled the greatest enthusiasm and put at our disposal a mass of millions. And the enthusiasm in the occupied Eastern territories would have had its reaction on the strength of resistance of the Red Army. It would have been easily attainable to have the Red Army man say to himself: "I fight for a system that is throughout worse than that which awaits me in the case of defeat. I will be better off in every respect among the Germans than I have been until now." If the Red Army man had become convinced of his well-being, the war would have been at an end very soon.

Knowing this the Main Department for Politics believed it to be its primary duty to assist our combat troops with all their power by a propaganda campaign aimed at crippling the power of resistance of the Red Army and to shorten the war in this way. For the attainment of this goal there are, among the measures proposed, two of the utmost importance: the Agrarian Law and Religious Freedom, which is the antithesis of Bolshevism.

Considering the exceptionally great significance of the agrarian question in the Soviet Union, the Main Department for Politics was demanding even before the beginning of the Eastern campaign, that the Kolchos be dissolved and private property be introduced again. This proposal was turned down by the Four Year Plan with the remark that organic changes were not to be considered during the war. Not until 1st August (1942) was an increase of the farmland successfully put through. . . .

The new Agrarian Decree came out shortly before the spring planting and was greatly played up in the territories by the Press and Propaganda Department of Main Department I. It succeeded; the population put in a hitherto inconceivable amount of work during the spring planting, which could be carried out in spite of unfavourable conditions. However, no lasting effect on the enemy has so far been noticeable. Naturally, enemy propaganda countered our Agrarian Decree with every means. . . . This propaganda found support in the very slow execution of the Agrarian Decree. . . . The agricultural co-operatives were installed only a short time ago, and according to the directives of the farmers' leader, Koerner, no more than 10 per cent of the land will have been transferred to them by August of this year. It is therefore understandable that large sections of the Ukrainian peasantry . . . have lost belief in the earnestness of our intentions.

The granting of religious freedom likewise called for large-scale propaganda. After months-long negotiations, it was eventually decided not to announce freedom of religion ceremoniously, but to let it come into existence as quietly as possible. The propaganda effect was consequently lost.

When the Main Department for Politics noticed the reluctance over the Church question, it searched for a propaganda substitute: the restitution of private property. . . . To the unbounded astonishment of the populace, however, the German administration decided to play the role of receiver of the goods stolen by the Bolshevists. . . .

Again a real weapon in the fight for the disintegration of the enemy front had been twisted out of our hand, a weapon whose effect cannot be undervalued. For the unrecompensed expropriation of private property by the Bolshevists had aroused at the time not only the dismay of Russian bourgeois circles, including the more prosperous peasants, but also of the entire civilized world. The world, including the labourers and peasants in the Soviet Union, who were disillusioned by Bolshevism, now expected a clear policy on this question from Germany. Enemy propaganda made obvious use of Germany's silence and effectively persuaded the Soviet masses that Germany had no intention of restoring individual property.

The Main Department for Politics has always emphasized that the Eastern people must be informed in concrete terms about their future. . . . It has accordingly often directed the attention of the Wehrmacht units to the expediency of having the Slavic Eastern peoples receive calming assurances about their future from the German authorities. As the best means, the establishment of a sort of counter-régime to Stalin with a captured Red general was indicated; or, if the word government should be avoided, just a rebellious general somewhat after the model of de Gaulle. . . . The correctness of this conception has been confirmed . . . by countless statements by prisoners of war, who have all said independently that the worst might be feared if Germany remained silent on the future of Russia. Many would like to desert, but they did not know to whom to turn. Under the banner of a recognized counter-revolutionary leader they would gladly and bravely fight against the Bolshevist régime.

All the respective suggestions were rejected in their essentials. Permission for front-line duty was given only for groups of Turki and Caucasian peoples and finally, after several refusals, also for the Estonians. . . . Only in the last few weeks . . . was the formation of native units allowed and that only for combatting the partisans. But even this measure will remain ineffective from the propaganda viewpoint unless combat units are activated and a personality with a resounding name is put in command.

(Here follows an outspoken condemnation of the German slave labour policy and their treatment of prisoners of war, measures which led directly to the strengthening of the Red Army's power to resist and the spreading of the partisan danger. The Memorandum then continues:)

If this danger which threatens the German people is to be prevented at the last moment, then the following is necessary:

1. For the Ukraine an absolutely positive policy is necessary.... The populace must sincerely feel that Germany is its friend and liberator.... The Russian people must be told something concrete about their future....

2. ... If we accomplish the proposed change in policy, it will certainly result in the decomposition of the Red Army. For the power of resistance of the Red Army man will break when he becomes convinced that Germany brings him a better life than he has led under the Soviets. ...

The problem is too serious to be allowed to remain undecided. It concerns the future of the German race, its future existence or doom. The consistent theses of the Main Department for Politics have proved themselves correct: a quick victory cannot be attained by arms alone, but only in conjunction with a great political offensive. That the administration of the occupied Eastern territories is almost entirely composed of personnel not acquainted with Russia is probably one of the reasons why these theses have not been translated into practice. These gentlemen slowly grope their way into the problem, and the majority still require interpreters. Nevertheless, it is today already certain that wide circles of the minor administrative executives in the Ukraine are plainly frightened of the policy laid down by the higher echelon. However, they are not allowed to have their way. So much the more reason why one should trust the Main Department's conception, which is based on the best technical and sociological information. The Department is even today convinced of a speedy victorious conclusion of the war provided its political conceptions are adopted.

Berlin, 25th October, 1942

(sd) BRAEUTIGAM

BIBLIOGRAPHY

AMERY, Julian: *Sons of the Eagle, A Study in Guerilla War*. London, 1948.
AMERY, Julian: *Of Resistance*. In: The Nineteenth Century and After, March, 1949.
ANDERS, General W.: *Hitler's Defeat in Russia*. Chicago, 1953.
ANISIMOV, Oleg: *The German Occupation in Northern Russia during World War II, Political and Administrative Aspects*. Research Program on the U.S.S.R. New York City, 1954.
BAKER-WHITE, Colonel John: *The Red Network*. Lower Hardress, 1953.
BAKER-WHITE, Colonel John: 'The Armies of Communism'. In: *Military Digest*, General Staff, Army HQ, New Delhi, July 1954.
BAUDOUIN, Paul: *Neuf mois au gouvernement, Avril-Décembre 1940*. Paris, 1948.
BOHN, Helmut: Book Review. In: *Ost-Probleme*, Bad Nauheim (Germany), 23rd October, 1954.
BOURRET, Général: *La tragédie de l'armée française*. Paris, 1947.
BRÄUTIGAM, Dr.: 'Memorandum on the German Political Aims in Soviet Russia'. (1942) In: *Nazi Conspiracy and Aggression*, vol. iii, Office of the United States Chief of Counsel for Prosecution of Axis Criminality. Washington, 1946.
BURNHAM, J.: *The Coming Defeat of Communism*. London, 1950.
CHASSIN, Général L.-M.: *La conquête de la Chine par Mao Tse-tung (1945-9)*. Paris, 1952.
CHURCHILL, Sir Winston: *The Second World War*. London. Vol. ii, 1949; vol. iii, 1950; vol. iv, 1951.
Comintern Appeal of the 1st May, 1940.
COOKRIDGE, E. H.: *Soviet Spy Net*. London, 1955.
COT, Pierre: *Triumph of Treason*. Chicago, New York, 1944.
DANJOU, Guy: *La révolution Communiste*. Paris, 1939.
DIMITROFF, G.: *Communism and the War*. London, 1939.
DIXON, G. Aubrey, and HEILBRUNN, Otto: *Communist Guerilla Warfare*. London, 1954; New York, 1954; Oslo, 1954; Paris, 1955.
DWINGER, Edwin Erich: *General Wlassow, Eine Tragödie unserer Zeit*. Frankfurt, 1951.

EINSIEDEL, Count Heinrich von: *The Shadow of Stalingrad*. London, 1953.
FAURE, Paul: *Communist Activity in France*. London, 1940.
FEDOROV, A.: *L'Obkom clandestin au travail*. Paris, 1951.
FISCHER, George: *Soviet Opposition to Stalin*. Cambridge, Mass., 1952.
FLICKE, W. F.: *Agenten funken nach Moskau*. Kreuzlingen, 1954.
FOLEY, Charles: *Commando Extraordinary*. London, New York, Toronto, 1954.
FOOTE, Alexander: *Handbook for Spies*. London, 1949.
FORDE, Colonel H. M.: Book Review in: *The Army Combat Forces Journal*, October 1954.
GAMELIN, Général: *Servir, Les armées françaises de 1940*. Paris, 1946.
GENEBRIER, R.: see: P. MAZÉ.
GOERLITZ, Walter: *Der Zweite Weltkrieg, 1939–45*. Vol. ii, Stuttgart, 1952.
GREINER, Helmuth: *Die Oberste Wehrmachtsführung, 1939–43*. Wiesbaden, 1951.
GUILLAUME, General Augustin: *Soviet Arms and Soviet Power*. Washington, 1949.
HALDER, General Franz: *Hitler as War Lord*. London, 1950.
HALDER, General Franz: *Diaries*. Vol. vi, February to August, 1941.
HEERESGRUPPE NORD, Führungsabteilung: *Feldzug gegen die Sowjetunion der Heeresgruppe Nord*, Kriegsjahr 1943. 1944.
HEILBRUNN, Otto: see: DIXON, C. Aubrey.
Herald Tribune: 'The Threat of Red Sabotage'. New York, 1951.
HESSE, Fritz: *Hitler and the English*. London, 1954.
HOETTL, Wilhelm: *The Secret Front*. London, 1953.
IGNATOV, P. K.: *Partisanen. Aus dem Russischen übersetzt von Manfred von Busch*. Berlin, 1953.
IGNATOV, P. K.: *Partisans of the Kuban*. Translated from the Russian by J. Fineberg. London, New York etc., 1945.
KAPETANOVIC, Nikola: *Tito and his Partisans*. Belgrade, 1950.
KHOKHLOV, Nicolai E.: 'I Would Not Murder for the Soviets'. *Saturday Evening Post*, 20th, 27th November, 4th and 11th December, 1954.
Khokhlov Briefing Papers. Prepared at the Offices of the United States High Commissioner in Bonn, April 1954.
KINTNER, William R.: *The Front is Everywhere*. Oklahoma University Press, 1951.

KLEIST, Peter: *Zwischen Hitler und Stalin*. Bonn, 1950.
KORIAKOV, Mikhail: Book Review in: *The New York Times Book Review*, 5th December, 1954.
KOUSOULAS, Dimitrios G.: *The Price of Freedom*. Syracuse University Press, 1953.
LAZITCH, Branko: *The Tragedy of General Mihailovitch*. London, 1946.
LEEPER, Sir Reginald: *When Greek meets Greek*. London, 1950.
LENIN, V. I.: ' "Left Wing" Communism, An Infantile Disorder'. In: *Selected Works*, London, 1947, vol. ii.
LENIN, V. I.: 'Conditions of Affiliation to Communist International'. In: *Selected Works*, London, 1943, vol. x.
LENIN, V. I.: *Collected Works* (1918–9), New York, 1945.
LEVERKÜHN, Paul: *German Military Intelligence*. London, 1954.
MACLEAN, Brigadier Fitzroy: *Eastern Approaches*. London, 1949.
MANSFIELD, Captain Walter R.: 'Marine with the Chetniks'. In: *The Marine Corps Gazette*, January and February, 1946.
MAO TSE-TUNG: *Aspects of China's Anti-Jap Struggle*. Bombay, 1948. Also in the translation by Colonel Samuel H. Griffith in: *The Marine Corps Gazette*, 1940.
MAO TSE-TUNG: 'Strategic Problems of China's Revolutionary War'. In: *Selected Works*. London, 1954.
MAO TSE-TUNG: *On People's Democratic Dictatorship*. Peking, 1951.
MARTIN, David: *Ally Betrayed*. New York, 1946.
MARTIN, Lt.-General H. G.: Book Review in: *Daily Telegraph*, 9th April, 1954.
MAZÉ, P., et GENEBRIER, R.: *Les grandes journées du procès de Riom*. Paris, 1945.
MEISSNER, Boris: 'Die sowjetische Deutschlandpolitik'. In: *Europa Archiv*, 1951.
General Mihailovitch, *The World's Verdict*. Gloucester, 1947.
MIKSCHE, Lt.-Colonel F. O.: *Secret Forces*. London, 1951.
A Military History of World War II, by Members of the Department of Military Art and Engineering, United States Military Academy, edited by T. Dodson Stamps and Vincent J. Esposito, vol. i. New York, 1953.
MILLER, H.: *Menace in Malaya*. London, 1954.
MURATOFF, Paul: 'The Third Russian Summer-Autumn Campaign, July-November 1943'. In: *Message*, Belgian Review. January 1944.
Nazi Conspiracy and Aggression, vols. iii and iv. Washington 1946.

PALLIS, A. A.: *Problems of Resistance in the Occupied Countries.* London, 1947.
PAPEN, Franz von: *Memoirs.* London, 1952.
Partisan Handbook (Soviet), 1942.
Partisan Operations: Chapter xvii of the Field Service Regulations of the Red Army, 1944.
PIYADE, Mosha: *About the Legend that the Yugoslav Uprising owed its Existence to Soviet Russia.* London, 1950.
'Protocol "M" '. In: *Der Kurier*, Berlin, 15th January, 1948.
PUTTKAMER, Jesco von: *Von Stalingrad zur Volkspolizei.* Wiesbaden, 1951.
REYNAUD, Paul: *La France a sauvé l'Europe.* Paris, 1947.
ROEDER, Dr. M.: *Die Rote Kapelle.* Hamburg, 1952.
ROOTHAM, Major Jasper: *Miss Fire.* London, 1946.
ROSSI, A.: *Les Cahiers du Bolshevisme pendant la campagne 1939-40.* Paris, 1951.
ROSSI, A.: *Les Communistes français pendant la drôle de guerre.* Paris, 1951.
ROSSI, A.: *A Communist Party in Action.* New Haven, 1949.
Royal Commission on Espionage, Commonwealth of Australia. Official Transcript of Proceedings, Melbourne, 1954 and 1955.
Royal Commission to Investigate the Facts relating to . . . the Communication of Secret and Confidential Information to Agents of a Foreign Power. Report. Ottawa, 1946.
SAMARIN, Vladimir D.: *Civilian Life under the German Occupation, 1942-4, Research Program on the U.S.S.R.* New York City, 1954.
SHERWOOD, Robert E.: *Roosevelt and Hopkins.* New York, 1948.
SHERWOOD, Robert E.: *The White House Papers of Harry L. Hopkins.* London, 1948.
SCHUMAN, Frederick L.: *Soviet Politics at Home and Abroad.* London, 1948.
SETON-WATSON, Hugh: *The Pattern of Communist Revolution, A Historical Analysis.* London, 1953.
Soviet World Outlook, A Handbook of Communist Statements, prepared by the Division of Research for U.S.S.R. and Eastern Europe, Office of Intelligence Research, Department of State, for the Co-ordinator of Psychological Intelligence, U.S. Information Agency, 1954.
STEVENS, Vice-Admiral Leslie C.: *Life in Russia.* London, New York, Toronto, 1954.

'Swiatlo Story, The'. In: *News from behind the Iron Curtain*, vol. iv, No. 3, March 1955.
TARACOUZIO, T. A.: *The Soviet Union and International Law*. New York, 1935.
TESKE, Hermann: *Die silbernen Spiegel*. Heidelberg, 1952.
THORWALD, Jürgen, *Wen sie verderben wollen*. Stuttgart, 1952.
Trial of the Major War Criminals before the International Military Tribunal at Nuremberg. Washington.
Trial of Mihailovic, Stenographic Record and Documents. Belgrade, 1946.
Trials of the War Criminals before the Nuremberg Military Tribunals, vol. xi, Washington, 1950; vol. xii, Nuremberg; vol. xiii, Nuremberg, 1953.
War Crimes Trials (British) against Field Marshal von Manstein.
War Crimes Trials (U.S.) against Field Marshal von Leeb et al.
War Crimes Trials (U.S.) against Field Marshal List et al.
War Crimes Trials (U.S.) against von Weizsaecker et al.
WHEELER-BENNET, John W.: *The Nemesis of Power*. London, 1953.
WILLOUGHBY, Major-General Charles A.: *Sorge: Soviet Master Spy*. London, 1952.
WOODHOUSE, Colonel C. M.: *Apple of Discord*. London, 1948.
YOURICHITCH, Evgueniye: *Le procès Tito-Mihailovitch*. Paris, 1950.
Yugoslavia Emergency Committee (British): *The Story of the Partisans of Free Yugoslavia*. 1944.

INDEX

A

Abwehr: Cf. Counter-intelligence, German; Intelligence, German Military
Action 'Zeppelin', 151 seq., 170
Agents:
  German P.O.W.s, 79, 151
  Legal Aspects, 167 seq.
  Partisan, 50, 54 seq., 90
  Russian P.O.W.s, 151 seq., 159 seq.
Albania, 101, 102, 103, 108, 122
Amery, J., 9, 99, 102 seq., 113
Anders, General W., 163
Anisimov, O., 54, 55, 162, 164, 165
Anti-Partisans, 94 seq., 99, 153, 164
Atomic weapons, 10, 11, 12, 168, 180
Australia, 13, 81: see also Royal Commission, Australia

B

Baker White, J., 73, 138
Bandera, 157
Baudouin, P., 72
B.B.C., 65 seq., 109, 149, 150
Beaverbrook, Lord, 35
Beck, Col.-General, 59
Bentivegni, Lt.-General, 160
Bielgorod, 44, 45, 47
Blanchard, General, 71
Bohn, H., 177
Bourret, General, 71
Braeutigam, Dr., 162, 163, 165, 200 seq.
Brandenburg Regiment, 88, 158 seq.
Bulganin, Marshal, 15 seq.
'Bund, Der', 21, 22
Burnham, J., 9

C

Cahiers du Bolchevisme, 60, 61, 63
Canada: see Royal Commission, Canada
Caucasus, 40, 41, 42, 89 seq.
Central Party Committee of the Soviet Union, 77, 132, 139
Chassin, General, L. M., 142 seq.
Chetniks, 106 seq.
Chiang Kai-shek, 142
China, 138, 140 seq.
Churchill, Sir Winston, 35, 36, 41, 42, 72, 110, 116
Clausewitz, C. von, 100
Co-existence, 14 seq.
Collingwood, Mr. Justice, 168
Cominform, 84, 128, 131, 134, 138, 192
Comintern, 58, 64, 69, 101, 102, 128, 131, 173, 196 seq.
Commanding General in Serbia 107 seq.
Communist Party:
  France, 56, 58, 60, 61, 62, 70, 73, 82
  Intelligence, 30, 134
  Organizational Chart, 134
  Organization of Partisan Warfare, 89, 138 seq.
Communist Radio transmissions, 64 seq., 76, 109
'Consul I', 157
Cookridge, E. H., 85, 133, 135, 136
Coro, 28
Cot, P., 71
Counter-Intelligence:
  German, 23, 24, 25, 26, 34 seq., 44
  Swiss, 27
Czechoslovakia, 21, 28 seq., 137

INDEX

D

Daily Telegraph, 21, 110
Daladier, 67
Danjou, G., 69, 73
de Gaulle, General C., 125, 163, 203
Denmark, 129
Dimitroff, G., 60, 61, 69
'Director', Soviet Military Intelligence, 25, 27, 36, 39, 42, 43, 44, 46, 47
Dixon, C. A., 10, 54, 55, 85, 138, 179
Duclos, 30, 69
Dwinger, E. E., 163

E

East troops, 93, 150, 163 seq.
EDES, 122 seq.
Einsiedel, Count von, 91, 92, 93
Eisenhower, President, 17
ELAS, 122 seq.
Enbom, F., 86 seq.
Espionage, Soviet, 21 seq., 33 seq., 130 seq.
Espionage trials, 21, 22, 30 seq., 86
L'Étinelle, 83

F

Factory Sabotage Groups, 81 seq., 134
Faure, Paul, 56
Fedorov, A., 51
Field Service Regulations of the Red Army, 51 seq., 92 seq., 183 seq.
Fifth Column, 13
Fischer, G., 163, 165
Flicke, W. F., 23, 25, 26, 27, 36, 37, 38, 41, 42, 43, 45
Foley, C., 160
Foote, Allan, 22, 23, 25, 27, 28
Forde, Colonel H. M., 55

France, 56 seq., 101, 125, 138, 139, 164, 176, 177, 180, 196 seq.
'Free Germany' Movement, 78
Freies Deutschland, 77
French National Defence Council, 30, 180

G

Gamelin, General, 71
Gehlen, General, 108, 114
Genebrier, R., 71
Geneva Conventions, 167 seq.
German Army Groups:
  A, 41
  Centre, 44, 76, 79, 178
  North, 93 seq.
  South, 44
German Federal Republic, 82, 83 seq., 87, 99, 177, 192 seq.
German General Staff, 10, 33, 35, 40, 44, 108, 156
German Intelligence Services: *see* Intelligence, German
German Ministry for the Occupied Eastern Territories, 162 seq., 200 seq.
German Officers' Bund, 76
German political warfare, 159
German propaganda, 148 seq.
German rearmament, 177 seq.
German sabotage activities, 158 seq.
German subversive activities, 157 seq.
Gilbert, 28
Glasgow Herald, 55
Goerlitz, W., 156, 159
Goernant, C., 123
Great Britain, 57, 59, 60, 61, 63, 67, 79, 103, 119, 120, 124
Greece, 102, 122 seq.
Greiner, H., 44
Griffith, Colonel S. H., 140
G.R.U.: *see* Red Army Intelligence,
Guerillas: *see* Partisans
Guide Book for Partisans, 53
Guillaume, General A., 46

H

Hague Convention, 49, 167 seq.
Halder, Col.-General, 10, 33, 38, 40, 41, 147
Handbook for Partisans, 50 seq.
Heilbrunn, O.: see Dixon
Hess, R., 36
Hesse, F., 79
Hitler, 36, 40, 47, 58, 61, 66, 70, 76, 77, 80, 115, 148
Hoettl, W., 151
Home Army (Poland), 124 seq.
Hopkins, Harry, 36
Hostages, 112 seq., 168
L'Humanité, 63, 64, 73, 82
Hungary, 137

I

Ignatov, P. K., 88 seq.
Imperialists, 60, 61, 63, 69
Infiltration, Soviet: Cf. Red Orchestra; Red Three, and page 172
Intelligence:
　British, 34
　German Military, 44, 108, 111, 114, 147, 151, 156 seq.
　German Naval, 34 seq.
　German Political, 151 seq., 159
　Groups, Soviet, 132, 134, 135
　Soviet, 125, 127, 130 seq., 134; see also: 'Director'; Partisans; Red Orchestra; Red Three; Sofia; Sorge
International Law and the New Warfare, 17, 167 seq.
Italy, 73, 101, 115 seq., 125, 164, 177

J

Japan, Soviet spy ring: see Sorge
John, O., 180

K

Kapetanovic, N., 104, 109
Kent, 28
Kharkov, 44
Khokhlov, N. E., 12, 82, 85, 129 seq., 135, 136 seq.
K.I., 136
Kislitsin, 13, 81
Kleist, P., 79
Koriakov, M., 55
Kousoulas, D. G., 123

L

Lahousen, General, 158
Laycock, Major-General Sir R., 160
Lazitch, B., 109, 115, 121
Leeper, Sir R., 122
Lenclud, General, 71
Lenin, 15, 16, 17, 57, 60, 61, 174
Leningrad, 167
Leverkuehn, Dr. P., 22, 23, 26, 158, 159

M

MacLean, Brigadier F., 104, 114, 120, 121
Macmillan, Harold, 16
Malaya, 99, 140
Mansfield, W. R., 121
Mao Tse-tung, 140 seq.
Martin, D., 109
Martin, Lt.-General H. G., 55
Marx, Karl, 11
Marxism, 11
Mazé, P., 71
McDowell, Colonel, 119, 122
McNeil, H., 83
Meissner, B., 79
Melnik, 157
Mihailovitch, D., 104 seq.
Miksche, F. O., 139
'Military History' (West Point), 38, 41, 42, 45, 58

Military Intelligence:
　German: see Intelligence
　Soviet, 125, 127, 130 seq., 134; see also: 'Director'; Partisans; Red Orchestra; Red Three; Sofia; Sorge
Miller, H., 140
Molotov, 10, 58, 59
Moscow, 39, 79, 155
Muratoff, P., 47
Mussolini, 115
MVD:
　Chief Directorates, 129 seq., 135, 136, 137
　Counter-Intelligence, 134 seq.
　Factory sabotage, 81 seq.
　Fifth Column organization, 13, 134
　History, 127, 130
　Intelligence, 130 seq.
　Ninth Section for Terror and Diversion, 82, 85, 129 seq., 134, 136 seq.
　Organizational Chart, 134
　Partisan Warfare, 139
　Preparation of Partisan warfare, 136 seq.
　Sabotage cells, 85 seq.
　Special Action tasks, 85, 137

N

National Committee for Free Germany, 76 seq.
NATO appraisals, 13
NATO capabilities studies, 14
Naval Intelligence, German, 34 seq.
'Nazi Conspiracy and Aggression', 34, 200 seq.
Neue Zuercher Zeitung, 28, 29, 31
New York Herald Tribune, 81
Nineteenth Century and After, 123
Ninth Section for Terror and Diversion, 82, 85, 129 seq., 134, 136 seq.
NKVD, 127, 130, 139, 153
Nuclear warfare, 10, 11, 12, 168, 180

O

Organization of the New Warfare, Soviet:
　Chart, 134
　Intelligence, 130 seq.
　Partisan warfare, 138 seq.
　Preparation of partisan work, 136 seq.
　Propaganda and Agitation, 128
　Sabotage and Terror, 129 seq.

P

Pallis, A. A., 123,
Panyushkin, Lt.-General, 136
Papen, F. von, 27, 132
Partisans:
　Agents, 54 seq.
　Albania, 101, 102 seq., 122
　China, 140 seq.
　Contact with Red Army, 51, 54, 90, 96, 139, 178, 179, 186, 187
　France, 101, 125, 138, 139 seq., 176, 177
　Field Service Regulations, 51 seq., 92 seq., 183 seq.
　Greece, 102, 122 seq.
　Guide Book, 53 seq.
　Handbook, 50 seq.
　Intelligence, 49 seq., 179, 184 seq.
　Italy, 101, 125, 177
　Losses, 97
　Malaya, 138, 140
　Organization, 138 seq.
　Organizational Chart, 134
　Preparation for partisan warfare, 13, 128, 136 seq.
　Poland, 101, 102, 124 seq.
　Reconnaissance tasks, 50 seq., 91, 179
　Revolutionary wars, 101 seq.
　Sabotage activities, 88 seq., 96 seq., 184 seq.
　Strategic function, 12
　Strength, 93 seq.

Training, 50 *seq.*, 88 *seq.*
U.S.S.R., 138 *seq.*, 177, 178, 179
Warfare, 88 *seq.*, 128, 178
Yugoslavia, 101, 102, 104 *seq.*
Paulus, Field Marshal, 43
Petrov, 85, 130, 131, 133, 135
Petrova, Mrs., 13, 81, 85, 136
Piekenbrock, Lt.-General, 157, 160
Piyade, M., 105, 106, 108
Poland, 101, 102, 124 *seq.*, 137, 158, 164
Political warfare, 75 *seq.*, 159
Prague Manifesto, 165
Prisoners of War as agents:
  Legal aspects, 167 *seq.*
  Moral, 161
  On German side, 151 *seq.*, 159 *seq.*
  On Soviet side, 78, 151
Propaganda and Agitation, 128, 134
Protocol 'M', 83 *seq.*, 192 *seq.*
Psychological warfare, 75 *seq.*, 148, 168 *seq.*
Puttkamer, J. von, 77, 78

R

Radio transmissions:
  Communist, 64 *seq.*, 76, 109
  German, 148 *seq.*
Rado, A., 22, 23, 27
Reconnaissance: *see* Partisans
Red Army:
  Contact with Partisans, 51, 54, 90, 96, 139, 178, 179, 186, 187
  Field Service Regulations, 51 *seq.*, 92 *seq.*, 183 *seq.*
  German aggression, 10 *seq.*, 35, 37
  German campaign, 33 *seq.*
  Intelligence, 21 *seq.*, 33 *seq.*, 127, 130, 132 *seq.*
  Organizational Chart, 134
  Partisan reconnaissance for, 49 *seq.*, 90, 139, 179, 186 *seq.*
Red Orchestra:
  Agents, 23, 26, 27
  Cipher, 28
  'Director', 25, 27, 36, 39, 42, 43, 44, 46, 47
  Discovery, 23
  German counter-intelligence, 23, 24 *seq.*
  Network, 22
  Resident Director, 27 *seq.*
  Short wave transmissions, 23, 24, 28
  Signals, 41
  Soviet infiltration, 26, 31, 172
  Transmissions, 23 *seq.*
Red Three:
  Agents, 23, 25, 26, 27
  Cipher, 28
  Couriers, 28
  'Director', 25, 27, 36, 39, 42, 43, 44, 46, 47
  Discovery, 23
  German counter-intelligence, 23 *seq.*
  German infiltration, 25
  Network, 22
  Resident Director, 27 *seq.*
  Short wave transmissions, 23, 24, 28
  Signals, 36, 38, 40, 42, 44, 45, 46
  Soviet infiltration, 26, 32, 33 *seq.*, 172
  Transmissions, 23 *seq.*
Reich Security Main Office, 151
Resident Director: *see* Red Orchestra; Red Three
Requin, General, 71
Reynaud, P., 64, 65, 67, 71
Riom Trial, 70
Roeder, Dr. M., 28, 41
Roessler, 21, 28 *seq.*, 180
Rootham, J., 121
Rossi, A., 60, 61, 63, 64, 71, 73, 130
Royal Commission, Australia, 13, 82, 130, 133, 135, 136
Royal Commission, Canada, 28, 128, 131, 132, 133
Rumania, 137
Russian Freedom Station, 149

S

Sabotage, 81 *seq.*, 128, 129 *seq.*, 173 *seq.*, 184 *seq.*
Sabotage cells, 85 *seq.*, 134
Samarin, V. D., 163
Sarraut, A., 64, 68
Schellenberg, SS Major-General, 151 *seq.*
Schulenburg, Count W., 75
Schuman, F. L., 76
Security risks, 179
Serbia: *see* Yugoslavia
Seton-Watson, H., 124, 125
Seydlitz, General von, 78
Shankar's Weekly, 175
Sherwood, R. E., 36
Skorzeny, 159, 160
Sofia, Soviet spy ring, 27, 132, 134
Sorge, Dr., 27, 28, 38 *seq.*, 132, 172
Soviets:
   Atomic weapons, defence against, 10, 12
   Broadcasts to Germany, 76 *seq.*
   Cold warfare, 11, 17
   Contacts with German Resistance, 75 *seq.*
   Defence, 10, 11, 12
   Embassies, 27, 86, 87, 131 *seq.*, 134
   Espionage, 21 *seq.*, 33 *seq.*, 130 *seq.*
   German attack, 10 *seq.*, 33 *seq.*, 37, 39 *seq.*
   German campaign, 26, 33 *seq.*
   Infiltration, 172: *see also* Red Orchestra; Red Three
   Operational conception, 10, 11
   Organization of the New Warfare, 127 *seq.*
   Pact with Germany, 58, 59
   Partisans: *see* Partisans
   Peace offers, 79
   Political warfare, 75 *seq.*
   Propaganda, 78, 79, 128, 134, 179 *seq.*
   Revolutionary wars, 101 *seq.*
   Sabotage, 81 *seq.*, 129 *seq.*, 134, 173 *seq.*, 184 *seq.*

Satellite espionage, 31
Spy rings: *see* Red Orchestra; Red Three; Sofia; Sorge
Subversion, 56 *seq.*, 172 *seq.*, 196 *seq.*
Soviet World Outlook, 16, 59, 173, 174
Special Action tasks, 85, 137
Stalin, 16, 34, 35, 36, 41, 42, 57, 58, 66, 79, 148, 172, 173, 175, 176
Stalingrad, 40, 41, 42, 43, 44, 46, 47, 76, 156
State Security Committee, 134, 136
Stevens, Vice-Admiral, L. .C, 161
Stolze, Colonel E., 157 *seq.*, 160
Strike weapon, 13, 82 *seq.*, 192 *seq.*
Subversion, 56 *seq.*, 172 *seq.*, 196 *seq.*
Sunday Times, 17
Sweden, espionage, 31, 86 *seq.*
Swiatlo, J., 125
Swiss Federal Police, 23, 25, 47

T

'Tamara', 158
Taracouzio, T. A., 173
Tass, 130
Terracini, 177
Teske, H., 179
Thorez, M., 61, 62, 64, 68, 69, 73, 82
Thorwald, J., 163
Time and Tide, 123
Times (London), 10, 12, 13, 15, 16, 17, 30, 31, 71, 86, 135, 136
Tito, Marshal, 17, 104 *seq.*
Trials: *see* War Crimes Trials; Espionage trials

U

Ukraine, 147, 150, 157, 158
'Ulm' Undertaking, 156
U.S.A., 61, 79, 81

U.S.S.R.: *see* Cominform; Comintern; Intelligence; Military Intelligence; MVD; Partisans; Red Army; Red Orchestra; Red Three; Soviets

V

Vlassov, General, 150, 163 *seq.*
Vyshinsky, 174, 176

W

'Walli', 156
War Crimes Trials:
    Field Marshal von Leeb et al, 167
    Field Marshal List et al., 106 *seq.*, 122, 123, 168
    Major War Criminals, 157, 158, 169, 170
    Field Marshal von Manstein, 168

General Mihailovitch, 109 *seq.*
Riom, 70
von Weizsaecker et al., 147, 151 *seq.*, 170
Warsaw, 124 *seq.*
Weygand, General, 68, 72
Wheeler-Bennett, J. W., 76, 77
Willoughby, Major-General C. A., 27, 38, 39, 132
Workers' Militia, 83
Woodhouse, Colonel C. M., 122 *seq.*

Y

Yourichitch, E., 116, 118
Yugoslavia, 101, 102, 104 *seq.*
Yugoslavia Emergency Committee, 109

Z

'Zeppelin': *see* Action Zeppelin
Zervas, Colonel, 122, 123

For Product Safety Concerns and Information please contact our EU representative GPSR@taylorandfrancis.com
Taylor & Francis Verlag GmbH, Kaufingerstraße 24, 80331 München, Germany

www.ingramcontent.com/pod-product-compliance
Lightning Source LLC
Chambersburg PA
CBHW052112300426
44116CB00010B/1639